ASIAN MODELS OF ENTREPRENEURSHIP
From the Indian Union and Nepal to the Japanese Archipelago

Context, Policy and Practice

2nd Edition

ASIA-PACIFIC BUSINESS SERIES **(ISSN: 1793-3137)**

Series Editor
Leo-Paul Dana
Professor of International Entrepreneurship
Groupe Sup de Co Montpellier Business School, France

Published

Vol. 1 Guanxi and Business
by Yadong Luo

Vol. 2 From Adam Smith to Michael Porter: Evolution of Competitiveness Theory
by Dong-Sung Cho & Hewy-Chang Moon

Vol. 3 Islamic Banking and Finance in South-East Asia: Its Development and Future (2nd Edition)
by Angelo M. Venardos

Vol. 4 Asian Models of Entrepreneurship — From the Indian Union and the Kingdom of Nepal to the Japanese Archipelago: Context, Policy and Practice
by Leo-Paul Dana

Vol. 5 Guanxi and Business (2nd Edition)
by Yadong Luo

Vol. 6 Islamic Banking and Finance in South-East Asia: Its Development and Future (3rd Edition)
by Angelo M. Venardos

Vol. 7 From Adam Smith to Michael Porter: Evolution of Competitiveness Theory (Extended Edition)
by Dong-Sung Cho & Hwy-Chang Moon

Vol. 8 Catalyst for Change: Chinese Business in Asia
edited by Thomas Menkhoff, Hans-Dieter Evers, Chay Yue Wah & Hoon Chang Yau

Vol. 9 Asian Models of Entrepreneurship: From the Indian Union and Nepal to the Japanese Archipelago: Context, Policy and Practice (2nd Edition)
by Leo-Paul Dana

Asia-Pacific Business Series – Vol. 9

ASIAN MODELS OF ENTREPRENEURSHIP From the Indian Union and Nepal to the Japanese Archipelago

Context, Policy and Practice

2nd Edition

LÉO-PAUL DANA

Groupe Sup de Co Montpellier Business School, France

World Scientific

NEW JERSEY • LONDON • SINGAPORE • BEIJING • SHANGHAI • HONG KONG • TAIPEI • CHENNAI

Published by

World Scientific Publishing Co. Pte. Ltd.
5 Toh Tuck Link, Singapore 596224
USA office: 27 Warren Street, Suite 401-402, Hackensack, NJ 07601
UK office: 57 Shelton Street, Covent Garden, London WC2H 9HE

Library of Congress Cataloging-in-Publication Data
Dana, Leo Paul, author.
Asian models of entrepreneurship : from the Indian Union and Nepal to the Japanese archipelago : context, policy and practice / Leo-Paul Dana (Groupe Sup de Co Montpellier Business School, France). -- Second edition.
pages cm. -- (Asia-Pacific business series ; vol. 9)
Includes bibliographical references and index.
ISBN 978-9814590259 (hardcopy : alk. paper)
1. Entrepreneurship--Asia. I. Title.
HB615.D29 2014
338'.04095--dc23
2014003421

British Library Cataloguing-in-Publication Data
A catalogue record for this book is available from the British Library.

In-house Editor: Chye Shu Wen

This book is dedicated to
Jakob Theodore, Naomi Josephine & Teresa Elizabeth

Foreword

Five years after Lehman Brothers' collapse, the world's economy has started to recover slowly with equity markets in America reaching record highs. Fears of a double dip recession are lessening as even nations like Japan, long mired in a deflationary spiral, are seeing their strongest growth in decades. The recovery though has largely been uneven, generally favouring the rich. Millions of people remain unemployed throughout the world and even more remain chronically underemployed. Spain's official unemployment rate is 26.6% as of September 2013. The pain is even more dramatic for the world's youth as the jobs they do find are not preparing them for long, successful careers.

Policy-makers around the world have debated whether quantitative easing or price caps on core products like oil and rice is the way out of the economic morass. Some academics like Ian Bremner have argued for the rise and success of state capitalism in nations like China—where large state-owned banks can flush capital through the system to state-owned enterprises and force them to continue to hire people, regardless of profits.

Far too few have looked at the role entrepreneurship can have in jump-starting employment rolls. Over the past three decades, over 50% of job growth in the United States has come from companies with fewer than 50 employees. In *Small Business Economics*, Alex Coad and Martin Binder have shown that entrepreneurs in the United Kingdom have higher job satisfaction than wage earners. Similarly, Wim Naude has found countries like Denmark and Sweden that score high in the Global Economic Development Index (GEDI) also score high in overall happiness.

The initial economic miracle in China that has lifted hundreds of millions out of poverty was not due to state planning as many believe—the growth was triggered by entrepreneurs in the southern province of Guangdong building small factories to produce trinkets to sell to the western world. Once proven a successful model for economic growth without threatening the primacy of the Communist Party, Chinese central government leaders started rolling out economic reforms throughout the country.

One reason why Asia overall has weathered the financial crisis better than western nations is its reliance on entrepreneurship to power growth. Entrepreneurs are more nimble than large corporations to react to changing market conditions and, due to closer ties in the company, are less likely to fire people just to hit quarterly earning targets. This has kept consumer confidence numbers higher in Asia than anywhere else.

Thus we come to Léo-Paul Dana's landmark book which is important for policy-makers and academics to read to learn what success factors were needed in Asia for entrepreneurship to rise. Dana argues there is no homogeneous entrepreneurs' model, or even an Asian one. He shows there are key elements needed to create an entrepreneurial environment from the Doi-Moi model to the Royal Cambodian one, to China's gradual one. Professor Dana analyses the successful factors behind entrepreneurship in 15 different nations in Asia and the cultural and political reasons underlying the differences in growth. These lessons can be applied by policy-makers in their home countries to spur not just job creation but good job creation. The book also shows why Asia's economic rise will continue and why more economic and business models will emerge from there. Western nations will have to adapt to the new competitive order or else go extinct.

The book also serves as an important guide for would-be entrepreneurs. One of Dana's strengths is his ability to bring together theoretical analysis as well as actionable learnings. I know Dana's lessons first-hand—15 years ago, I took one of Professor Dana's courses on entrepreneurship in Asia and first read his book, *Entrepreneurship in Pacific Asia: Past, Present & Future*. Reading this book, and taking his course, I quickly saw myself as an entrepreneur like the ones he profiles. I quickly decided that a career as an entrepreneur was far more desirable than working in a large corporation and used Dana's book as a guide on how to plan my own career. 15 years later, I have since started several companies and invested in dozens of others as a venture capitalist and angel investor.

Dana's book is an invaluable contribution to scholars, policy-makers and businessmen bitten by the entrepreneurial bug.

Shaun Rein
Shanghai, China
Founder,
China Market Research Group

Preface

I was born the second son to the daughter of an entrepreneur. Both her parents were born in Asia as were their ancestors as far back as they can be traced. My paternal grandfather was also an entrepreneur. Like his brothers, my late father was an entrepreneur too; when he learned of my birth, he was in Asia. Perhaps it is not a random event that I have such a keen interest of entrepreneurship in Asia.

In Dana (1993b) I noted that Professor Shigeru Fujii of Kobe University pioneered applied education in entrepreneurship. In 1998 I took up residence in Singapore where I taught at Nanyang University.

Three centuries earlier, India's share of world income was about 23%, approximately the same as Europe's (Singh, 2006). Over time, imperial powers prospered further. Today, "India's middle class is bigger than the entire 300 million population of the US (Johnson, 2006, p. 1)." Indeed demographics have changed dramatically.

In 2013, Grandadam reported, "10 years ago, China's labour costs were 200 times lower than Mexico's (2013, p. 45)." The same article reported that by 2013, hourly salaries had become 19.6% higher in China than in Mexico. Indeed, Asia is changing. A fascinating place, it appears to be getting increasingly interesting; hence, I was delighted when World Scientific Publishing approached me to write this second edition.

Throughout this book, unless otherwise specified, statistics were provided by government sources. The symbols $ and ¢ refer to the currency of the United States.

Happy reading.

Léo-Paul DANA,
Professor,
Groupe Sup de Co Montpellier Business School, France
and Visiting Scholar,
Kansai University, Japan

Acknowledgements

The research leading to this book was conducted on location, in Asia. For travel to Asia, the author received funding from McGill University, Nanyang Technological University, the University of Oxford, and the University of Pittsburgh.

In the process of preparing the manuscript, each chapter was sent to experts for review. The following kindly volunteered their time, providing inspiration, encouragement and constructive comments:

- Vishwanath V. BABA, Editor, *Canadian Journal of Administrative Sciences*, McMaster University, Canada
- Lady BORTON, author of *After Sorrow*
- Kevin B. BUCKNALL, Griffith University, Brisbane, Australia
- David P. CHANDLER, Professor Emeritus, Monash University, Melbourne, Australia
- Florence CHANG, Department of Business Administration, National Changhua University of Education, Changhua, Taiwan
- Jason C. H. CHEN, Graduate School of Business, Gonzaga University, Spokane, Washington, USA
- CHEW Soon Beng, Professor of Economics & Programme Director of MSc in Applied Economics, Nanyang Technological University, Singapore
- Yongho CHOI, Professor of Economics, Kyungpook National University, Korea
- Myrna R. CO, Open University of the Philippines
- Saroj Kumar DATTA, Dean, VIT Business School, VIT University, India
- Heidi DAHLES, Department of International Business and Asian Studies, Griffith University, Australia
- Evelyne DOURILLE-FEER, Economist, CEPII, Paris, France

- Sophal EAR, University of California at Berkeley, California, USA
- Rakesh GUPTA, Griffith University, Australia
- Masaaki HIRANO, Waseda University Business School, Tokyo, Japan
- Earl Dwight HONEYCUTT Jr., Professor of Marketing & Chair, Department of Business Administration, Old Dominion University, Norfolk, Virginia, USA
- Glenn HOOK, Professor of Japanese Studies, University of Sheffield, UK
- Ming-Wen HU, Tamkang University, Taiwan
- Masahiro ISHIGURO, The Small & Medium Enterprise Agency, Japan
- Takayuki ITO, Good Samaritan Club, Japan
- Jan JOHANSON, Professor of International Business, Centre of International Business Studies, University of Uppsala, Sweden
- Katsuyuki KAMEI, Professor, Kansai University, Osaka, Japan
- Raymond KAO, Founder, *Journal of Small Business and Entrepreneurship,* Canada
- W. F. Fred KIESNER, Conrad Hilton Chair of Entrepreneurship, Loyola Marymount University, Los Angeles, USA
- Philippe LASSERRE, Professor Emeritus, INSEAD, France
- Byoung-Hoon LEE, Chung-Ang University, Seoul, Korea
- Julie MALLET, Open Universiteit, Heerlen, The Netherlands
- Nancy K. NAPIER, Professor of International Business, Boise State University, Idaho, USA
- Kenichi OHKITA, Associate Professor, Kagawa University, Kagawa, Japan
- Michael J. G. PARNWELL, Professor of South East Asian Development, University of Leeds, UK
- David. P. PAUL III, Monmouth University, West Long Branch, New Jersey, USA
- Michael PENG, Jindal Chair of Global Strategy, University of Texas at Dallas, USA
- Jozef R. RACO, Universitas Katolik De La Salle, Manado, Philippines

- Suneeporn SUWANMANEEPONG, Policy Researcher, National Science and Technology Development Agency, Phathumthani, Thailand
- David I. STEINBERG, Distinguished Professor, Georgetown University, Washington DC, USA
- Tulus TAMBUNAN, Trisakti University, Indonesia
- Mitsuru TANAKA, Professor Emeritus, Kansai University, Osaka, Japan
- Sarah TURNER, Department of Geography, McGill University, Canada
- Michiel VERVER, Vrije Universiteit, Amsterdam, The Netherlands
- Takashi YAMAMOTO, Centre for Entrepreneurship and Leadership Studies for Regional Economies, Akita International University, Akita, Japan
- Yung-Kai YANG, National University of Kaohsiung, Taiwan
- Henry Wai-Chung YEUNG, Department of Geography, National University of Singapore
- Joseph J. ZASLOFF, Professor Emeritus, University of Pittsburgh, Pittsburgh, Pennsylvania, USA

In addition, I deem it appropriate to acknowledge the influence that Confucius has had on me.

> ***If one learns from others, but does not think,***
> ***one will be bewildered.***
>
> ***If one thinks, but does not learn, one will be in peril.***
>
> — Confucius (551–479 BC)

Contents

Chapter 1

Introduction[1]

Richard Cantillon (1755) described entrepreneurs as absorbing uncertainty caused by changing conditions, and thus contributing to the welfare of society. The aristocrat industrialist, Jean Baptiste Say defined the entrepreneur as the agent who "unites all means of production and who finds in the value of the products...the re-establishment of the entire capital he employs, and the value of the wages, the interest, and the rent which he pays, as well as the profits belonging to himself (Say, 1816, pp. 28–29)."

In this book, entrepreneurship refers to economic undertaking; this is based on the classical definition of the word, which can be traced to the German *unternehmung* literally translated as undertaking. The agents of entrepreneurship are entrepreneurs, from the French *entre preneurs,* literally meaning "between takers." The flagships of entrepreneurship are small and medium enterprises (SMEs).

While large corporations can greatly increase their efficiency and profitability, by outsourcing to specialised enterprises of lesser scale, entrepreneurs can benefit by focusing on niche markets. When having an economy of scale is not an issue, small firms may even have comparative advantages (*vis-à-vis* larger ones) in assembly, mixing or finishing. Thus, entrepreneurs need not compete with large firms. Instead, large and small firms can form symbiotic relationships (Dana, Etemad and Wright, 2008), offering complementary services, thus improving a society's bearing capacity. Given that the flexibility of entrepreneurs, in the absence of excessive bureaucracy, helps them respond quickly to changing needs, entrepreneurship can also contribute to social development by providing local employment with relatively low levels of investment.

---

[1] The chapter draws on previous publications by the same author.

Today, it is widely accepted that entrepreneurship contributes to development, with a positive effect on society, creating employment, economic expansion, a larger tax base, and more consumer well being. This is increasingly supported by research, and governments around the world have acknowledged this.

Although interest in entrepreneurship as an academic discipline has spanned the globe, the phenomenon itself is expressed differently around the world. Furthermore, each government's policies affect entrepreneurship in different ways.

As will be shown, entrepreneurship differs greatly across Asia. Cultural values, government policy and a variety of other factors, including a nation's colonial experience, affect entrepreneurship.

Even the definition of "small business" varies. In Indonesia, for example, the government defines small industries as units of production with five to 20 workers. In Malaysia, "a small or medium industry" is defined as "a manufacturer with up to 2.5 million ringgits in owner's equity." Environments with unlike histories and public policies shape entrepreneurship differently.

The East

> ***The East is a career.***
>
> — Benjamin Disraeli, Prime Minister of England (1868, 1874–1880)

The concept of "Asia" originates from the ancient civilisation of Mesopotamia and the eastern shores of the Mediterranean Sea. In Assyrian, *asu* means "east." It is likely that ancient Greek entrepreneurs adopted the term from Phoenician merchants, thus designating the land to the east. That was probably between 600 and 500 BC.

The Greeks cultivated relations with Asians, and trade expanded considerably. Both land and sea routes were further developed under the Romans, mostly to the Indian sub-continent. The Venetian explorer, Marco Polo, wrote accounts of his 13th century travels to India, China, and beyond. Before the arrival of the Europeans, there were many independent empires in Asia — at least a dozen in Southeast Asia alone.

Beginning in the 16th century, European colonialism began to impose a new economic structure, and new patterns of trade emerged. Coffee, rubber and tea plantations were introduced. These being labour-intensive, workers were imported, thereby causing significant demographic shifts and changing ethnic distribution. Whereas Asia had formerly exported finished products, the colonies became exporters of raw materials and importers of manufactured goods. The emphasis on cash crops caused a move away from traditional self-sufficiency.

The mid-20th century saw a return to independence. In 1944, the Japanese declared Indonesia independent, effective at the termination of the war. The independence of the Philippines was declared on July 4, 1946. Ho Chi Minh declared Vietnam independent, on September 2, 1946. Laos, which was declared an associate state of the French Union in 1949, was granted full independence in 1953. Also in 1953, Cambodia declared its independence, which was recognised in 1954. Malaya became independent in 1957. Singapore obtained self-government from London in 1959, and independence from Malaysia, in 1965. However, nations continued to be influenced by their historical experiences.

Cultural and religious differences are also important. Mahayana Buddhists (of the northern school) adopted the name "Greater Vehicle." They called the Theravada (southern) school the "Lesser Vehicle." The state religion in Cambodia is Hinayana Buddhism. In contrast, the principal religion of Vietnam is Mahayana Buddhism. In Tibet, the *Srunmas* are guardians of their faith.[2] In Malaysia, the religion is Islam. Singapore is officially multi-denominational, recognising Baha'i, Buddhist, Christian, Hindu, Jewish, Muslim, Sikh, Taoist and Zoroastrian religions.

Asia covers more area than North America, Europe and Australia combined. Nations of western Asia — Israel, Jordan, Lebanon, Palestine, Syria, and Turkey — are treated in Dana (2000b). Countries of Central Asia — Kazakhstan, the Kyrgyz Republic, Tajikistan, Turkmenistan and Uzbekistan — are the focus of Dana (2002). The geographic focus of this book is the group of Asian countries from India to Japan, including Cambodia, China, Indonesia, Korea, Laos, Malaysia, Myanmar, Nepal, the Philippines, Singapore, Taiwan, Thailand and Vietnam.

Heterogeneity

Westerners sometimes speak of an Asian model of business or management, without considering the wide divergence within this vast geographic region. Yet, entrepreneurship, today, is shaped by cultural

---

[2] See Rock (1935).

and historical factors. Not surprisingly, peoples with unlike experiences exhibit different approaches to management and entrepreneurship.

The Chinese and Indian minorities in Pacific Asia demonstrated a strong propensity for entrepreneurship. The same is true for Jews from Iraq (Dana, 2010) and also for Armenians. Some chose entrepreneurship because they were unable to integrate into their host society; others did so because cultural values made it socially desirable for them. In other cultures, entrepreneurship is considered to be a less desirable option. Haley and Haley (1998) wrote that while merchants are exalted in Japanese culture, they are reviled in Chinese tradition.

Attitudes toward entrepreneurship and entrepreneurs vary not only among countries but also within them. There are important differences among people of one nation. Goodnow suggested that the physical environment was among the causal variables, and he described China as "two countries in one (1927, p. 651)." The Chinese speak a variety of dialects and different dialect groups have their own clan associations, resulting in unique networks of entrepreneurs with distinct patterns of entrepreneurship. While most Chinese in Vietnam are Cantonese, 77% of the Chinese in Cambodia are Teochew, and 85% of the Chinese in the Philippines are Hokkien (Haley, Tan and Haley, 1998).

Within Indonesia, the Balinese are more tolerant of Chinese entrepreneurs than are the orthodox Muslims of Sumatra. Among the Indigenous hill-tribes of Sumatra, women are in charge of possessions, and traditionally a man's assets were passed on to a sister rather than to a spouse (Moore, 1930).

In Kelantan and in Terengganu — on the east coast of the Malay Peninsula — pork-eating is not tolerated in public, as this act is considered offensive to the Muslims of this Malaysian province. In contrast, compatibility in religion, social customs and culinary habits allowed Chinese entrepreneurs to integrate easily into Thai society.

Also important is the fact that attitudes and behaviours are not always static. About Japan, Griffis wrote, "When feudalism had been abolished, in 1871, and the once-despised merchant was given honor and opportunity, he unfolded the pinions of a towering ambition and looked abroad to capture the markets of Asia (1923, p. 419)."

A characteristic which reappears across Asia is the existence of entrepreneurship networks that bind together entrepreneurs, based on trust. Numerous enterprises work together as a team, with little concern about core competencies. Group conformity prevails over individualism, and relationships prevail over constraints. Entrepreneurship networks transcend the limits of a small-scale enterprise. Redding (1990) focused on Chinese enterprise — prominent in East Asia. The economic dominance of Chinese entrepreneurs often led to tensions. In response to ethnic discrimination, Chinese entrepreneurs often chose to have a low profile. Rather than develop their own brands, they usually preferred to act as subcontractors, wholesalers and retailers. As will be shown throughout this book, there is no one best approach to entrepreneurship; rather, different nations adopt policy models, which are relevant to their respective history and culture.

Economic Sectors

Where governments have clung on to socialist ideology, there tends to be a large sector of the economy that is state-controlled, and it operates along side the traditional bazaar and the more modern firm-type sector. It is useful, therefore, to distinguish among these very distinct sectors of economic activity, which co-exist across Asia. The bazaar, the state-controlled planned sector, and the firm-type sector are components of the formal economy, some of the features of which are summarised in Table 1.1. In addition, the parallel economy includes informal economic activity; internal economic activity with no transaction; covert economic activity; and fictitious economic activity. Discussions of these shall follow.

The Bazaar	State-Controlled Planned Sector	Firm-Type Sector
Focus on personal relations	Focus on bureaucracy	Focus on impersonal transactions
Segmentation refers to producers	Segmentation not considered	Segmentation refers to the market
Competition refers to tension between buyer and seller	Competition is deemed unnecessary, as the state declares a monopoly	Competition is an activity which takes place among sellers
Prices are negotiated	Prices are dictated by the state	Prices are indicated by the vendor

Table 1.1 Sectors of the Formal Economy.

The Bazaar

The bazaar is a social and cultural system, a way of life and a general mode of commercial activity, which has been in existence for millennia. In the bazaar, economic transactions are *not* the focus of activities; instead, the focus is on personal relationships. In this scenario, consumers do not necessarily seek the lowest price or the best quality. An individual gives business to another with whom a relationship has been established, to ensure that this person will reciprocate. *Reciprocal preferential treatment reduces transaction costs.*[3] The multiplicity of small-scale transactions, in the bazaar, results in a fractionalisation of risks and therefore of profit margins; the complex balance of credit relationships is carefully managed, as described by Geertz (1963). Prices in the bazaar are negotiated, as opposed to being specified by the seller. In contrast to the firm-type sector, in which the primary competitive stress is among sellers, the sliding price system of the bazaar results in the primary competitive stress being between buyer and seller (Parsons and Smelzer, 1956). The lack of information results in an imperfect market and with few exceptions, such as basic food staples, retail prices are not indicated; rather, these are determined by negotiations. The customer tests price levels informally, before bargaining begins. It is often the buyer who proposes a price, which is eventually raised. As discussed by Geertz, the "relatively high percentage of wholesale transactions (*i.e.*, transactions in which goods are bought with the express intention to resell them) means that in most cases both buyer and seller are professional traders and the contest is one between experts (1963, p. 33). Once a mutually satisfactory transaction has taken place, the establishment of a long-term relationship makes future purchases more pleasurable, and profitable. As noted by Webster (1992), building long-term relationships can be viewed as a social and economic process. Unlike Western relationship marketing, which is customer-centred, whereby a seller seeks long-term business relationships with clients (Evans and Laskin, 1994; Zineldin, 1998), the focus in the bazaar is on the relationship itself. In the bazaar, *both* the buyer and the seller seek a personal relationship. Firms in the bazaar are not perceived as rivals of one another. There is minimal — if any — brand differentiation among merchants. Vendors do not necessarily seek to optimise monetary gain. Economic rationality is not always obvious.

[3] For a discussion of transaction costs, see Williamson (1985; 1996).

Figure 1.1 Typical Bazaar; photograph by Léo-Paul Dana.

In contrast to the Occident, where segmentation refers to the market, in the bazaar economy, segmentation refers to the clustering of producers and retailers; street-names reflect this. In Yangon — formerly Rangoon — the Chamber of Commerce and Industry is located on Merchant Street. The street-map of Hanoi includes Broiled Fish Street, Coffin Street, Fish Sauce Street, Gold Street, Jewellers Street, Paper Street, Silk Street, Sweet Potato Street, and Tin Street. Long gave an account of his observations in Hanoi, "Street names in the teeming native-Chinese section are a guide to the shopper. Each bears the name of the product traditionally sold there — silk, tin, scales, spice, brass, paper, jewelry (1952, pp. 315–316)."

Likewise, Passantino described the bazaar in Kunming, China, "There is also a street of beggars...There are streets for pig auctions and for prostitutes; there is one for banks...(1946, p. 142)." Even today, in the bazaar economy, shops still are clustered according to the goods offered therein.

When examining the bazaar, it is important to understand the relationships among the players within it, their organisation and their economic principles. The bazaar is a hub of information exchange. Buyers and sellers express intentions, and an intricate network of relationships facilitates transactions. As explained by Christian, "News spreads rapidly in a Shan States bazaar. Within the hour I was offered a half a dozen old pistols (1943, p. 504)."

While the entrepreneur described by Schumpeter (1912; 1928; 1934; 1939; 1942; 1947; 1949) is an innovator who causes disequilibrium to profit therefrom, the entrepreneur of the bazaar may simply identify an opportunity for profit — rather than create one. In this way, the entrepreneur of the bazaar corresponds to that of the Austrian school (Kirzner, 1973; 1979; 1982; 1985). Geertz (1963) and Dana (2000b) discuss, in detail, phenomena of the bazaar. Dana, Etemad and Wright (2004) note similarities between the bazaar and the New Economy.

The State-Controlled Planned Sector

In transitional economies, state firms are remnants of the communist model — a doctrine first published in German (Marx and Engels, 1848), then in Russian in 1882, and in English in 1888. This model assumed that a central office was in the best position to balance supply and demand. The focus of the state-controlled planned sector is thus neither on transactions nor on relationships, but rather on the state bureaucracy.

When the state produced everything, centralisation ruled out competitors. Barriers to trade, coupled with an import-substitution policy, ensured that competition is not a factor. Since demand exceeded supply, marketing was not necessary and segmentation was not considered. Prices became a function of the government's bureaucracy. Dalgic (1998) reported on an empirical study, which found that state-owned firms had much less of a market orientation, than did private companies.

Figure 1.2 Working for the State; photograph by Léo-Paul Dana.

The Firm-Type Sector

The firm-type sector is an economic institution, which involves a mode of commercial activity such that industry and trade take place primarily within a set of impersonally defined institutions, grouping people according to organisation and specialisation. It is assumed that profit-maximising transactions will occur based on rational decision-making, rather than the nature of personal relationships. The focus is transactions and these tend to be impersonal. Weber's (1924) thesis applies here. In this sector of the economy, the decision space is occupied by product attributes; the buyer and seller are secondary, if not trivial, to the transaction decision. The interaction between the buyer and the product is deemed more important than that between the buyer and the seller. Transactions are based on economic rationality and are therefore impersonal in nature. Competition is an activity that takes place between sellers, who engage in segmentation, in order to partition the market into like-groups of predictable consumers. Prices are tagged, reflecting market forces. While Western marketing principles (Gronroos, 1989) apply to this sector, market-orientation is linked to the maturity of the industrialisation process (Seglin, 1990). Where industrial development is limited, the framework for economic transition may have to rely more on new ventures and on joint initiatives.

Figure 1.3 Firm-Type Sector; photograph by Léo-Paul Dana.

The Parallel Economy

Under central planning, the lack of a legal market economy led to permanent shortages. Survival strategies often involved the emergence of entrepreneurs in the parallel economy, where inefficient regulations could be circumvented. According to Grossman (1977), this underground activity increased the overall efficiency of resource allocation under central planning. The problem is that a mind-set evolved, equating efficiency with the evasion of regulation.

Recent years have been characterised by economic reform, regulatory reform, and change in the mind-set of people. However, change in mind-set has not kept up with changes in regulatory framework (North, 1990). Since these have not been evolving at the same pace, new problems have become associated with transition. As a consequence of their experience under central planning, people came to equate entrepreneurship with the avoidance of communist law. When new regulations were introduced to usher in market economics, people continued to circumvent business law. As noted by Feige and Ott (1999), during transition, evasion and non-compliance with new rules renders them ineffective. Thus, where economic reform has been faster than the ability of people to adapt, inertia has delayed actual transition. Štulhofer (1999) used the term *cultura inertia* to describe a collectivist legacy that has survived from the past. Especially among the elderly, there is still a distrust of the state, of banks and of legal institutions. Conditions in transitional economies thus make the parallel sector very popular, avoiding all forms of taxation. In transitional economies that lack developed market institutions, it is common to have a high proportion of underground activities. O'Driscoll, Holmes and Kirkpatrick (2001) reported a black market in Laos, larger than the formal economy.

The popularity of the parallel economy is no surprise, considering the low initial role of legitimate private enterprise, coupled with a high degree of liberalisation, and hindered by the lack of macro-stability in the absence of a sufficiently developed legal framework. As illustrated in Table 1.2, the parallel economy may be informal; internal; covert; or fictitious.

Category	Examples
Informal Economic Activity (with business transaction)	Barter, street vending, unrecorded cash sales
Internal Economic Activity (with no business transaction)	Subsistence agriculture, hunting, fishing
Covert Economic Activity (with illegal business transaction)	Prostitution, smuggling, trade in illegal drugs
Fictitious Economic Activity	Foreign devil company

Table 1.2 Activities of the Parallel Economy.

Informal Economic Activity

Barter, selling from an impromptu stall and itinerant vending are considered forms of informal economic activity. Unrecorded cash sales circumvent taxation as well as regulation. In some economies, private enterprise is concentrated in the informal sector. This is illustrated by the large numbers of self-employed vendors in the profitable distribution of goods and services. The law is often bent, but authorities generally tolerate the sector. A relevant discussion from Dana (1992) is presented concisely by Chamard and Christie (1996). For some entrepreneurs in transitional economies, legal transactions may be limited to informal barter. The transition from such a traditional system to a modern cash economy will require cognitive innovation. A prerequisite will be for people to internalise new notions of measurability, to encourage the use of cash. New elements of formality, and impersonal structure, will have to be introduced and internalised, before new institutions can function effectively. At the World Economic Forum in Davos, Somavia (2006) argued that cultural barriers often hinder transition from the informal economy to the formal sector.

Figure 1.4 Informal Repairman; photograph by Léo-Paul Dana.

Figure 1.5 Informal Itinerant Vendor; photograph by Léo-Paul Dana.

Internal Economic Activity

This category of economic activity is best described as internal, because *no business transaction* takes place. Wealth is created, but nothing is sold for profit. That which is created is consumed or saved for personal use. In transitional economies, internal subsistence activity is often necessary, as a means to adapt to rapid reform.

Examples of internal economic activity include subsistence agriculture, and subsistence fishing. Both are legal, but involve no market transaction external to the producer. These are, therefore, forms of internal economic activity.

While internal economic activity exists, as an activity of choice — even amid the most advanced and industrialised backdrop (Dana, 1995a) — for some people in transitional economies, this is the only strategy for survival.

Figure 1.6 Subsistence Fishing; photograph by Léo-Paul Dana.

Figure 1.7 Subsistence Harvest; photograph by Léo-Paul Dana.

Covert Economic Activity

This category of economic activity involves business transactions, which are illegal, and therefore conducted in a covert way, in order to avoid punitive measures from law-enforcing authorities (Haskell and Yablonsky, 1974; Henry, 1978). Prostitution, which Cantillon (1755) considered a form of entrepreneurship, often falls in this category.

Covert activity promises fast cash. Glinkina (1999) predicted the growth of covert economic activity, in some environments. In Cambodia, illegal logging has been an economically significant covert activity. In Myanmar, smuggling has been on the rise (O'Driscoll, Holmes and Kirkpatrick, 2001).

Fictitious Economic Activity

Fictitious economy has been created to facilitate circumvention of the law; this "implies speculative transactions and different kinds of swindles with a view to receiving and transferring money, including contrived rent-seeking (Glinkina, 1999, p. 102)." In Vietnam, for instance, "foreign devil" companies have been used to set up fictitious economic activity.

Melting Pot Pluralism and Structural Pluralism

Where groups with unlike spheres of values co-exist, the result is a pluralistic society. Norwegian anthropologist Frederik Barth[4] placed great emphasis on the existence of different spheres of values. Central to his discussion is the concept of the entrepreneur being an essential broker, mediating boundary transfers in this situation of contacts between cultures. By being active in the transformation of a community, entrepreneurs are the social agents of change.

Enterprise is very much influenced by the nature of pluralism. It is, therefore, important to distinguish between **melting pot pluralism**, and **structural pluralism.** When people, from different cultures, share activities in a secular mainstream arena, the expression of cultural differences tends to be limited to private life. Often, employment is shared in a common sphere of life, while cuisine, customs, languages and religion are a domestic concern. This form of socio-economic pluralism is referred to as **melting pot pluralism**, and this is descriptive of the situation in Singapore.

In contrast, **structural pluralism** involves a society with different cultures that do *not* share a secular mainstream arena. In such a case, there is minimal interaction across cultures. Rather, each ethnic group has its distinct institutions, and members of a given community have a lifestyle that is incompatible with that of people from other backgrounds. This type of pluralism is prevalent in Xinjiang (China).

---

[4] See Barth (1963; 1966; 1967a; 1967b; 1981).

Toward an Understanding of Transition

Cambodia, China, Laos, Myanmar and Vietnam are among many countries referred to as being in transition to a market economy. As China prospers, it is useful to keep in mind that transition requires more than funding and infrastructure. Transition also involves mind-set. Business takes place between people, and the interaction between the parties does not take place in a vacuum, but rather it is part of a social system, as discussed by Hakansson (1982).

Central to transactions are the cultural assumptions of a social system. In the West, these are implicit because it is assumed that everyone knows about them; marketing takes place in the context of a firm-type economy. In transitional economies, environmental factors must not be ignored. As discussed by Huntington (1996), globalisation has not led to a single world culture.

The move to a market economy — transition — is process-driven, and this necessitates the understanding of people and their culture. The focus of the following chapter, therefore, is culture.

Chapter 2

Culture and Enterprise[1]

Introduction

Globalisation may have given rise to a global village, but has not produced a homogeneous world culture. Instead, there are different belief systems, each with its set of customs. This is important because culture shapes managerial assumptions. While that which goes on around the negotiation table is important, everything that surrounds a deal is equally influential — spoken or unspoken.

Many managers report frustrations when doing business in Asia, particularly when delaying tactics appear during negotiations. Du Ding-Ping, in his book about how to do business with Americans, explains that delays help the Chinese during negotiations with Westerners. Perhaps knowing this may be a good reminder of the Western notion that "patience is a virtue" and that it might be beneficial to adhere to this virtue when doing business with Asians. Developing the ability to be patient and tolerant can surprisingly speed up negotiations; inflexibility and haste may, more often than not, lead to a bad relationship, what the Chinese call *guanxi gao jiang*.

Business increasingly involves interaction with foreign suppliers, employees, distributors, clients and government officials. Each operates in a particular environment, where interactions involve implicit and explicit assumptions. This is a function of the complex belief systems, cultural values and attitudes that dictate accepted norms of conduct.

It is of crucial importance for people in business to understand cultural differences. Yet, many Westerners often fail to acknowledge the extent to which culture affects enterprise.

---

[1] This chapter draws heavily on material published in an article commissioned by the *Financial Times* (Dana, 2000c).

It is not a matter of noting the "different ways" that "those" people have; it is considerably more useful to understand the rationale behind these ways. Everything has a reason, and actions may have implications. In contrast to the short-term focus of many companies in the West, Asians often have a longer-range plan. Also, Asian entrepreneurs are generally reluctant to share their implicit assumptions with outsiders.

Many Asians have mastered the comprehension of Western culture and have developed the ability to adapt to it; they have built on the knowledge conveyed to them by a variety of sources. In contrast, Westerners seldom have the patience to master an Asian language, let alone one of its cultures. Complex cultural environments require fluency not only in words, but also more importantly in understanding of what is not said — and this takes time, patience and dedication to learn. Westerners may argue that time is money and they cannot afford to learn everything it takes before even discussing a deal. In the long term, however, more knowledge does pay off.

The Chinese Experience

The dominant culture in Asian business is that of the Chinese. This is not surprising, considering that ethnic Chinese are well represented in the realm of business around the world and very concentrated in Asian countries. In Ho Chi Minh City — formerly Saigon — for instance, 12% of the population is ethnic Chinese, and this group controls half of the local economy.

Given the widespread influence of Chinese culture, one would think that it is appropriate for Western businesses to take the time to learn something about this culture and how it affects business; yet, even large and global players have made costly errors. In 1979, Northern Telecom was approached to provide new switching equipment for China. The communications giant underestimated the importance of "face" and embarrassed Chinese officials. When the company tried to get a deal with China in 1987, the Chinese officials remembered that Northern Telecom had "walked away from negotiations in 1979." This time, the tables were turned: although Northern Telecom was eager to do business, the Chinese negotiators were not.

Networking as Viewed from the Occident

Networking involves calling upon a web of contacts for information, support and assistance. Aldrich and Zimmer (1986) integrated social network theory into the study of entrepreneurship. They linked entrepreneurship to social networks. Carsrud, Gaglio and Olm (1986) also found networks important to the understanding of new venture development. Aldrich, Rosen and Woodward (1987) studied the impact of social networks on profit, as well as on business creation; they found network accessibility significant in predicting new venture creation. Likewise, Dubini and Aldrich (1991) found networks central to entrepreneurship. Gomes-Casseres (1997) focused on the alliance strategies of small firms. Anderson (1995) and Johanson and Associates (1994) studied the effect of business networks on internationalisation of firms. Indeed, networks can influence a firm's degree of internationalisation (Dana, Etemad and Wright, 2000).

Boissevain and Grotenbreg (1987), in their study of the Surinamese in Amsterdam, suggested that access to a network of contacts is an important resource for entrepreneurs. They noted, for instance, that networks could provide introductions to wholesalers and warnings of government inspections. In their study of Asians in Atlanta, Min and Jaret (1985), found family networks to be a source of manpower for entrepreneurs. Analysing Asian entrepreneurs in Britain, Aldrich, Jones and McEvoy found that their sample benefited from "certain advantages denied non-ethnic competitors (1984, p. 193)." They found a strong internal solidarity in the ethnic enclave. Given that the possibility of exploiting opportunities appears to be linked to the internal organising capacity of a group — such as creating an ethnic network — Auster and Aldrich (1984) concluded that the ethnic enclave reduces the vulnerability of small firms, by providing an ethnic market and also general social and economic support, including credit. Others who focused on ethnic minority enterprise include Aldrich and Waldinger (1990), Cummings (1980), Dana (1995a), Jenkins (1984), Light (1972; 1984), Light and Bonacich (1988), Min (1984; 1986–7; 1987), Portes and Bach (1985), Portes and Jensen (1987; 1989; 1992), Sanders and Nee (1987), Waldinger (1984; 1986a; 1986b), Waldinger and Aldrich (1990), Waldinger, Aldrich and Ward (1990), Waldinger, McEvoy and Aldrich (1990), Ward (1987), Ward and Jenkins (1984) Wong (1987), and Wu (1983).

Networking in Asia

Aspects of networking reflect historical, cultural and demographic factors. In contrast to the situation prevailing in many industrialised countries, where voluntary migration prompted members of some immigrant minorities to create networks to help other members of their community (Acs and Dana, 2001; Boissevain and Grotenbreg, 1987; Brenner and Toulouse, 1990; Dyer and Ross, 2000; Iyer and Shapiro, 1999; Light, 1984), much of the demographic shifting in Asia resulted from forced migration.

Migration to Central Asia was largely the result of civil engineering, rather than a voluntary migration of entrepreneurs with a high need for achievement (McClelland, 1961). Today, Muslims in western China have networks of like-minded co-ethnics in neighbouring countries, and this has enhanced opportunities for trade. International transactions are facilitated by the fact that members of ethnic networks speak the same language, and share similar values, influenced by the same religion.[2]

Figure 2.1 Muslim in China; photograph by Léo-Paul Dana.

[2] For a discussion of how religion influences entrepreneurship, see Dana (2009).

In spite of the political divide, which separated the Kazakhs in China from those in the Soviet Union, the Kazakhs in China feel that they have more in common with their co-ethnics in the republics of Central Asia, than with the Han-Chinese who rule them. The Han-Chinese read Mandarin and eat dishes that include pork. The Kazakhs — like the Uygurs and other Muslims in China — are often trained in Arabic script, and of course they would feel uncomfortable at a table where pork has been served. Indeed, entrepreneurs are comfortable doing business with like-minded people, whom they understand, and with whom they get along. Inevitably, entrepreneurs form networks (Dana, 2001a). Where civil servants are poorly paid, it is no secret that bribes are welcome. In these scenarios, business networks include government officials, as well as entrepreneurs.

Roles in Society

Confucianism teaches that people are *not* equal. To this day, people in China are defined by their role in society and contribution to it. Status is influenced by relationships and these are attached to implicit duties and obligations. People are viewed as relation-oriented beings, regulated by cardinal relationships that dictate an individual's obligations — *renqing* — toward other people. Observance of proper relationships is essential for the smooth functioning of society.

In Laos, for instance, the ethnic Chinese have become highly successful entrepreneurs, partly thanks to the lack of a local entrepreneurial culture. Business activities in this country have not been traditionally associated with high social status. Stemming from religious beliefs, cultural values in Laos emphasise the elimination of desire. Since commerce was traditionally perceived as a means to satisfy desire, social forces discouraged enterprise, and trade has usually been the role of those with inferior social standing. The communist takeover further discouraged entrepreneurial spirit. In Laos, culture makes it important to extinguish unsatisfied yearnings. An important doctrine, here, focuses on suffering caused by unsatisfied wishes. Assuming that an unsatisfied craving causes suffering, then suffering can be eliminated if its cause — desire — is suppressed. According to this ideology, a respectable person strives to eliminate a perceived material need, rather than working toward the satisfaction of materialistic wants. Not surprisingly, ethnic minorities, especially the Chinese, dominate private enterprise, in Laos.

Guanxi

In the Chinese realm of business, a special relationship — *guanxi* — involves the exchange of favours, usually involving position or rank. It is similar to insurance, inasmuch as favours are registered — like premiums — so that benefits may be obtained if and when required. *Guanxi*, composed of two words, *guan* — meaning "to close up" — and *xi* — "to tie up" — expresses the notion of being an insider to a relationship network that involves obligations. *La guanxi* refers to the act of getting on one's good side.

While Western business-people usually have a general understanding of this concept, relatively few Westerners realise that the mutual obligation is a function of one's ability to help, explaining why the weaker party accepts to receive more, in exchange for less. Furthermore, *guanxi* is not easy for Westerners to develop. *Guanxi* is intuitive, rather than rational, and it is not limited to business hours.

In the West, relationship marketing — the pursuit of customer loyalty — involves the fostering of long-term alliances with customers; in a similar fashion, *guanxi* involves building a long-term relationship, based on trust and mutual exchange, in order to secure customer loyalty and good working relations. *Guanxi* forms a bond among buyers and sellers and between suppliers and producers.

Westerners seeking joint venture partners in China should seek the ideal partner using connections maintained through *guanxi*; simultaneously, the foreigner would benefit by linking up with a company that has enough *guanxi* to get things done efficiently in China. For companies regulated by legislation such as the American Foreign Corrupt Practice Act, this is not an easy task; difficulty increases if and when a joint venture is established and the venture must maintain the *guanxi* of counterparts in China. Furthermore, it is important to look at the whole — not simply the parts.

Guanxi has long been important in Chinese business circles. The West has known contract law since the 1700s; the purpose of such legislation is to give business an assurance that deals will be honoured. In the absence of an elaborate contract law, the Chinese have relied on *guanxi* for the same assurance. When a relationship is more valuable than a transaction, then it is likely that the transaction will be smooth. Who would tarnish a relationship for a single transaction? No contract is necessary. The sense of obligation would come from the relationship, rather than a piece of paper.

On the other hand, in the absence of a strong relationship, there exists the possibility that one of the parties might ignore a contract. For example, although it had 18 years remaining on its lease, McDonald's was evicted from a Beijing site in favour of a newcomer with stronger *guanxi*. In Chinese circles, it is therefore more crucial to monitor a relationship than a transaction. Where a strong relationship exists, problems can always be solved. The long-term benefit of *guanxi* becomes obvious. During the process of cultivating *guanxi* within business relationships, customer loyalty evolves naturally, while bonds are created with suppliers and with creditors. *Guanxi* rests on the moral premise of *renqing*, as a justification for social exchange. In a Chinese cultural setting, *guanxi* is the norm for carrying on business.

Adapting to the Environment

One might argue that Western companies also value relationships and that these hold mutual obligations. There is, however, an important difference between the Chinese and Western views of relationships.

> *In the West, successful transactions lead to good relationships. In Chinese circles, one builds relationships in order to initiate transactions; the common belief is that if a relationship is built properly, then profitable transactions will follow.*

As explained by Peng and Heath (1996) reciprocal preferential treatment reduces transaction costs.

Every region has a predominant culture and there are many intricacies intertwined into each one. Just as Europe hosts many different cultures,[3] there is neither one single culture nor one single way of doing business in Asia. The key for those attempting business there is to have patience and to learn as much as possible about what is important to each company, manager and worker.

As stated so well by Lasserre and Schütte, "The West cannot expect to compete successfully with Asia as long as the Asians know more about the West than the West knows about Asia (1995, p. xv)."

---

[3] See Dana (2005; 2006).

Chapter 3

Cambodia[1]

Indochina

This chapter is about Cambodia, one of the countries (the other two being Laos and Vietnam[2]) of the land which was formerly referred to as *Indochine française* — French Indochina. There are some important differences, as well as similarities, among the constituents of this region. As explained by Moore and Williams, China and India were the cultural parents of Indochina, making it a "mosaic of Indian and Chinese cultures (1951, p. 462)." Hindu Brahmans sparked the native genius of the early Khmers, while Chinese officials lent their culture to the Annamese. Under colonial rule, the whole region used the same currency, the Indochinese *piastre* — issued by the *Banque de l'Indochine*.

Traditionally, in Cambodia, the ownership of land was strongly individual in nature. In contrast, a tradition of communally owned land existed among the Vietnamese. Long observed:

> Unlike Viet Nam, which took China as its teacher, Cambodia and Laos received much of their art, religion, and language from India. Both countries resemble Thailand more than they do their Indochinese neighbor...Nor has Cambodian writing been changed to Roman letters like Viet Nam's; it uses graceful, rounded lines of Sanscrit (1952, p. 312).

---

[1] This chapter is based on information obtained from a variety of sources, including the Ministry of Commerce and the Ministry of Economy and Finance of Cambodia. The chapter includes historical material that first appeared in Dana (1999b; 2002).

[2] Literally, Vietnam means "people of the south."

Figure 3.1 Currency of the *Banque de l'Indochine.*

Indeed, in contrast to the adjacent area — today corresponding to southern Vietnam — which had its status changed to that of a colony and its alphabet changed to the Roman one, Cambodia had relatively little Occidental influence. Cambodia retained its monarchy and its script.

Williams wrote, "Between the India of unrest and stormy China is an oasis of peace and beauty — French Indo-China, composed of one colony and four protectorates (1935, p. 487)." Zasloff (1988) examined post-war Indochina. Vietnam became independent on September 2, 1945, Laos on July 19, 1949, and Cambodia on November 9, 1953.

In the 21st century, there are still important differences to be found when comparing the Kingdom of Cambodia, the Lao People's Democratic Republic, and the Socialist Republic of Vietnam. Their paths to transition follow quite unlike models.

In Cambodia, a true veritable transition has taken place. This involves complete "restructuring" under the constitutional monarchy. Cambodia has already privatised most state-owned enterprises, and import licenses have been abolished for most items. O'Driscoll, Holmes and Kirkpatrick (2001), described Cambodia as being freer[3] than any other transition economy of Asia. They showed that the government in Cambodia is less of a fiscal burden than is the case in the other countries of Indochina. Nevertheless, as observed by Prasso, "compared to neighboring Laos and Vietnam, which have also struggled to recover from an era of war and bloodshed, Cambodia remains far behind in its ability to establish the most basic building blocks of economic recovery…. Domestic savings rates are stunningly low compared to other Asian countries (2001, p. 2)."

O'Driscoll, Holmes and Kirkpatrick (2001) described Cambodia as having less black market activity than any other transitional economy in Asia. These authors also revealed that the economies of Laos and Vietnam each had more government intervention than is the case in Cambodia. While Cambodia has fewer restrictions on foreign direct investment, than other countries described in this book, Laos was imposed the most.

In contrast to situation in Laos, where transition was centrally planned by a heavy bureaucracy, Cambodia embraced free enterprise, with significant restructuring. In Vietnam, the Communist Party has taken steps, to "renovate" the economy with some transitional measures; yet, there has been no attempt to "restructure."

Cambodian law has included legislation influenced by the United Nations Transitional Assistance in Cambodia (UNTAC), as well as royal decrees. In contrast, the legal system of Laos is largely based on traditional customs and Soviet practice. The law in Vietnam blends communist theory with the French Civil Code.

In addition to differences among the countries of Indochina, there is also heterogeneity *within* each country. Most noticeable is the ethnic Chinese minority, very active in enterprise. Over half a century ago, Moore stated, "keen traders, Indochina's 500,000 Chinese dominate many businesses (1950, p. 508)." Centrally planning has since come and gone, and the Chinese are still involved in entrepreneurial activity.

---

[3] Beach and O'Driscoll defined economic freedom, as "the absence of government coercion or constraint on the production, distribution, or consumption of goods and services beyond the extent necessary for citizens to protect and maintain liberty itself (2001, pp. 43–44)."

Cambodia

Cambodia covers 181,035 square kilometres. It lies on the Gulf of Siam, bordering Laos, Thailand, and Vietnam. Although Cambodia is a target for Chinese investment, it remains among the least developed countries in the world. Traditionally, the people of Cambodia — known as Khmers — were not inclined to become entrepreneurs, as enterprise was not seen as contributing to Buddhist society. A merchant class developed after independence, but during the 1970s, the Khmer Rouge — officially the Communist Party of Kampuchea — extinguished private enterprise in this country. More recently, the ownership of property was legalised, and the nation embarked on a comprehensive programme of transition to a market economy. In Cambodia, today, ethnic Chinese largely comprise the upper and middle class that is active in commerce. In setting up ventures, they rely largely on family and co-ethnics (Verner, 2012; Verner and Dahles, 2013).

Figure 3.2 Entrepreneurial Spirit; photograph by Léo-Paul Dana.

Figure 3.3 Change in the Air; photograph by Léo-Paul Dana.

Historical Overview[4]

About 2,000 years ago, much of that which is Cambodia today belonged to the Kingdom of Funan — a prosperous nation frequented by merchants travelling between India and China (for a detailed account, see (Chandler, 1999)). At the time, Mahayana Buddhism flourished alongside the religion and culture of the Hindus.

[4] This section benefited greatly from the personal assistance of David P. Chandler, PhD, Professor *Emeritus* of History, at Monash University, and Adjunct Professor of Asian Studies at Georgetown University. Professor Chandler is recognised as the leading authority on Cambodian history.

During the 6th century, the Kambu'jas — literally "those born from Kambu" — established a kingdom in the interior of present-day Cambodia. Chinese travellers knew this kingdom as Chenla. Its people associated themselves with Kambu, a figure of Indian mythology and the nation became known as Kampuchea, a derivative of Kambu'ja.[5]

In 802, a Khmer prince declared himself a universal monarch, and founded a dynasty that lasted until Angkor was abandoned in the 16th century (Chandler, 1999). During the Angkorian period — 9th to 15th century — the civilisation stretched into parts of today's Laos, Thailand and Vietnam. Indravarman, who ruled from 889 to 910, built an elaborate irrigation system. Jayavarman VII, who ruled from 1181 to 1201, built a new capital — Angkor Thom.[6] During the 13th century, the nation gave up Hinduism, in favour of Buddhism. The official language of the Hindu priests was also abandoned.

Over the next two centuries, several tributary states — in what is now Thailand — declared their independence and invaded Cambodian territory (Chandler, 1999). The capital city shifted away from Angkor to the region of Phnom Penh.

In 1860, King Norodom ascended to the throne. Fearful of nearby Siam — as Thailand was then known — in 1863, King Norodom asked France to provide protection, and he subsequently signed a treaty with Napoleon III, making Cambodia a French protectorate. In 1904, King Norodom was succeeded by King Sisowath, who reigned until 1927.

King Sisowath was succeeded by King Monivong, who died during the early phases of Japanese occupation. Prince Norodom Sihanouk — born on October 31, 1922 — was crowned king, in 1941. After the Japanese surrender, in 1945, France made Cambodia an autonomous state within the French Union — but retained control over its diplomatic, financial and military affairs. In 1953, the *Royaume du Cambodge* — Kingdom of Cambodia — declared its independence, which was recognised in May 1954 by the Geneva Conference. Self-sufficient in food, the new kingdom enjoyed economic growth and became a net exporter of rice (Ear, 1995; Prud'Homme, 1969; Steinberg, 1959). In 1955, Sihanouk abdicated, but remained for 15 years the leading political figure in Cambodia.

---

[5] The Portuguese later modified *Kambu'ja* to *Camboxa*. The French adapted it to *Cambodge*. When anglicised, the name became "Cambodia."

[6] *Angkor* means "the city," in Khmer, while *Thom* means "large."

Although Cambodian-American relations deteriorated after Cambodia rejected the American economic and military aid programme, in November 1963, Cambodia remained officially "neutral." Radio Phnom Penh subsequently stepped up anti-American propaganda (Abercrombie, 1964). For a lucid account of Sihanouk's policy of neutrality, see Hamel (1993).

In 1969, the United States began bombing suspected communist camps in Cambodia. The population of Phnom Penh was slightly more than half a million at the time, and Cambodia was agriculturally prosperous.

In March 1970, General Lon Nol staged a successful *coup d'état*. Sihanouk was deposed and moved to Beijing. The country was renamed the Khmer Republic. Chantrabot (1993) gave a detailed account of that era.

On April 30, 1970, American and South Vietnamese troops attacked Cambodia. During the following years, hundreds of thousands of people were killed, and many fled from rural areas to Phnom Penh. By 1975, the capital city was home to two million people.

On April 17, 1975 the Khmer Rouge, a group whose goal was to transform the nation into an agrarian peasant-dominated Maoist co-operative, overran the republic. Under the leadership of Saloth Sar — who used the pseudonym Pol Pot[7] — the Khmer Rouge transformed the nation (Jackson, 1989), as the new regime confiscated private property, banned currency and changed the name of the country to Democratic Kampuchea. Millions of city dwellers were ordered to evacuate their homes and to migrate to the countryside; they were told that these measures were being taken in order to avoid bombings by the United States.

Cambodians interviewed by the author explained that the Khmer Rouge communists slit the throat of their prisoners, in order to save ammunition. Women's nipples were removed with pliers, and victims were left to scorpions.

Border clashes between the Khmer Rouge and the Vietnamese led to an invasion by Vietnam on December 25, 1978. On January 7, 1979, Vietnam toppled the Khmer Rouge regime. Again, the name of the country was changed, this time to the People's Republic of Kampuchea. Currency was re-introduced and people were again permitted to reside in towns.

---

[7] For a discussion, see Chandler, Kiernan and Boua (1988).

Figure 3.4 French Colonial Architecture; photograph by Léo-Paul Dana.

Figure 3.5 Buddhist Monk in Phnom Penh; photograph by Léo-Paul Dana.

Many ethnic Chinese landlords escaped to France and the United States before the Khmer Rouge take-over, but the Khmer Rouge killed remaining urban landlords. When people returned to Phnom Penh, rice fields were abandoned; famine followed. During the 1980s, the Soviet Union and Vietnam contributed food to Kampuchea.

In 1991, the United Nations brokered a peace accord known as the Paris Agreement, which was signed in October that same year. On October 31, the United Nations Security Council agreed to establish the United Nations Transitional Assistance in Cambodia (UNTAC).

The Khmer Rouge continued fighting in the jungle, and in January 1992, riots broke out in Phnom Penh — with the return of nominal Khmer Rouge leader, Khieu Samphan. On February 28, 1992, the United Nations Security Council voted to send a force of 22,000 to Cambodia.

Figure 3.6 Landlords Gone; photograph by Léo-Paul Dana.

Although the signing of the peace accord strengthened the riel, the influx of United Nations peacekeeping troops contributed to higher prices and subsequent devaluation. Profiteers took advantage of the situation (Verver, 2012). Retailers and even government ministries began refusing local currency. Inflation, in 1992, was 177%, while per capita GNP was $150. Government employees were earning low wages and often pursued sideline opportunities. The 1993 constitution re-established the monarchy. Norodom Sihanouk was crowned king, once again, on September 23. In 1994, the literacy rate edged up to 35%. During the first weekend of July 1997, a *coup d'état* by Hun Sen — holding the position of Second Prime Minister — overthrew Prince Norodom Ranariddh, the so-called Prime Minister. The nation was scheduled to join the Association of Southeast Asian Nations (ASEAN) — along with Laos and Myanmar — on July 23, 1997. However, on July 10, the members of ASEAN decided to postpone admitting Cambodia into the association.

The last Khmer Rouge fighter surrendered in December 1998. On April 30, 1999, Cambodia officially joined ASEAN. The other members were Brunei, Indonesia, Laos, Malaysia, Myanmar, the Philippines, Singapore, Thailand and Vietnam.

The 2001 land act allowed people to claim land they had cultivated for 30 years. This led to new problems (Hughes and Un, 2011).

In 2006, New Zealander Jane Nye, the 28-year-old editor of the *Cambodian Scene* magazine, had her throat slashed during a robbery at a bar in Phnom Penh. The entrepreneur who owned the bar was stabbed to death. In 2010, a new law governing foreign ownership expanded the rights of foreigners to own property in Cambodia.

Changing Policies and the Royal Cambodian Model

Under colonial rule, Cambodia's public policy was dictated by France, which was actually more interested in neighbouring Cochin-China — the area around Saigon, as Ho Chi Minh City was then known. In Cambodia, the French left the economy to market forces, but taxes raised in Cambodia were used to develop Cochin-China. Large-scale rubber plantations in Cambodia — which belonged to Europeans — imported workers from the area known today as Vietnam, justifying this by a claim that the local people were less productive. Since Cambodia, Laos and the other constituents[8] of French Indochina used the same *piastre*, this facilitated such "imports."

French control ended with the independence of Cambodia. The *Banque National du Cambodge* (National Bank of Cambodia) introduced the local currency — the riel, which was pegged to 23.3905 mg. of gold. From 1953 to 1970, Sihanouk implemented a policy of national socialism. In the 1955 elections, the *Sangkum Reastr Niyum* (People's Socialist Community) won every seat in parliament. Although socialist policies were introduced, about 80% of the farmers remained the proprietors of the land that they farmed. Most of the farmers cultivated rice, and many raised animals. In urban areas, the ethnic Chinese controlled the economic sphere; 77% of these were Teochew Chinese from Guang Dong Province, in China.

Sihanouk introduced his first economic plan in 1956. It was a two-year plan, the budget of which the United States paid 57%, China 23%

---

[8] These were Annam, Cochin-China, and Tonkin, later consolidated as Vietnam.

and France 17%. Only 3% of the budget was raised by Cambodia. The two-year plan emphasised the role of capital, but ignored private investment and entrepreneurship. The plan was renewed for another two years, beginning in 1958. After that, the Planning Ministry began to set longer plans. The first of these covered 1960 to 1964.

In 1963, private banks were nationalised and austerity measures resulted in many tariffs being doubled. A new economic plan covered the period 1964 to 1968 and another the years 1968 to 1972. In April 1975, the Khmer Rouge implemented an unprecedented policy reform. During the last two weeks of April, the Khmer Rouge evacuated Phnom Penh, forcing every urban resident out of the city and into slave-labour camps in the countryside.

The regime proclaimed 1975 as Year Zero (Ponchaud, 1977). Private property, in theory and in practice, ceased to exist. The Central Bank was blown up, other banks were closed, currency was abolished, postal service ceased to exist, and the regime caused the death of over 1.5 million[9] Khmers — out of a national population of about seven million — eliminating intellectuals, landlords, entrepreneurs and the business sector. Market activities were banned and all commercial transactions were outlawed. In addition to a change in clothing, individuals were allowed only two items of private property, namely a bowl and a spoon. The urban areas, including the capital city, Phnom Penh, were depopulated and would remain empty for over three years. All flights to and from Democratic Kampuchea were halted — except a fortnightly flight linking Phnom Penh with Beijing. The regime designed a four-year plan for the period 1977 to 1980. In 1977, people were required to participate in communal cooking and eating, as Pol Pot banned the private ownership of pots and pans.

When the Khmer Rouge regime was driven from power in 1979, trade resumed, but in the absence of a national currency; commerce relied on barter or foreign money. Only in March 1980 was currency reintroduced, and then only within the context of a socialist economy. Cigarettes, condensed milk, kerosene, rice, soap and sugar were subsidised by the state, but goods were rationed. During the 1980s, the government devalued the Kampuchean currency. In 1984, $1 bought 7 riels; by the end of the decade, $1 was worth 380 riels.

---

[9] Vietnamese sources claim the figure to be 3 million.

After the 1989 withdrawal of the Vietnamese from Cambodia, reforms enhanced the economic environment for entrepreneurs to operate in the private sector. The local authorities divided farmland and distributed it to those living on it. In the urban areas, the Law of Private Ownership allowed persons to claim title to property occupied, and even to sell it.

In August 1991, the National Assembly passed the Law on the Management of Exchange, Precious Metals and Stones. This legislation contained 20 articles governing foreign exchange, precious metals and gems. In November, the Foreign Exchange Decree supplemented this law.

By 1992, three quarters of the economy was in private hands. Some entrepreneurs operated from their homes, while others lived in their shops. Smaller-scale vendors set up impromptu stalls. Petrol was sold on roadsides, in used soda-pop bottles. Entrepreneurs were required to pay a signage tax and, therefore, many merchants opted to have no sign.

Figure 3.7 Tiger Beer Could Afford Signs; photograph by Léo-Paul Dana.

A new constitution introduced the Royal Cambodian Model in 1993. Article 56 specified that the kingdom would have a market economy. In an attempt to improve the inadequate infrastructure, in November 1993, the kingdom participated in the formation of Royal Air Cambodge, to supplement the operations of state-owned Kampuchea Airlines. Royal Air Cambodge was established as a joint venture, 60% owned by the government and 40% by a Malaysian affiliate of Malaysia Airlines (MAS). Linking Phnom Penh with Bangkok, Guangzhou, Ho Chi Minh City, Hong Kong, Kuala Lumpur and Singapore, Royal Air Cambodge became the largest airline in Cambodia. Yet, between 1994 and 2001, the firm lost over $30 million. In September 2001, flights to Ho Chi Minh City were suspended. On October 16, 2001, the airline stopped flying.

In August 1994, liberal laws were implemented to encourage entrepreneurship in the kingdom. A very lenient implementation of public policy allowed corruption to persist (Ear, 2011). Also in 1994, special zoning laws were introduced, to limit development in the area of Siem Reap; only small-scale ventures were allowed near Angkor Wat, and large hotels were required to be four kilometres away. Nevertheless, entrepreneurs could bribe officials and obtain exemptions. In the French daily *Figaro,* Desjardins (1997) dubbed Cambodia the "Kingdom of Corruption."

In 1994, the dollar traded at 2,400 riels and the inflation rate fell to 26%, but fighting escalated. Brown and Zasloff (1999) provided a detailed account of peacekeeping efforts. In 1995, although the Khmer Rouge continued to control its stronghold — in the northwest of the country — economic growth approached 5%; per capita GNP was $215, while inflation stood at 3.5%. The average value of $1 was 2,451 riels in 1995, 2,624 riels in 1996, and 2,938 riels in 1997. Then came the Asian Financial Crisis. By 2006, $1 bought 4,230 riels. (In 2013, the rate was around 4,100 riels per dollar.)

The Nature of Entrepreneurship

Entrepreneurship in Cambodia developed rapidly after independence from France. In 1955, there were 650 small and medium-scale factories in Cambodia. By 1968, there were almost 4,000. Most entrepreneurs, however, were not industrialists. Many were speculators who tried to make fast money in alcohol, beef, gold, land, tobacco, salt and other commodities. These people also contributed to economic instability. The economy collapsed during the era of the Khmer Republic, which lasted from 1970 to 1975. Manufacturing declined due to shortages of inputs. The republic financed its deficit by printing money and imposing a 60% Value Added Tax (VAT) on cigarettes.

White (1982) reported on covert economic activity in Cambodia. The article described entrepreneurs dealing in contraband goods smuggled to Kampuchea from Thailand. These included cigarettes, medicines, soap and watches. A decade later, the *Far Eastern Economic Review* ran a cover story (Chandra and Tasker, 1992) describing the widespread activities of Thai entrepreneurs who were extracting gems from Cambodia.

In 1995, the *Washington Post* described Cambodia as a "pre-emerging market." That same year, *Paris Match* reported that prostitution was Phnom Penh's leading industry, with 10,000 prostitutes in town and another 10,000 elsewhere in the country. The prominent French magazine explained that virgins were rented for 2,500FF[10] before being discounted to 200FF. While opium was worth 150FF per gram, a bag containing 200 grams of cannabis cost 10FF. Marijuana was traded openly and commonly added as flavouring, in soups. Meanwhile, some entrepreneurs made 6-year-old children work in factories. Other children became entrepreneurs themselves, taking advantage of arbitrage opportunities, selling food and drinks to long-distance travellers on boats, buses and trains. Desjardins (1997) described how government employees in Cambodia were selling, for personal gain, rubber and wood that belonged to the state, in addition to medicines donated by foreign parties, and meant for free distribution.

On March 7, 1999, the *Japan Times* (1999) described poverty-driven Cambodian entrepreneurs dealing in rare animals and their products. In Phnom Penh, an entrepreneur offered an endangered sun bear for sale, for $600.

Entrepreneurship in Cambodia tends to take the form of micro-entrepreneurship, and this is compatible with the traditional way of life here. Most enterprises in this country are family-based.

For entrepreneurs wishing to expand their enterprises, VisionFund Cambodia provides business training and small loans. During 2013, 1.3 million Cambodians had micro-finance loans.

---

[10] The French franc (FF) was the currency of France until the introduction of the euro (€) on January 1, 2002. The euro was valued at 6.55957 FF.

Figure 3.8 Dehydrated Mammals For Sale; photograph by Léo-Paul Dana.

Pluralism

The Chinese always had a significant impact on the economy in Cambodia. Gold, silver and coins were introduced to Cambodia by the Chinese, and Chinese traders flourished at Angkor. Immigrants from China came to dominate the realm of business.

Traditionally, the ethnic Khmers tended to be attracted to occupations related to agriculture, government service, and monastic life; commerce and industry were occupations that were left to ethnic minorities. Muslims controlled the cattle trade, commercial fisheries and the weaving industry. The ethnic Chinese engaged in international trade and in retailing.

Abercrombie reported on the situation during 1964, "Nearly a third of Phnom Penh's population of 403,500 are Chinese. Together with Vietnamese importers, shopkeepers, and moneylenders, they dominate the city's — and the country's — commerce. In the shops strange goods caught my eye: dogmeat sausages, incense sticks, begging bowls... (1964, p. 518)." Notice that the above account does not mention Khmer entrepreneurs. Elaborating on the ethnic Chinese, in Cambodia, Abercrombie explained, "Rarely holding citizenship, they maintain their own language, customs, and schools (1964, p. 526)."

Although Cambodia is less heterogeneous than other countries in Asia, it does have important minority groups. The ethnic Chinese community is concentrated in entrepreneurial activities. The Vietnamese in Cambodia are often associated with fishing-related occupations. Although both of these minorities have suffered persecution in Cambodia — especially the Vietnamese — the Chinese are emerging as an important economic force, and Chinese aid is crucial to the well being of the current regime. Cambodia is also home to some 200,000 Cham Muslims and members of the Khmer Loeu hill-tribe.

Dahles and Ter Horst (2012) observed that key commercial positions in the Cambodian silk trading networks are dominated by the Chinese. Their paper explains how their business practices and representations may develop into an institution that is both a model of and for conducting business.

Toward the Future

Average tariff rates are lower in Cambodia than in China and elsewhere. There is less official government intervention in Cambodia than in many other countries. Comparing the fiscal burden of governments, Cambodia scored very low on the list. Yet, further investigation suggests that this may be an optimistic picture. Wright and Innes-Brown (2009), hint at challenges ahead.

Naranhkiri Tith, Professor of International Economics and Asian Studies, at John Hopkins University, explained to the author: "Tax burden is low because of the inability to tax and not because of the willingness not to burden the tax payers; tariff is low because room must be left for corruption...and the official government intervention is less but corruption—a form of unofficial government intervention — is pervasive."

Although most enterprises in Cambodia are privately held, entrepreneurship in this kingdom is concentrated in grey or black market areas. Casinos and shady banks are said to launder money. Can causal variables be identified? One explanation is that the historical experience of this nation makes immediate gains more attractive than waiting for an uncertain future. All middle-aged Cambodians can remember the day money was made useless; the result is a predisposition to reject currency as a medium for savings and for large purchases, Cambodians often used the *damleung* (1.2 ounces of gold) to buy property, and *the chi* (0.13 ounces of gold) for items such as televisions (Prasso, 2001).

Figure 3.9 Grey Market Activity; photograph by Léo-Paul Dana.

Entrepreneurship in Cambodia is largely short-term in nature, due to high risks and uncertainty. People use a young tree for firewood, as they are impatient to wait seven years for it to produce rubber. Yet, younger entrepreneurs are setting up firms with a long-term orientation (Verver, 2012). Entrepreneurship remains largely the realm of the political elite, and of the large informal sector including ethnic Chinese, Sino-Khmer, and Vietnamese owners of micro-businesses. The layer of middle class entrepreneurs is thin and often under pressure by various forces acting to the disadvantage of this segment.

Figure 3.10 Toward the Future; photograph by Léo-Paul Dana.

Case Study: No. 8 Wire Entrepreneurialism

New Zealand's geographic isolation meant that ordering spare parts for vehicles traditionally took long periods of time. Enter Kiwi ingenuity and No. 8 wire.

Until the 1970s, it was relatively difficult for New Zealanders to buy an automobile, and when they had one, they took care of it! Until the 1980s, damaged car parts were panel-beaten, rather than disposed of and replaced. Today, New Zealand has skilled craftsmen who know how to restore and even reconstruct classic cars. This has been a competitive edge for Christchurch-based Auto Restorations Ltd.; motor vehicles from around the world are shipped to this firm in New Zealand, where they are restored before being sent back to their owners.

Located on Stewart Street, in Christchurch, Auto Restorations Ltd. had a sophisticated facility where cars are restored for customers in Australia, Europe, Japan, the United Kingdom, and the United States, as well as New Zealand. Managing Director Bruce Pidgeon had his team of talented craftsmen make carburettors, cylinder blocks, inlet manifolds, oil coolers, and superchargers. A staff of 23 took care of body-building, machining, mechanical work, and panel-beating. Some specialised jobs are linked to specific parts of cars. Local beech is used to make the wooden framework standard in many vintage automobiles. When mechanical parts cannot be repaired, new ones are produced, sometimes starting out with a wooden pattern, and making a casting in a local foundry. Some castings are in bronze.

Others in the business include Bruce McIlroy (in Ashburton), Dave Brown's Classic Car Developments (in Invercargill) and Derek Prentice Classic Cars (in Christchurch). In an attempt to increase business from Europe, Derek Prentice Classic Cars has formed a strategic alliance with Upper Classics BV, a collectable car specialist in the Netherlands.

Also in this lucrative sector is Gerhard Heins, who was a medical doctor, in Germany, before coming to New Zealand where he launched Dr. Heins Classics Ltd., in Christchurch. Among Gerhard's fulltime staff is Richard Findlay, who is Chief Restorer. Much business is conducted with customers overseas.

Rather than concentrating on restoring old vehicles, engineer Dave Brown produces replicas. He begins researching a car six months before starting production; he obtains original factory drawings and ensures accurate reproductions. Whereas an original Jaguar C-type may sell for $1 million, Dave can sell a replica for $100,000. He sources some parts from overseas, and recently opted to develop a client base in the United States.

Case Study Assignment

A New Zealand man married to a Khmer woman is living in Phnom Penh. Given that salaries are low in Cambodia, he may be interested in restoring vehicles in Cambodia and exporting them to the world. Be his consultant and advise him who he might wish to network with and explain why. Also, prepare for him a business plan.

Figure 3.11 Restored 1957 Ford; photograph by Léo-Paul Dana.

Chapter 4

China[1]

Introduction

The People's Republic of China (PRC) — commonly referred to as mainland China, or simply China — covers 9,596,960 square kilometres, neighbouring Afghanistan, Bhutan, India, Kazakhstan, the Kyrgyz Republic, Laos, Mongolia, Myanmar, Nepal, North Korea, Pakistan, Russia, Tajikistan and Vietnam. China has shores along the East China Sea, the South China Sea, and the Yellow Sea. Since the 1970s, liberalisation of the Chinese economy led to dynamism among SMEs (Wang and Yao, 2002). Unlike the situation prevailing in Eastern Europe, in Cambodia and in other states that have abandoned communist ideology in favour of capitalism, entrepreneurship in the PRC was introduced by the government as a supplement to the socialist economy.

China is vibrant with entrepreneurial energy. In 2012, real GDP growth in China was 7.8%. The exchange rate in 2013 was approximately 6 RMB per dollar. In 2014, China was encouraging entrepreneurship, with a more selective approach than was the case in the past.

[1] This chapter is based on information obtained from a variety of sources, including: the China Council for the Promotion of International Trade (CCPIT); the CITIC Group; and the Ministry of Agriculture. Travel to China was funded by Nanyang Business School. The chapter includes historical material that first appeared in Dana (1998a; 1999a; 1999b; 1999d; 1999e; 2002).

Despite its success, in June 2001, China's Prime Minister Zhu Rongji declared that he was slowing down transition in the PRC, due difficulties created by economic reform. Ahlstrom and Bruton (2002) suggested that entrepreneurial firms employ specific tactics in order to navigate China's often hostile institutional environment. According to Minniti, Bygrave, and Autio (2006), the prevalence rate of informal investors is higher in China than in Thailand.

While the *guoying qiye* — literally, state-run enterprise — is the Chinese term to describe a collective enterprise, the *siying qiye* is defined as a private enterprise owned by entrepreneurs and providing employment for eight or more people. Smaller firms, with fewer than eight people, are referred to as *getihu*.

Figure 4.1 Entrepreneurship as a Supplement; photograph by Léo-Paul Dana.

Figure 4.2 Vibrant with Energy; photograph by Léo-Paul Dana.

Historical Overview

China's first dynasty, the Xia, was established over 4,000 years ago. In 221 BC, Emperor Qin Shi Huang of the Qin dynasty (221 BC to 206 BC) united China, centralised his authority over the nation, banned slavery, and initiated the transition to feudalism.

The Hans (206 BC to 220 AD) entrenched the feudal system in China[2] and allowed the export of silk. During a horse-buying mission in 138 BC, Han-Chinese traders realised that Central Asian merchants were willing to pay a high price for silk, and this soon became China's main export. Agriculture, handicrafts, shipbuilding and weaving were developed during the Han dynasty. Also during this era, the armillary sphere and the seismograph were invented in China. Table 4.1 summarises Chinese history according to dynasties.

[2] See Edwards (2004).

Dynasty/Era	Period	Type of Economy
Xia (Hsia)	2205 BC to 1766 BC	Slavery
Shang	1766 BC to 1122 BC	Slavery
Western Zhou	1122 BC to 770 BC	Slavery
Spring & Autumn Period	770 BC to 476 BC	Transition
Warring States Period	476 BC to 221 BC	Transition
Qin (Ch'in)	221 BC to 206 BC	Feudalism
Han	206 BC to 220 AD	Feudalism
Wei	220 to 265	Feudalism
Jin	265 to 420	Feudalism
Southern & Northern	420 to 589	Feudalism
Sui	590 to 617	Feudalism
Tang	618 to 907	Feudalism
Five Dynasties	907 to 960	Feudalism
Song	960 to 1279	Feudalism
Yuan (Mongol)	1279 to 1368	Feudalism
Ming	1368 to 1644	Feudalism
Qing (Manchu)	1644 to 1911	Feudalism
Modern Era	1911 to 1949	Bourgeois
Post-war Era	1949 to 1952	Rehabilitating
Planned Economy	1953 to 1978	Centrally planned
Opening Policy	1979 to 1992	Planned-commodity
Transitional	1993 to date	Socialist-market

Table 4.1 Historical Periods in China.

Chinese entrepreneurship developed without institutional support. Rather than foster entrepreneurship, several emperors attempted to discourage the activities of entrepreneurs. Traditional Chinese law, influenced by Confucian principles, forbade merchants from wearing nice clothes in public. The law also forbade them from riding horses or from travelling on wagons. For many years, international trade occurred not because of encouragement by rulers, but rather in spite of state intervention. Boulnois (1963) gave an account of Huang Ch'ao, who massacred 120,000 traders in China — Christians, Jews, Mazdeans and Muslims. The same author cited the Arab writer Abu Zaid Al-Hasan who wrote about China banishing Western merchants — Christians, Jews and Nestorians. In 1424, Emperor Hung-Hsi of the Ming dynasty banned foreign expeditions, and in 1426[3] China closed its borders to keep out foreign influence. Emperor K'ang-hsi of the Qing dynasty banned foreign travel.

The first Westerner to sail into China's Pearl Delta was Captain Jorge Alvares, in 1513. There, he found Guangzhou (Canton), already a great trading city at the time. In 1553, officials in Guang Dong accepted bribes from the Portuguese who wished to conduct trade in Macao. When the Portuguese discovered that the Japanese were willing to buy Chinese silk while the Celestial Empire prohibited business dealings between Chinese and Japanese merchants, Portuguese entrepreneurs prospered as middlemen between the two.

In 1557, China allowed Portuguese merchants to establish homes and warehouses in Macao. The Portuguese supplied ivory from Africa and cotton from Goa, as well as cannons, clocks and mirrors from Europe. In exchange, Chinese entrepreneurs brought porcelain, seed pearls, and silk. Exporting silk from Macao to Japan proved to be highly profitable for the Portuguese entrepreneurs who were happy to be paid in silver. They then used the silver to pay for Chinese goods, which they sold in Europe.

During the 1600s, English entrepreneurs decided to get silk and tea directly from China. A problem, however, was that Chinese consumers wanted nothing from England. This obstacle was resolved when Chinese entrepreneurs gave English traders silver in exchange for opium from India. The silver was then used to acquire silk and tea in China. Toward the end of the 18th century, the English also purchased from Chinese merchants a fine cotton fabric known as nankeen. In 1821, the English began using Hong Kong as a base for opium vessels.

The year 1839 marked the start of the Opium War between China and the English. In 1841, the latter occupied Hong Kong Island, and in 1842 the Treaty of Nanking[4] ceded Hong Kong to the British. In 1860, Queen Victoria also acquired the Kowloon Peninsula and later leased the New Territories for a period of 99 years. In 1887, Portugal forced China to sign the Draft Agreement of the Sino-Portuguese Meeting. This was followed by the Sino-Portuguese Treaty of Peking,[5] allowing Portugal perpetual administration of Macao.

---

[3] For a discussion of the Chinese military defeat of 1426, see Lamb (2004).

[4] Nanking is known today as Nanjing.

[5] Peking was Romanised from Beijing.

The Sino-Japanese War that lasted from 1894 to 1895 resulted in a shift of dominance from China to Japan (Scidmore, 1910). By signing the Treaty of Shimonoseki, China agreed to stay out of Korea, ceded a large portion of eastern Manchuria to Japan, and gave up its sovereignty over Taiwan.

By 1898, Shanghai was one of the world's great trading centres (Bishop, 1899). Large numbers of Jews from Iraq settled in Hong Kong, Ningbo, Shanghai and Tianjin. Among the prominent Jewish entrepreneurs in China were the Kadoories and the Sassoons. In 1903, Sir Jacob Sassoon, brother of Sir Edward Sassoon and son of Elias, donated the Ohel Leah Synagogue, part way up Victoria Peak. Sir Matthew Nathan, governor of Hong Kong became president of the synagogue, and the main street in Kowloon — Nathan Road — was named after him. Large numbers of Ashkenazi Jews began arriving in China during the Russo-Prussian War of 1905; many settled in Harbin, Manchuria. Simpich called Manchuria the "promised land of Asia (1929, p. 379)."

In 1911, overseas Chinese entrepreneurs financed Dr. Sun, Yat-Sen's bourgeois-democratic revolution, which overthrew the Qing dynasty. On December 25, 1914, Yunnan[6] Province announced its separation from the Chinese Empire (Passantino, 1946). After WWI, many thousands of Chinese men chose to go to France to work at restoring the French republic (Williams, 1919).

A great famine came about in 1920.[7] The Communist Party of China was established in 1921. Chitty (1922) discussed economic life in China at the time. China was exporting up to 4,800 tons of silk annually. Things changed, however, when three quarters of its silkworms were found to be diseased in 1923 (Boulnois, 1963). Chinese sericulture was no longer a major force in international markets. In order to re-establish a significant market presence, the International Committee for the Improvement of Sericulture in China then purchased healthy silkworms in France and Italy. Yet, the 1920s were bleak. A revolution took place in 1926,[8] followed by the Agrarian Revolutionary War that lasted until 1937. In 1928, Nanjing became the nation's capital city, and the name of China's former capital, Peking, was changed to Peiping (Moore, 1933).

---

[6] For a details about the Nashi, Indigenous people of Yunnan, see Rock (1924; 1930).
[7] For a discussion, see Robinson (1923).
[8] For a discussion, see Chapman (1928).

Figure 4.3 Former Ghetto in Shanghai; photograph by Léo-Paul Dana.

When the Japanese arrived in 1931, Manchuria was home to 13,000 Jews, many of these entrepreneurs with an impressive network, including two Jewish banks. Yet, these Jews did not mix with the Indigenous Jews of China.[9] Williams (1935) correctly described China during the 1930s as stormy, in more ways than one. During 1932, Harbin was flooded for several weeks; Coville noted, "Many Russian and Chinese boatmen ferried across ...to make a little pocket money rowing people around town (1933, p. 243)."

Another Sino-Japanese War began in 1937.[10] Between January and September 1938, nearly 200,000 Chinese worked on the Burma Road,[11] an all-weather highway linking Kunming, with Rangoon. Outram and

---

[9] For a discussion of the Indigenous Jews of China, see Bainbridge (1907).
[10] For a discussion, see Eigner (1938).
[11] For a discussion of 21st century opium trade along the Burma Road, see Webster (2003).

Fane described how the "opening of the Burma Road turned sleepy Kunming into a bustling metropolis. Capital and largest city of Yunnan Province, the ancient community slumbered half-forgotten until 1939... Suddenly trucks by the hundreds poured into the city, which became a distributing center for the Chinese armies (Outram and Fane, 1940, p. 654)." The Japanese occupation of Burma was tragic since Burma had been the principal base for Allied aid to China (Christian, 1943).

By the time the war was over, in 1945, millions of Chinese had been killed. Brown (1944), Stewart (1944) and Lowdermilk (1945) gave detailed accounts of wartime China. When Hong Kong fell to the Japanese, many entrepreneurs fled from occupied Hong Kong to China. In 1945, capitalists in western China declared the independence of the Turkestan Republic. Following the National Liberation War — which lasted from 1945 to 1949 — on October 1, 1949, Mao Zedong proclaimed the establishment of the PRC. Turkestan was subsequently absorbed into the PRC.

From 1949 to 1952, the PRC focused on "the task of rehabilitating the national economy (Hong, 1990, p. 11)." The First Five-Year Plan (1953–1957) gave rise to a centrally planned economy. Entrepreneurship in the PRC was eliminated, in favour of a system of state production and co-operatives. By mid-1950, about 20,000 refugees poured in every week to Hong Kong (Long, 1954). With 80,000 seats, the Peking Workers' Stadium was completed in 1959 (Shor, 1960). Until 1978, business was production-oriented, based on a plan. Prices were fixed and advertising was banned.

The Chinese Model of Gradual Transition

In 1978, Deng Xiaoping declared that the PRC needed to "reform and open up," thus setting the nation on the road to economic liberalisation — with an open-door policy. The state moved away from Maoism, reduced its control of the economy, and business became increasingly oriented toward sales. Private enterprises — including foreign participation — were permitted. Some prices were allowed to float. Advertising was legalised.

In 1979, the State Council of China officially endorsed a policy allowing entrepreneurship to contribute to economic development, not as a replacement of central planning, but rather as a supplement to the socialist economy. Regulatory reform legalised entrepreneurship, and by 1980 there were over one million entrepreneurs in China.

The government also recognised *zhuanyehu* — "specialised households." These were families who were given permission to operate family businesses. Enterprises included animal husbandry, carpentry, construction, embroidery, and fish farming. Self-employed farmers were permitted to cultivate apples, beans, corn, grapes, pears, persimmons, rice, sorghum, soya beans, sugar beets and tangerines. A new constitution was adopted on December 4, 1982. Taxation was subsequently introduced (Wei, 2001).

The Chinese proverb, "A single spark can start a prairie fire," led to the "Spark" Programme, an important scheme that was launched in 1986, to promote entrepreneurship in rural areas of China. Through this programme, the State Science and Technology Commission encouraged the establishment of several thousand new ventures. Special incentives were offered to entrepreneurs who harnessed a technology deemed to be appropriate for rural industry. This included enterprises involving agriculture, aquaculture, food processing, light industry, textile manufacturing, and the production of components. In 1992, the Fourteenth National Congress of the Communist Party of China proposed the establishment of a socialist market economy. During the early 1990s, annual growth reached 13.4%, as the orientation of firms was shifting toward the market. In 1993, the China Council for the Promotion of International Trade hosted a world conference in Beijing to encourage entrepreneurship. Devaluation of the yuan, in 1994, helped Chinese entrepreneurs increase their competitiveness in export markets. The state also introduced a variety of incentives for entrepreneurs who export. This included tax exemptions and easy access to financing via specialised banks. An overview of entrepreneurs in China, during the early 1990s, appears in Chow and Tsang (1995).

In 1995, legislation declared 339 cities and counties open areas in which entrepreneurship could thrive, as a supplement to socialism. The Financial Security Law came into effect in October 1995. This legislation affects entrepreneurship inasmuch as it covers different forms of security: deposit, guarantee, lien, pledge and mortgage. Land-use rights and social facilities were placed on the list of assets, which could be mortgaged.

Figure 4.4 Entrepreneurship Thriving as a Supplement; photograph by Léo-Paul Dana.

Figure 4.5 In the Informal Sector; photograph by Léo-Paul Dana.

Figure 4.6 Using Traditional Scale; photograph by Léo-Paul Dana.

Figure 4.7 Earning Well; photograph by Léo-Paul Dana.

Figure 4.8 Selling Live Poultry from the Farm; photograph by Léo-Paul Dana.

The All-China Federation of Industry and Commerce — established in 1953 and with more than 80,000 members — opened its Information Centre in 1995. Its major functions are: to provide assistance to foreign entrepreneurs, in finding Chinese partners for joint ventures; to perform market analysis; to provide consulting services to foreign entrepreneurs; to organise trade shows; to organise technology exchanges; and to assist foreign entrepreneurs. The federation also publishes periodicals of interest to entrepreneurs.

Until April 1996, foreign entrepreneurs benefited from Value Added Tax (VAT) exemptions and exemptions from customs duties on imported capital equipment. These were then withdrawn, thus putting foreign and local entrepreneurs on equal footing with regards to investment incentives.

Figure 4.9 Ambulant; photograph by Léo-Paul Dana.

In 1997, domestic growth in the PRC slowed down, and in 1998, the state responded by launching an elaborate programme of government spending on infrastructure. In 1998, the State Economic and Trade Commission of China was restructured such as to include a Department of Small and Medium Enterprises.

From a level of 43% in 1997, average tariffs were significantly reduced; yet, imports remained subject to VAT. However, Chinese entrepreneurs are often exempted from sales tax. Thus, it may be said that the effective tariff rate is close to 40%, thereby protecting local entrepreneurs.

In July 2001, President Jiang Zemin made news with his declaration that the Communist Party of China should recruit capitalists. He said this would boost the "influence and cohesiveness" of the party. That same month, the PRC passed new rules on intellectual property. Anderson, Li, Harrison and Robson (2003) noted the increasing role of small businesses in China.

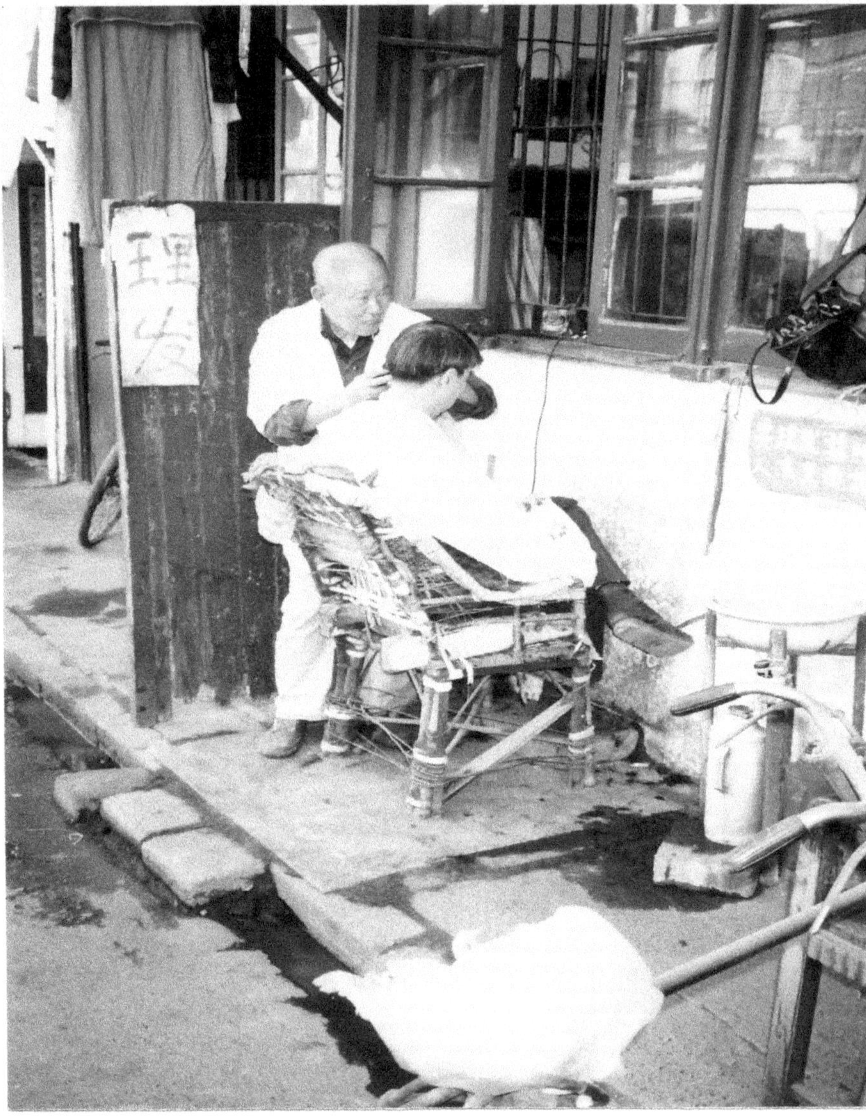

Figure 4.10 In the Tertiary Sector; photograph by Léo-Paul Dana.

In 2005, the State Council released 36 articles on non-public economy. For the first time, the central government supported the entry of non-public firms into sectors previously reserved for monopolies. A three-tier system exists in China today:

1. Consumer staples, raw materials and industrial materials are supplied by the state and prices dictated by the government. This is truly a state-controlled planned sector.
2. For other products — as determined by the state — prices can vary within a range dictated by *guojia wujia guanliju,* the State Price Bureau. This may be described as a hybrid sector.
3. In contrast to the state-controlled planned sector, a free-market system allows the market to establish prices of some products.

Figure 4.11 In Hong Kong; photograph by Léo-Paul Dana.

One Country, Two Systems

In 1984, the Sino-British Agreement pronounced the reversion of British Hong Kong to China, effective July 1, 1997. This was conditional on the PRC creating a Special Administrative Region, conforming to the concept of "one country, two systems." Hong Kong reverted to Chinese rule, but the Special Administrative Region of Hong Kong was allowed to keep its own legal and judicial system, as well as capitalist economy, until 2047.

Along the same lines, in April 1987, Portugal signed the Joint Sino-Portuguese Declaration and Basic Law. This allowed the PRC to take back Macao, on December 20, 1999.

There are, nevertheless, important differences between Hong Kong and Macao. Although both were built on entrepreneurship, their industrial sectors evolved differently. Entrepreneurs in Hong Kong benefited from the government's *laissez-faire* policy, including favourable tax treatment. In contrast, beginning in 1981, Macao adopted an increasingly interventionist approach.

Hong Kong has at least 300,000 small and medium enterprises, which are flexible, and cost-effective. While their product mix is increasing, the typical size of an order is shrinking.

Many entrepreneurs in Hong Kong are concentrated in the service industries. Others have manufacturing plants, outside Hong Kong. Entrepreneurs from Hong Kong have financed over 170,000 joint ventures in China, and these employ some 10 million people — twice the labour force in Hong Kong. According to unpublished sources at the Hong Kong Trade Development Council, two-fifths of the exporters in Hong Kong, have operations in two or more economies.

The Trade Development Council of Hong Kong operates the SME Service Centre. This is a one-stop shop for entrepreneurs in search of information about technology acquisition and internationalisation.

In contrast, entrepreneurs in Macao tend to be small-scale producers of low-technology goods, including artificial flowers, ceramics, clothing, electrical products, electronics, firewood, footwear, furniture, machinery, optical devices, plastic goods, textiles and toys. Dana (1999e) provided a detailed contrast of differences between entrepreneurship policy and practices in Hong Kong and those in Macao.

Pluralism

While the Han-Chinese comprise the majority of China's population, the country is also rich with minority groups (see Wong, 1984). There are 55 recognised national minorities in the PRC.

In Xinjiang (see Dana, 1998b), the largest administrative region in China, the Han-Chinese are a minority, and most people are Muslims. The Indigenous people in Xinjiang are Uygurs — Muslims with Indo-European features. Members of different ethnic communities have distinctly different tastes. A particular favourite among the Hui is soup made of flour. In contrast to the Hans who use chopsticks, the Kazakhs in Xinjiang eat with their hands; these people enjoy smoked meat and horse intestines as well as mutton with noodles eaten without utensils. The Kirghiz prefer eating rice mixed with milk, and they exhibit a preference for horse's milk. A popular meal among Uygurs consists of hand-pulled noodles mixed with bits of lamb and vegetables, savoured with strong tea. They enjoy fried *sanzi* — made from dough — and a variety of steamed foods including buns and dumplings; they also like roasted cubes of mutton on skewers. They eat rice with their fingers. The Mongolians, the Uygurs and the Xibe drink milk-tea. As for the Kazakhs and the Kirghiz, their favourite drink is fermented mare's milk, known in Central Asia as *koumis*, and in China as *manaizi*. In major centres, Western food has also made inroads, with chains such as Kentucky Fried Chicken (Dana, 1999d).

A Muslim Uygur, in Xinjiang, sells *nan*, flat bread with *plov* — rice mixed with religiously prepared halal mutton — along with *shashlik, i.e.,* halal mutton broiled on charcoal. On another street, Han entrepreneurs sell tofu, noodles, dumplings, dogmeat, fried vegetables, white rice and eggs cooked in tea. Pluralism is structural in nature, as members of the different ethnic groups do not share a secular mainstream arena. Whereas the Han-Chinese introduced a firm-type economy to Xinjiang, the non-Han sphere of activity is concentrated in the bazaar economy.

Among the non-Han peoples in Xinjiang are Kazakh and Kirghiz minorities; these are also Islamic, with a Turkic language. In contrast to the Uygurs who have been cultivating the land, the Kazakhs and Kirghiz have retained their traditional nomadic lifestyle, which includes breeding camels[12] and horses, both of these for meat and for milk as well as for transport.

Among the Kazakhs, horseback courtship is still practised, as a suitor must kiss his woman, on the gallop. Although Kazakhs, in Xinjiang, engage in agriculture on a limited scale, many are herdsmen, and their entrepreneurial spirit is strong. Clark (1954) described the thousands of families of Kazakhs in Xinjiang who opted to trek 3,000 miles, in order to escape communist control in China.

While the Hans speak Mandarin, the Uygurs speak a Turkic tongue, written with an Arabic script. The Uygurs have more in common with their Turkic neighbours of the formerly Soviet, Central Asian republics, than with the Han-Chinese. Perhaps because they are often looked down upon by Han-Chinese, the Uygurs do not generally identify with Chinese nationality, but rather consider themselves to be under Chinese occupation.

Rather than wearing Chinese slacks, Uygur women sport colourful dresses or skirts with matching, brightly coloured scarves. Among the Uygurs, both men and women wear a colourful head cover. Daggers are fashionable among Uygur, Kazakh, Kirghiz and Mongolian men.

The Uygurs continue to cultivate cotton, grapes and melons. Local green grapes are still dried in the traditional manner, producing export-quality raisins with no pits. At local markets, such as that in Turpan, donkey-carts wait for local loads. Closer to the Kyrgyz Republic, trucks at the Kashgar market represent major international business. While some Uygurs have opted to urbanise, many have decided to remain in rural areas, residing in rectangular farmhouses with scuttles on flat roofs.

Recently, a new class of international merchants has been emerging with a pan-Turkic scope. Rather than doing business with Han-Chinese, the Muslims of Xinjiang express a preference to trade with co-religionists from the Turkic republics of the former Soviet Union. While the majority of the world's international trade takes place in the firm-type economy, Uygur traders thrive in the bazaar.

Perhaps the most striking bazaar is at the Horgas Pass, to the south-west of Bortala. Like other towns of the Silk Road,[13] the settlement was impoverished when caravans stopped passing through it. In 1971, all

---

[12] Wulsin (1926) provided a comparison between camels owned by Chinese people and those owned by Mongols in China.

[13] This term refers not to one road *per se*, but to a web of inter-weaving paths that linked towns and bazaars.

international activity was banned here, as the border with the Soviet Union was closed. The local inhabitants had no electricity, no running water, and no trade.

In 1983, the border was re-opened. The following year, entrepreneurs carried 20 million kilogrammes of goods across this border, according to information obtained by the author during an interview in Kazakhstan. The demise of the Soviet Union meant little to the average Chinese individual. However, the independence of the five formerly Soviet Central Asian states — Kazakhstan and the Kyrgyz Republic in particular — had a great symbolic lift for Uygurs, for Kazakhs and for Kirghiz in Xinjiang. These Turkic-speaking minorities had historical, religious and cultural links with their Turkic-speaking neighbours in the Commonwealth of Independent States(CIS).

Uygur entrepreneurs in Xinjiang began to rebuild commercial links between east and west. In Khorghus, formerly a Silk Road town, now on the Kazakh side of the Kazakhstan-Xinjiang border, a new bazaar is sprawling. A unique feature along the border of China and Kazakhstan is "The Bazaar for Entrepreneurs from Both Sides." This market has an entrance in Xinjiang and another in Kazakhstan. Uygur entrepreneurs from Xinjiang bring beer, vodka, sugar, candies, clothing, leather goods, sporting apparel, toys, house-wares, tools, cigarettes and jewellery, all of which they sell to buyers from Kazakhstan, including Kazakhs and Russians, most of whom arrive by bus. Thus, pan-Turkic trade is on the rise, as Muslims in Xinjiang conduct business with Muslims in republics of the CIS.

Although the bazaar is not simply a means to monetary reward, it is producing wealth among the Uygurs. More importantly, it allows Uygurs to socialise among others sharing similar cultural values. The flow of commerce is still fragmented into numerous transactions between individuals, just as it was generations ago. This allows the sharing of cigarettes over tea, and it helps to spread risks.

Officially, all of China has only one time zone, which is the same as that of Beijing. Uygurs function according to their own unofficial time zone. Uygur entrepreneurs, in Xinjiang, are more concerned with conducting business with Kazakhstan and the Kyrgyz Republic, than with pleasing politicians in China's capital; although Han-Chinese in Xinjiang respect Beijing time, most Uygurs set their watches two hours behind the official time of China. This presumably facilitates pan-Turkic trade between Uygurs and entrepreneurs in Kazakhstan and in the Kyrgyz Republic; more importantly, it is a highly symbolic gesture.

Given that the Uygurs have a Turkic culture and that they speak a Turkic language, this has facilitated trade with bazaar entrepreneurs in the rapidly developing, newly independent republics of Central Asia.

Toward a More Selective Approach

Yu and Stough noted that "the Chinese government that not only implemented a successful top to bottom economic reform, but also preserved much of its socialist political system, is taken as the most influential determinant of entrepreneurship development (2006, p. 48)." A widespread conclusion has been that China has adopted a particularly innovative and welfare-enhancing blend of reform policies that delayed the privatisation of state firms, while solving efficiency and social issues by encouraging new ventures by private parties (Rodrik, 2007).

Across the PRC, entrepreneurship has become a supplement to socialism and industrialisation is viewed as a complement to agriculture. Unlike other economies, which rapidly abandoned communism, the PRC is liberalising its economy slowly, thus avoiding spiral inflation. As well, its township enterprises are helping the nation industrialise, while avoiding uncontrolled urbanisation. In the longer term, sustained growth will likely require privatisation of state enterprises and a free flow of labour. Meanwhile, local and foreign entrepreneurs are playing an important role in the economic and social development of China despite tight control by Beijing. Heavy investment has been pouring in from overseas Chinese entrepreneurs, and the PRC today has the world's second largest GDP.

China's model of transition is likely to bring increasing prosperity to its people. MacDonald warned, however, "But development has been uneven and the losers number in the hundreds of millions. Their growing dissatisfaction with their plot poses a threat to China's stability and economic progress (2005, p. B.2)." As Becker stated, "China's race to riches comes at a high cost to both land and people (2004, p. 69)." At the World Economic Forum, in Davos, Bhagwati (2006) cautioned not to assume that China's rapid growth was sustainable. As noted by Rein (2012), rising costs of real estate and of labour are prompting some factories to move up the value chain or else close or relocate; Rein observed that Chinese people prefer to buy iPhones rather than make them for others to buy. Rising incomes are encouraging a restructure of the economy toward the domestic market. Shi and Dana (2013) examined the relationship between entrepreneurship in China and market orientation.

In its endeavour to establish a technology-intensive economy, the government is hence encouraging more value-adding activities than was the case in the past, while reducing labour-intensive production by cutting off credit to targeted firms. In contrast, the new policy favours entrepreneurial firms at higher levels of the value chain. Almor and Yeheskel (2013) suggested that skilled, professional entrepreneurs from Israel — sojourning entrepreneurs have the ability to overcome liability of foreignness and the ability to engage both networks in the home country and in the host country to further the entrepreneurial venture in the host country. The future may benefit from such mutual gain.

Case Study : Joint Venture for Chocolate

Chocolate

For centuries before the arrival of the Europeans in America, the Aztecs of Mexico had used the fruit of the *cacauatl* — the "Tree of the Golden Pad" — as currency, as a drink, and as a religious offering. The English words cocoa and chocolate were later derived respectively from the Aztec words *cacauatl*, meaning cocoa tree, and *chocolatl*, the term used to refer to the drink traditionally prepared from the beans of *cacauatl*.

The manufacturing of chocolate involves a finely ground mixture of cocoa butter, cocoa mass, sugar and sometimes milk. Both cocoa butter and cocoa mass are produced from cocoa beans. The production of cocoa is widely spread across the Americas, Africa and Asia.

Ghana is one of Cadbury's most important suppliers of cocoa beans. Cocoa used by Cadbury in Tasmania were typically been sourced in Ghana, Malaysia and New Guinea. Cadbury chocolate produced in New Zealand contained cocoa beans from the Cook Islands, Ghana, Malaysia and/or Nigeria. Chocolate made in the Americas might instead be made from cocoa beans grown in Brazil, Costa Rica, Ecuador, Mexico, Venezuela, and/or the West Indies, Trinidad in particular. A manufacturing facility in India might use cocoa beans from Zaire as well as from Nigeria. Other sources of cocoa beans include Western Samoa and Vanuatu (formerly New Hebrides).

Beans arrive in bags at factories around the world. These are sometimes stored for many months, and must therefore be protected from humidity and from contaminants. The bags are tipped and the beans are cleaned by being passed over magnets, vibrating screens and air separators. Once cleaned, the beans are roasted, facilitating the removal of the shell from the nib. The beans are then cooled, and kibbled (cracked) by passing them through toothed rolls. The shells are removed from the nibs by winnowing machines in which air blasts are directed towards broken beans in order to blow away the pieces of shell. The unpalatable shells are sold, for use as fertiliser and soil conditioner. The remaining nibs consist of approximately 55% fat, which is locked inside the cellular mass of nibs. The fat is released by grinding, which ruptures the cell walls. The grinding apparatus consists of disc mills made of steel. The discs are mounted vertically with a central grooved disc rotating at a high speed, between two grooved steel faces, which are stationary. The nib is poured towards the centre of the discs, and collected at the outer edge. Water-cooling is provided to absorb the considerable heat generated by the grinding process.

The cocoa fat released by the grinding is then liquefied by frictional heat, and becomes a continuous phase in which the disintegrated cell particles are suspended. Continued disintegration releases more fat that reduces the viscosity of the paste until it becomes a fluid referred to as cocoa mass. Hydraulic pressing of cocoa mass yields cocoa butter, which is added to cocoa mass to produce chocolate and a by-product referred to as cake. This hard cake is pulverised and sifted to produce cocoa powder, which is sold as such.

Chocolate is produced by mixing and grinding a mixture of cocoa mass, cocoa butter, sugar and other ingredients, if any. It is the cocoa butter, which gives chocolate its quality of being firm at room temperature while dissolving in one's mouth without any waxy sensation. A good dark chocolate must have sufficient cocoa butter (added to cocoa mass and sugar) to enable the chocolate to set in block form, when moulded, or as a firm shell on confectionery centres. Furthermore, chocolate must not give any sensation of roughness. Fine texture is the result of grinding on machines with hollow water-cooled steel rolls. Since grinding increases the surface area of the solids, the fluidity of the paste is restored by adding extra cocoa butter and/or milk, which also softens the texture. The milk, however, must have most of its water removed.

The next phase after grinding involves the mixture being pummelled for hours, by large rollers of machines designated for this purpose. During this process, dark chocolate requires a higher temperature than needs milk chocolate. This reduces the viscosity of the chocolate. Milk chocolate may then be ready after twelve hours, but high-quality dark chocolate may need several days. At the end of this process, flavour, fruits, nuts or other ingredients may be added. The addition of cocoa butter adjusts the viscosity of the chocolate, depending on requirements.

Filled chocolates are made by first depositing tempered chocolate into moulds and cooling the chocolate shell. The filling (caramel, cream or syrup) is then deposited and finally, once this is cooled, the filling is covered with more chocolate and the whole bar is cooled. The centres for chocolate assortments are made by depositing liquid cream, fudge or other contents, into shallow depressions of trays covered with starch. The starch sucks out some of the moisture, forming a dry surface area. When these are firm enough to be handled, they are tipped out and the starch is brushed off.

For chocolate assortments or chocolate-covered bars, the centres are placed on a wire net, which is conveyed through a shallow pool of chocolate coating the bottoms. Then, the conveyer belt passes through a falling curtain of tempered chocolate, which flows continuously over the centres. The excess drips through the wire net and is recycled. The weight of the chocolates is adjusted by shaking and blowing on the wire net.

Once moulds are filled, they are shaken to release air bubbles and to spread the chocolate evenly. A cooler facilitates setting. Cooled centres may then be decorated manually, mechanically, or by blowing air.

To make solid chocolate bars, the chocolate is then cooled at a temperature below the crystallisation point of cocoa butter, in order for crystals to be formed. The temperature is lowered and the chocolate deposited into moulds, which are carried by a belt moving under the depositing machine. Due to its milk fat, milk chocolate requires cooling at a lower temperature than does dark chocolate.

The solidification of the chocolate causes the chocolate bar to contract away from the mould, such that it can easily be discharged. The mould thus remains clean. The final products are then transferred to embossed, moving belts, which imprint the chocolate with the brand name.

Packaging

The ideal package should be attractive to consumers, while maintaining the quality of its contents throughout shelf life. The packaging material must be free from any constituents, which might adversely affect the product. It should be strong enough to withstand packing methods and the hazards of transportation. The packaging should exclude light, which might accelerate oxidation. The packaging should also provide protection from the absorption of contaminants or odours, and it should protect against the absorption or loss of moisture.

In Australia, Cadbury chocolate bars have been cased in silver-coloured aluminium foil wrapping, while a gold-coloured foil has been used in England. In Canada, a purple foil has been chosen. In Egypt, a gold-colour foil was selected for wrapping Cadbury chocolate. In any event, extreme heat often makes nibbling on chocolate a sticky activity.

Whereas the traditional Australian package has a "best before" date, the new Singapore package has a "use by" date. Cadbury chocolate made in Kenya did not show a "use by" or "better before" date. Instead, a "sell by" date was shown.

Cadbury

It was 1824, when John Cadbury began his business career as a tea and coffee merchant in Birmingham, England. He was soon impressed by the chocolate lozenge, a product, which in 1826, J.S. Fry & Sons advertised as "a pleasant and nutritious substitute for food while travelling or when unusual fasting is caused by irregular period of mealtimes."

At a time when South America was the chief producer and exporter of cocoa anywhere in the world, John Cadbury established, in 1831, a firm to manufacture a range of cocoas in England. The product line was expanded under the leadership of John Cadbury's sons, George and Richard, who took over the family business. Richard was the artist who sketched the first pictorial chocolate boxes.

In 1865, Richard Hudson, an illiterate waif, orphaned at the age of nine, worked his passage from England to New Zealand on a sailing ship. Following the discovery of gold, Dunedin became New Zealand's leading city, and this is where young Richard established a biscuit bake-house. He visited Europe in 1884, returning with a chocolate plant, which eventually produced that which was claimed to be the first chocolate made in the South Pacific.

In 1905, Cadbury's "Dairy Milk" chocolate was introduced, followed by Cadbury's "Bournville" in 1910. In 1914, Cadbury's "Milk Tray" was launched, soon to become the first boxed assortment to achieve national popularity in England.

In 1921, the firm of J.S. Fry & Sons merged with Cadbury Brothers, forming Cadbury Fry, which the following year, began to open factories in Australia, Canada, India, Ireland, New Zealand, Nigeria, and South Africa. In 1930, Richard Hudson's R. Hudson & Co. Ltd. amalgamated with Cadbury Fry, in New Zealand, resulting in the creation of Cadbury Fry Hudson.

In 1969, Sir Adrian Cadbury, great-grandson of John Cadbury, joined forces with Lord Watkinson of Schweppes, paving the way for a new era. The merger created a large international business and thus a strong foundation for further expansion and extension of product lines. In Australia, Cadbury Schweppes Australia Limited was incorporated in May 1971, to merge Cadbury Fry Pascal Australia Limited and Schweppes (Australia) Limited. In New Zealand, Cadbury Fry Hudson changed its name to Cadbury Schweppes Hudson Ltd., which became known as the largest advertiser on New Zealand national television.

On January 22, 1986, Cadbury Fry Pascal Australia Limited announced that approval would be sought from shareholders at an Extraordinary General Meeting for the acquisition of Cadbury Schweppes Hudson Ltd. of New Zealand. A decade later, Cadbury decided to take over Toronto-based William Neilson Limited, in Canada.

"Fruit & Nut" was a Cadbury product, which has had a long history of being manufactured at several locations. Yet, although this chocolate bar had a somewhat similar name in different environments, its taste varied considerably as do its ingredients. The principal constituent of Cadbury's Fruit & Nut in the UK was milk; in Australia, it was more specifically full cream milk. In Canada and in South Africa, the primary ingredient was sugar. Containing 27% full cream solids, Fruit & Nut in Australia had a more milky taste, while Fruit & Nut in England has a noticeably darker colour. Fruit & Nut in Australia contained light yellow sultanas, while in England dark purple raisins were used instead. Nuts used in England's Fruit & Nut were blanched almonds, while in Australia, cashew nuts were added with almonds which are not blanched.

Although standardisation may yield economies of scale, it is sometimes better to adapt the package, the name, the product, the advertising and the promotion. Cadbury's 25-gram bar sold very well in Indonesia for example, while in Australia the 375-gram was quite popular; in Canada the 46-gram format was enjoyed, while in the United States, people often preferred the 5-oz. package. Product line also varies with markets, and ingredients reflect cost and consumer tastes. Furthermore, product names may change from one environment to another.

In Tasmania, the Cadbury Confectionery launched "Cadbury White," a bar made from sugar, full cream milk powder, cocoa butter, emulsifier (442), salt and "flavour." In New Zealand, "Cadbury Milky White" became popular, containing sugar, full cream powder, vegetable oil, emulsifiers (332, 476), salt and "flavour." Cadbury (Pty.) Ltd. in Port Elizabeth created a similar bar containing sugar, full cream milk solids, cocoa butter, vegetable fat, emulsifier and "flavouring agent," but no salt. Despite the similarity in product, to avoid racial tension, the South African company excluded the term "white" from the name of their product. The name "Cadbury's Creamy Bar" was selected.

Even when names are turned into another language, one translation may not be sufficient. In Canada, "Fruit & Nut" became known in French as "Fruit et Noix." New Zealand's "Fruit & Nut" was also translated into French, but reading: *Chocolat au lait aux raisins secs et aux amandes*.

In each market, a different assortment of Cadbury chocolates became available, at a variety of prices. In England, Cadbury's "Dairy Milk" was among the least expensive; Cadbury's "Fruit & Nut" was moderately priced, while Cadbury's "Turkish" was premium-priced. Other popular Cadbury's chocolates in the UK included: Bournville; Creme Egg; Double-decker; Fingers; Flake; Mounds; Snack; and Whole Nut.

In Australia, the Cadbury product line included: Crunchie; Cherry Ripe; Dairy Milk; Energy; Fruit & Nut; Hazelnut; Hazelnut Cream; Muesli Munch; Picnic, Sultana; Whip; and White. Very popular in Australia, was Cadbury Four Fruits, manufactured in Tasmania, with dark and white chocolate containing blackberry, raspberry, blueberry and strawberry. In 1992, a blended chocolate, Cadbury Gold Caramel, was introduced in Australia. Even though there was a Cadbury plant in New Zealand, a country that exported macadamia nuts, Cadbury Macadamia Nut was manufactured in Australia and exported to New Zealand.

Other favourites in New Zealand included: Cadbury Cashews; Crunch; Crunchie; Dairy Milk; Flake; Fruit & Nut; Milky White; Moro; Peach Cream; Peppermint, Picnic; Pinky; Red Fruit; and Strawberry. Note that New Zealand, like Australia, dropped the "s" from "Cadbury's."

In South Africa, best sellers included Cadbury's *Kasjoe-neut* (Cashew Nut); Creamy Bar; Dairy Milk; *Vrugte & Neute* (Fruit & Nut); and *Rum & Rosyne* (Rum & Raisin). Cadbury's Cashew Nut and Cadbury's Rum & Raisin were also exported to Lesotho. In Zimbabwe (formerly Rhodesia), Crystal Candy (Pvt) Ltd. of Harare (formerly Salisbury), chose to produce a very limited assortment of Cadbury chocolates.

Although Cadbury adapted and expanded in many parts of the world, Hershey Chocolate USA became a market leader in the United States, while William Neilson became increasingly dominant in Canada. Prior to the Cadbury-Schweppes merger, the Canadian subsidiary of Cadbury Limited used to manufacture chocolate in Canada, but had nothing to do with soft drinks. Eventually Cadbury Beverages Canada Inc. became responsible for the Schweppes line in that country. Yet, Cadbury stopped manufacturing chocolate in Canada. William Neilson Ltd. became the manufacturer of Cadbury chocolate in Canada, and the marketing of these became the responsibility of Cadbury Canada Marketing Inc., in Toronto. In the United States, where Cadbury chocolates were formerly produced by Cadbury, USA (a division of Cadbury Schweppes Inc., in Connecticut), Hershey Chocolates USA obtained the license to add Cadbury chocolates to its existing product line, although Hershey and Cadbury had traditionally been competitors. In the United States, Hershey Chocolate USA manufactured Cadbury's Fruit & Nut milk chocolate, raisins and almonds using the following ingredients: "milk chocolate (sugar, milk, cocoa butter, chocolate, lecithin, artificial and natural *flavors*), raisins and almonds" which were not blanched. In contrast, "Cadbury's Fruit & Nut Milk Chocolate with Sultanas and Almonds" in South Africa, was made with: "sugar, full cream solids (no milk), sultanas, cocoa butter, cocoa liquor, *blanched almonds*, vegetable fat, emulsifiers and *flavouring* agents." In Canada, William Neilson Limited opted to make Fruit & Nut with *chopped almonds,* corn starch, and "*artificial* flavour"; the Canadian product contained one and a half glasses of milk per 250 grams of chocolate.

It was decided that "Cadbury's Fruit & Nut Milk Chocolate with Raisins and Almonds" manufactured in Birmingham, England, for local consumption would contain a glass and a half of full cream milk in every half pound of milk chocolate. Ingredients were listed on the package as: "milk, sugar, raisins, almonds, cocoa butter, cocoa mass, *vegetable fat*, emulsifiers 442 and 476, flavourings" with "milk solids 20% minimum" and "cocoa solids 20% minimum." A "best before" date was indicated. In contrast, "Cadbury's Fruit & Nut Milk Chocolate with Raisins & Almonds" also manufactured in Birmingham but exported to Singapore showed a "use by" date and contains different ingredients: "milk, sugar, raisins, cocoa butter, almonds, cocoa mass, emulsifier E322, *artificial flavourings,*" with "milk solids 14% minimum" and "cocoa solids 25% minimum." (In Australia, where Cadbury milk chocolate was made from "full cream milk, sugar, cocoa butter, cocoa liquor, emulsifiers (322 and 442) and flavour," contents included 27% full cream milk solids.)

In Indonesia, a relatively small business, P.T. Cipta Rasa Primatama, manufactured "Cadbury's Fruit & Nut Milk Chocolate with Raisins & Almonds." Ingredients included "sugar, milk solids, cocoa liquor, cocoa butter, raisins, almonds, vegetable fat, lecithin, *permitted* and natural flavours."

In New Zealand, Cadbury products were produced by one of the country's largest companies. There, a glass and a half of full cream milk was used in every 250 grams of Cadbury chocolate.

All of the above "Fruit & Nut" variations contained almonds but no cashew nuts. "Cadbury Fruit & Nut Covered in Dairy Milk Chocolate," made by Cadbury Confectionery in Tasmania, Australia, contained milk chocolate, sultanas, cashews and almonds along with the equivalent of a glass and a half of *pure* full cream milk in every 200 grams of dairy milk chocolate. The package included a "best before" date.

Cadbury's "Fruit & Nut" manufactured by Cadbury Schweppes Kenya Limited, in Nairobi, contained "sugar, milk, cocoa butter, raisins, cocoa, cashew nuts, almonds, emulsifier and flavours." It contained less milk than its Australian counterpart: a glass and a half per 227 grams. A "sell by" date was provided rather than a "best before" date.

In striking contrast, Cadbury's Fruit & Nut manufactured by Hindustan Cocoa Products Limited in Bombay, India, opted to use "sugar, milk solids, cocoa butter, chocolate mass, raisins, *roasted* cashew nuts, roasted *apricot kernels* (no almonds), permitted emulsifying agent (synthetic lecithin) and artificial flavouring agents." Rather than supplying a "best before" or "sell by" date, it was been the norm in India to indicate a "package date," along with a maximum allowed retail price.

Whereas Singapore traditionally obtained its "Cadbury's Fruit & Nut Chocolate with Raisins and Almonds" from Cadbury Limited, in England, Cadbury Singapore Pte. Ltd. began importing Cadbury Fruit & Nut chocolate from the Cadbury Confectionery in Tasmania. In contrast to the England-made Fruit & Nut, which contained raisins and almonds, with "milk solids 14% minimum," the Australian-produced Fruit & Nut introduced to Singapore had sultanas with cashew nuts, in chocolate with 27% full cream milk solids.

J. H. Whittaker & Sons Limited

Whittaker's has been a famous chocolate in New Zealand since 1896. The product line was sold nationally and by J. H. Whittaker & Sons (Australia) Limited, in Australia.

Whittaker's contained high quality products. Its Fruit & Nut milk chocolate tablet was made with 33% cocoa solids and 30% whole milk, compared to Cadbury Fruit & Nut with 25% cocoa solids and 27% milk solids. By the 1980s, cocoa beans were the world's largest export crop, after coffee and sugar. J. H. Whittaker & Sons Limited used only cocoa beans sourced from West Africa; it could be argued, therefore, that the Whittaker product might be more consistent. Whittaker's Fruit & Nut chocolate tablet with roasted almonds in smooth milk chocolate was made from sugar, milk powder, cocoa butter, cocoa mass, soya lecithin and flavour.

Table 4A. Sampling of Ingredients of Cadbury Chocolate by Country of Origin.

Country	Name of Product	Manufacturer	Ingredients
Australia	Cadbury Fruit & Nut covered in dairy milk chocolate	Cadbury Schweppes Pty Ltd., main operating company of Cadbury Schweppes Australia Limited, Claremont, Tasmania, Australia	Full cream milk, sugar, cocoa butter, cocoa mass, cashews, almonds, emulsifier (soya lecithin), natural and artificial flavours
Canada	Cadbury's Fruit et Noix Pure milk chocolate, Raisins & Almonds	William Neilson Limited, Toronto, Ontario, Canada	Milk chocolate (sugar, milk ingredients, cocoa butter, chocolate, soya lecithin, natural and artificial flavour) raisins (corn starch, hydrogenated vegetable oil), chopped almonds
China	Cadbury Fruit & Nut	Cadbury Food Co. Ltd., East of Wanyuan Road, Yongwai, Beijing, China	Milk, sugar, raisins, cocoa powder, cocoa oil, cashew nuts, almonds, fermented milk, fragrance
Egypt	Cadbury's Milk Chocolate with Raisins & Almonds	Cadbury Egypt, 10th of Ramadan City, Arab Republic of Egypt	Sugar, raisins, milk solids, cocoa butter, cocoa mass, blanched almonds, lecithin, vanillin and natural flavourings
India	Cadbury's Fruit & Nut	Hindustan Cocoa Products Limited, Bombay, India	Sugar, milk solids, cocoa butter, chocolate mass, raisins, roasted cashew nuts, roasted apricot kernels, permitted emulsifying agent (synthetic lecithin) and permitted flavouring agents
Indonesia	Cadbury's Fruit & Nut Dairy milk chocolate with raisins & almonds	P.T. Cipta Rasa Primatama, Jakarta, Indonesia	Sugar, milk solids, cocoa liquor, cocoa butter, raisins, almonds, vegetable fat, lecithin, permitted and natural flavours

Table 4A.(Continued) Sampling of Ingredients of Cadbury Chocolate by Country of Origin.

Country	Name of Product	Manufacturer	Ingredients
Kenya	Cadbury Fruit & Nut	Cadbury Schweppes Kenya Limited, Nairobi, Kenya	Sugar, milk, cocoa butter, raisins, cocoa, cashew nuts, (chopped) almonds, emulsifier, flavcurs
Malaysia	Cadbury's Fruit & Nut	Buatan Cadbury Confectionery, Malaysia Sdn. Bhd., Shah Alam, Malaysia	Sugar, full cream dairy milk, cocoa mass, cocoa butter, raisins, roasted (unblanched) almonds, vegetable oil, contains permitted emulsifiers and flavours
New Zealand	Cadbury Fruit & Nut *Chocolat au lait aux raisins secs et aux amandes*	Cadbury Confectionery Ltd., Dunedin, New Zealand	Milk, sugar, raisins, cocoa butter, cocoa mass, roasted chopped almonds, skim milk powder, butter oil, emulsifiers (322 and 476), flavour
Republic of South Africa	Cadbury's Vrugte & Neute Milk chocolate with sultanas & almonds	Cadbury (Pty.) Ltd., Port Elizabeth, Republic of South Africa	Sugar, full cream milk solids, sultanas, cocoa butter, cocoa mass, blanched almonds, vegetable fat, emulsifiers, flavouring agents
United Kingdom	Cadbury's Fruit & Nut Milk chocolate with raisins and almonds	Cadbury Limited, Bournville, Birmingham, UK	Milk, sugar, raisins, blanched whole almonds, cocoa butter, cocoa mass, vegetable fat, emulsifiers (442 and 476) flavourings
United States of America	Cadbury's Fruit & Nut Milk chocolate, raisins & almonds	Hershey Chocolate USA Pennsylvania, U.S.A.	Milk chocolate (sugar, milk, cocoa butter, chocolate, lecithin, artificial and natural flavors), raisins, almonds

Case Study Assignment

As China's growing middle class prospered, there was increasing demand for chocolate in China. A popular chocolate was Fruit & Nut manufactured by Cadbury Food Co. Ltd., in Yongwai, Beijing. However the growing market had room for new entrants. Serena was born to a Chinese family in New Zealand and she longed to go to China and set up a new venture. New Zealand being an exporter of dairy products, she had contacts to source the milk. She had access to raisins from Xinjiang and with a friend who had a contact in Ghana for cocoa beans, she could produce chocolate in China. Advise her about her about establishing a joint venture to manufacture chocolate in China for the local market.

Chapter 5

India[1]

Introduction

Situated in southern Asia, the Indian subcontinent has over 7,000 kilometres of coastline along the Arabian Sea and the Bay of Bengal. The Republic of India is the world's fastest growing free market economy; it a vibrant country, covering an area of 3,165,596 square kilometres. The federation shares borders with Bangladesh (formerly East Pakistan), Bhutan, China, Myanmar (formerly Burma), Nepal and Pakistan.

As noted by Johnson, "India's middle class is bigger than the entire 300 million population of the US (2006, p. 1)." India is very tolerant of minorities and its multicultural society includes Hindus and Muslims living peacefully with people from many different religions.

Dana (2000a) observed that a combination of historical factors, including the caste system,[2] British occupation, cultural values and government regulations, formerly limited innovative entrepreneurship in India. Kanitkar and Contractor wrote, "handicaps to entry into business ownership have been far too many given the traditional, conservative, orthodox Indian society (1992, p. 5)." In recent years, however, efforts have focused on changing the mindset and creating entrepreneurs by giving youngsters the self-confidence to become high achievers. Raghavendra and Subrahmanya (2005) found that inter-firm co-operation increased collective efficiency in India, with a significant influence on capability.

---

[1] This chapter is based on information obtained from a variety of sources, including the National Bank for Agriculture and Rural Development, and the World Association for Small & Medium Enterprises, in Delhi. Travel to India was provided by the University of Pittsburgh. Travel within India was provided by the World Association for Small & Medium Enterprises. The chapter includes historical material that first appeared in Dana (2000a).

[2] For discussions of the caste system, see Gadgil (1959); Medhora (1965); and Weber (1958). Hazlehurst (1966) focused on merchant castes.

Figure 5.1 Entrepreneurial Spirit; photograph by Léo-Paul Dana.

Historical Overview[3]

The early history of India stretches back to Mohenjodaro and Harappan times with well laid-out cities, a script, and possible evidence of trade. During Vedic times — with the flourishing of philosophical treaties on life, and intricate writings about astronomy, mathematics, and medicine — the caste system classified individuals based on their birth. The four castes were: (i) the Brahmins or priestly class; (ii) the *kshatriyas* or warrior class; (iii) the *vaishyas* or merchant class; and (iv) the *shudras* or those at the bottom rung of this social hierarchy, who did menial tasks. The untouchables, or *harijans,* fell out of this system. The *shudras* and untouchables were those who would do work such as the burying of animal carcasses and the cleaning of waste, or in today's terminology waste management. The caste system resulted in occupational

[3] This section benefited greatly from the personal assistance of Edwina Pio incorporating material from Pio (2010).

specialisation, with the *vaishya* class becoming the merchants, the overland traders, the maritime investors for waterborne trade, and intermediaries between the European powers; today their scions form the top management and owners of many of the large industrial organisations and conglomerates in India.

During the Buddhist period of ancient India, along with the travelling monks were travelling merchants, whose wealth allowed the construction of caves for residence on the trade routes between various villages and cities. Such caves were often lavishly decorated, along with the carved images of deities and donors, and can still be viewed in states such as Maharashtra. The caves were the dwelling place for monks during the monsoon season, and also served as five-star hotels for the merchants. The Buddhist period also saw the flourishing of major universities such as Nalanda and Taxila, resulting in a wave of Chinese monks who came to India to study and take back their learnings and relics to China. Merchants also used the Silk Road of the first century, which served as a significant boost to trade with many countries. It was the traders and merchants who were the early entrepreneurs in India, and the *vaishya* class became and still is highly specialised in scanning the environment and setting up businesses. The early entrepreneurs developed intricate systems for credit and forward trading to further their entrepreneurial activities such as buying ships, goods, and investing in cargo and land. The *vaishya* class was largely the source for subcastes such as the Marwaris or Banias in northern, eastern and western India (Pio, 2010). In southern India the merchants were primarily the Nattukottai Chettiars (Pio, 2010).

In 1700, the East India Company established a formal system of government for Bengal. At the time, India's share of world income was about 23%, approximately the same as Europe's (Singh, 2006).

In 1784, the British government took control of the East India Company. Entrepreneurs from various lands saw commercial opportunities in India. In 1790, Shalom ben Ovadiah HaCohen — a well-known Mizrahi[4] Jew — moved from Aleppo (*Halab*), in Syria, to Bombay. He was followed by other Jewish entrepreneurs from Baghdad and from Basra; Jewish entrepreneurs also came to India from Persia and from Yemen.

---

[4] For a discussion of this ethno-cultural group, see Dana (2010).

In 1832, David Sassoon moved to Bombay where he became a magistrate of the cotton industry. His son Abdullah Sassoon revolutionised the weaving industry in Bombay, helping Bombay become an important manufacturing centre. In 1903, the Sassoon family built the Sir Jacob Sassoon School, next to the Magen David Synagogue, in a predominantly Jewish neighbourhood of Bombay.

Until the late 20th century, the Jewish Club, on V. P. Ghandi Road in Mumbai (formerly Forbes Street, Bombay), served as a meeting place for Jewish entrepreneurs. In 1985, Giani Zail Singh, president of India, graced the festivities celebrating the centennial anniversary of the Knesset Eliyahoo Synagogue, on V. P. Ghandi Road, and the Post Office issued a stamp for the occasion.

Figure 5.2 The Jewish Club; photograph by Léo-Paul Dana.

The Marwaris are a community who specialised in domestic trade. Their enterprises complemented those of English entrepreneurs, who allowed the Marwaris to become prominent in a diversified industrial economy. In contrast, other groups of Indian entrepreneurs had experiences of another kind. During the 1800s, the British discriminated against communities who competed with English entrepreneurs in international commerce. Many Indian entrepreneurs were thus pushed out of the business realm. During the 1880s, local firms with established reputations were defrauded by British partners, an action which led to more withdrawals from the business sector. Consequently, Nafziger concluded that "the lack of indigenous entrepreneurship… stems in part from the discrimination and duplicity of the British in the 19th century (1971, p. 30)." Nevertheless, until the turn of the century, Indian entrepreneurs were central to the geographic expansion of manufacturing industries (Medhora, 1965). Dilke (1894) gave a detailed account of India during the late 19th century. Between 1912 and 1945, industrial production, in India, doubled (Balakrishna, 1961). During the 1920s and 1930s, the Jains (especially the Marwari Jains) shifted their activity from trading to manufacturing.

Williams (1942) provided a war-time account of the British colony. "Tryst with destiny," were the words of India's first prime minister, Jawaharlal Nehru, to describe independence on August 15, 1947. India became a republic in 1950 and its constitution indicated specifically that the state — not entrepreneurs from the private sector — would play the decisive role in building up the national economy. The Small Scale Industry Organisation was established in 1954, for the purpose of planning the growth of small businesses as supplements to the efforts of large industries. Also in 1954, formerly French Pondicherry was transferred to India. Decimal system coinage was introduced in 1957. Goa, under Portuguese rule since 1510, was incorporated into India in December 1961.

Patel (1987) gave a historical account of entrepreneurship development in India. "The first programme to convert potential entrepreneurs into actual owner-managers of manufacturing businesses was held at Ahmedabad in April 1970 (Sebastian and Thakur, 1994, p. v)."

In 1975, unemployment in Rajasthan led to urbanisation. That year, Barefoot College began promoting rural handicrafts, providing artisans with access to credit and also marketing outlets. Barefoot College encourages people to take risks, to innovate, to improvise and to experiment.

Figure 5.3 British Colonial Architecture; photograph by Léo-Paul Dana.

Economic liberalisation took effect in 1991. The official exchange rate was abolished in 1993 and government focused on technological development. Wani, Garg, and Sharma (2003) suggested that "to develop and transfer technology for SMEs in India, effective interaction of academic institutions with this sector will be the first step (2003, p. 71)." Wani, Garg, and Sharma (2005) emphasised developing technology-based entrepreneurship. At the 2006 Meeting in Davos, India was a star player. In 2012, India's rice exports exceeded 9.5 million tonnes.

Troubles that were rooted in the past continue to have consequences. Singha (2013) showed that good infrastructure in Manipur has a positive impact on entrepreneurship, but the state was still lagging behind the national average in terms of trade and commerce. Thomas and Prasain wrote about Manipur, "It is endowed with rich bio-diversity and natural resources with potential for entrepreneurship to thrive. Yet, Manipur continues to be the most industrially backward state with hardly any industrial base (2013, p. 16)."

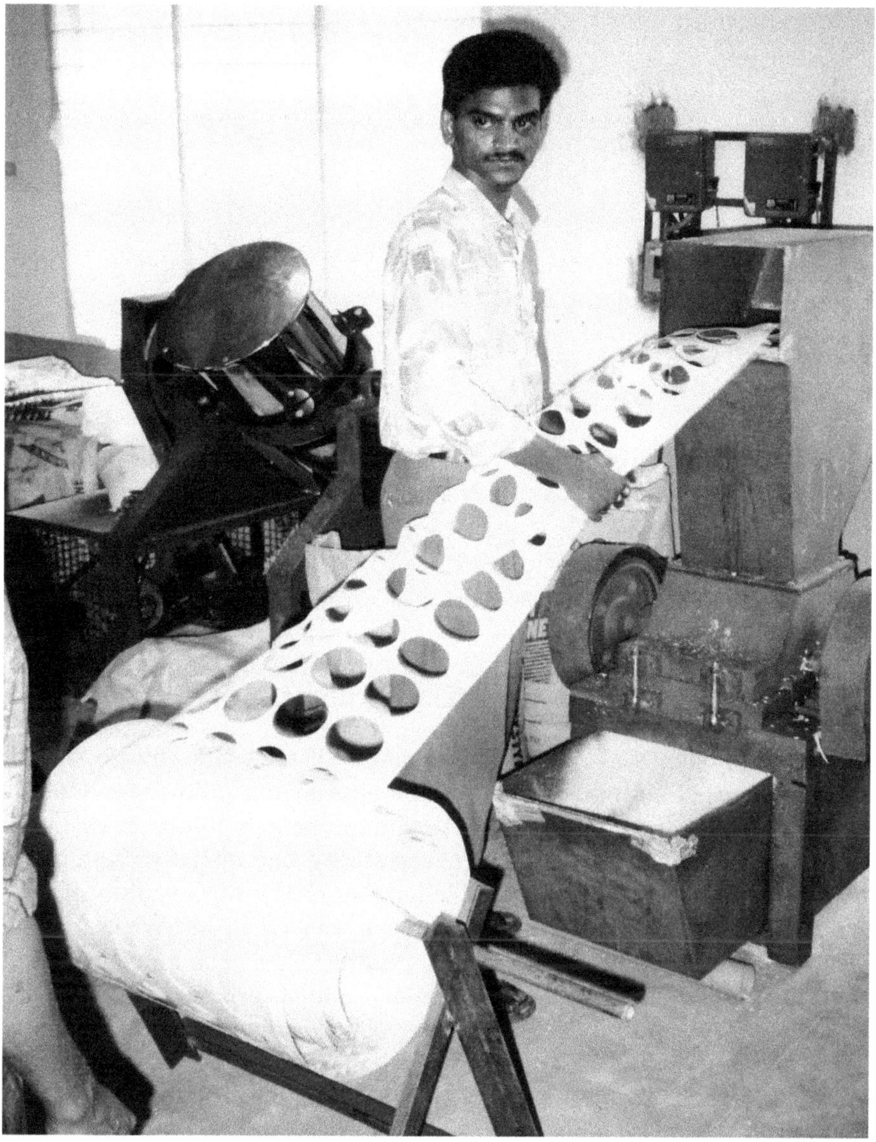

Figure 5.4 Small Firm Supplements Efforts of Large Industries; photograph by Léo-Paul Dana.

Figure 5.5 Rice Has Long Been Important; photograph by Léo-Paul Dana.

The Impact of Culture and Social Structure[5]

Pio (2005b) examined everyday Indianness of the work culture and the future dreams of an Indian export hub; it appears that culture continues to be an important force in the nature of entrepreneurship. Indeed, culture is central in explaining the social acceptability and perceived utility of entrepreneurship. Ever since McClelland's (1961) investigation of need for achievement, entrepreneurs have been viewed in the West as those with a high need to achieve. In contrast, the economy of India traditionally reflected Indian culture and social structure. Pio (2005a) explained how religious and philosophical concepts have practical applications in India; she argued that Indian culture does not segment the spiritual from the secular, and that spirituality is intrinsic to being Indian. She also explained that a person's *dharma* is interpreted through his/her role in life, and every role has certain expectations of *dharma* to be fulfilled (Pio, 2005a).

[5] This section benefited greatly from the personal assistance of Edwina Pio.

The Jains — ascetic religious group — became traders, not because of an entrepreneurial spirit based on materialism, but due to ritualistic reasons; trading was an occupation free from conflict with religious requirements. Observant Jains have become famous entrepreneurs dealing with textiles and diamonds in western India and abroad — even in Africa. Another group of Indians who have thrived on their business acumen are the Sindhis (from Sindh). Both the Jains and Sindhis are closely aligned to Hinduism in their beliefs. Other early entrepreneurs were merchants from the Islamic religion such as the Bohras from Gujarat, the followers of Zoroastrianism (religion of the Parsees), and Mizrahi Jews who settled in India. Under colonial rule, Marwari enterprises complemented those of English entrepreneurs who permitted them an important role in a diversified industrial economy. Today, Marwaris have the reputation of having business acumen and are considered to be a very enterprising group. Likewise, Banias are considered to be thrifty and with an eye on business opportunities.

As noted by Mishra, "In India there are many castes that are categorised as business castes... Most of the business castes (the erstwhile *vaishya*) are now classified under 'Other Backward Castes' for purposes of government regulations (2005 p. 305)." While the caste system reinforced the practice of following a family occupation, this impeded class mobility (Dana, 2000a). In fact, Nafziger (1971) noted that leading entrepreneurs often belonged to communities in which caste divisions were not rigidly observed.

In India, according to Kakar (1978), people are more sensitive to emotional affinity in the workplace than to work and productivity. According to Sinha (1978), work — as an end in itself — is not valued in India. Sinha (1984) explained that work is done with involvement only when done for a nurturing superior. This supported McClelland's (1975) suggestion that people in India generally performed their work as a favour to their employer.

"In India, the Planning Commission, central and state governments recognize that women should be in the mainstream of economic development. In particular, the development of microenterprise for women is seen as an appropriate way to attack poverty...(Ghosh, Gupta and Dhar, 1998, p. 158)." Yet, Porter and Nagarajan suggested that there "may be a bias in Indian culture against women who engage in entrepreneurial activities outside the home (2005, p. 41)." The practice of *purdah* keeps women at home.

Figure 5.6 Working with Spouse; photograph by Léo-Paul Dana.

A Holistic Approach to Entrepreneurship

Across India, there are countless advocates of holistic management. This is a philosophy which attempts to synergise basic elements, in order to get optimal results. The holistic approach, for instance, encourages an all-encompassing integration of the intellectual with the physical and the spiritual. Mental, material and moral aspects are involved.

Although schools teach facts, educational institutions are often lacking when it comes to personality development. It is the belief of many that entrepreneurship personality can be taught, and that this should be done at a young age. This could lead to more effective members in society.

Various agencies participate in holistic entrepreneurship development. To coordinate and oversee their activities, the Ministry of Industry established the National Institute for Entrepreneurship and Small Business Development (NIESBUD). Among the many programmes of this institute is one entitled, "Training Trainers for Barefoot Managers."

In line with the observation that over-population greatly nullifies the effect of overall development, it has been deemed in the national interest to promote birth control. For this reason, a non-governmental organisation, the Progress Harmony Development (PHD) Chamber of Commerce and Industry has become involved in propagating the message of population control. Its Rural Development Foundation has been organised to act with a holistic approach. Likewise, the Entrepreneurship Development Institute of India (EDII) takes a holistic perspective with very impressive results. Located near Ahmedabad, in Gujarat, the EDII promotes independent thinking, creativity, and a spirit of innovation. Its Rural Entrepreneurship Development division promotes micro-enterprise and provides micro-credit. The EDII sponsors research, provides education and training — including its own educational video series — and publishes an academic journal on entrepreneurship. Perhaps the most unique contribution of the EDII is its summer camp, an entrepreneurial adventure for youth to learn achievement, a concern for excellence, creativity, innovation, leadership, problem solving and systemic planning.

Figure 5.7 Attention to Detail; photograph by Léo-Paul Dana.

Figure 5.8 Work as a Favour; photograph by Léo-Paul Dana.

Toward the Future

Today's merchant princes include the Ambanis, Birlas and Tatas, the Premjis and Narayanamurthys, as well as the Indians of Silicon valley such as Kanwal Rekhi, many of whom are returning to India to invest and manage start-up as well as top performing IT companies. According to Skaria, "Indian family-run businesses have been developing rapidly from firms with limited goals that valued loyalty more than ability into dynamic professionally-managed corporates capable of taking on global competition (2006, p. 48)."

While India continues to be a patriarchal society, today there are a number of Indian women entrepreneurs many of whom are highly educated and run their own businesses, as well as the larger segment of Indian women who are starting their own micro-enterprises through micro-financing schemes. This is quite a change from the past; women in the early history of entrepreneurship are hard to find.

Traditionally, merchants would marry among their own caste, and even today one finds that arranged marriages, often to keep the wealth in the family, as well as to keep the "purity" of the caste, continue. Nevertheless, there is change in the air. Torri and Martinez (2014) explored the case of the Gram Mooligai Company, the first female community enterprise in India active in the herbal sector, entirely formed and managed by untouchables.

Figure 5.9 Rural Enterprise; photograph by Léo-Paul Dana.

With Manmohan Singh, the prime minister, calling for the 21st century to be the 'Indian Century,' the geopolitical ramifications of the country's rise are now attracting global attention (Johnson, 2006, p. 1). Challenges facing India, however, include the liberalisation of government regulation; this was discussed by James F. Hoge at the World Economic Forum, in Davos, (Hoge, 2006). At the same Forum, Bhagwati (2006) cautioned not to assume that India's rapid growth was sustainable.

Figure 5.10 Neighbourhood Fruit-mongers; photograph by Léo-Paul Dana.

Figure 5.11 Micro-enterprises; photograph by Léo-Paul Dana.

While some people run micro-enterprises, Internet entrepreneurs in Bangalore are preparing taxes for people in faraway places, reading X-rays for doctors around the world and tracing lost luggage. The national economy is growing. Jain reported, "organised retail is expanding at a rate of 40 to 45 per cent each year (2006, p. 4)." In the long run, this will have an impact on small neighbourhood shops. Despite constraints and restrictions, new generation entrepreneurs are emerging as leaders of the future.

Meanwhile, with a budget exceeding $1 billion, India is planning to put an astronaut in space. Already in 2013, India's first Mars orbiter was successfully launched. As suggested by Koster and Rai (2008), a focus of future policy should be increasing the quality of entrepreneurship.

Case Study: Nirula's

Figure 5.12 Nirula's; photograph by Léo-Paul Dana.

There are literally countless restaurants in India — 20,000 in Delhi alone. Most fast food, in India, comes from dhabas, which are roadside stands. Food is good, but may be covered with flies, and utensils may be crusty.

India's first fast-food chain, Nirula's was started by Mr. L.C. Nirula and his brother, Mr. M. Nirula, both originally from Lahore, when the city was still in India, prior to the creation of Pakistan. The brothers moved to New Delhi, and in 1934 established a restaurant with a twelve-room hotel. Later, they expanded with a cabaret. During the 1950s, Nirula's introduced fast-food burgers and chips (fries).

Lalit and Deepak Nirula, the sons of the founders, left India to study at the Cornell University School of Hotel Administration, and upon their return, they elaborated Nirula's menu, adding Indian food and 21 flavours of ice cream. They trademarked a logo with pink and white — almost identical to that of Baskin Robbins. A favourite ice cream flavour is *zafrani badaam pista*, a pungent blend of almonds, pistachio and saffron.

Nirula's grew to include numerous locations in New Delhi, feeding tens of thousands of people daily. The chain internationalised by opening outlets in Nepal. As huge international chains penetrated the Indian market, Nirula's began promoting itself heavily; it even embarked on joint-marketing campaigns with Lee (jeans). In contrast to foreign companies that paid a corporate tax rate of 48%, Nirula's benefitted when the corporate tax rate for local firms fell from 43% to 35%.

Today, Nirula's caters to an eclectic crowd; sari-clad women eat the vegetarian dishes, side-by-side with their children eating "Western" meals. Uniformed employees prepare curries, pizza, tandoori chicken, mutton-burgers and sandwiches. Other popular dishes include *dal* (a lentil dish) and *matar paneer* (a mixture of cheese with peas). Half the meals on the menu are meat-free, reflecting the fact that 80% of the population in India practice Hinduism, a religion for which the cow is sacred. A branch of this religion, the Jain sect, is opposed to killing all living beings.

With close to 300 outlets in India and battling for supremacy, in 2012 McDonald's announced it would launch all-vegetarian restaurants. In response, Indian firms were considering measures to compensate for lost market share. In 2014, an alternative for Nirula's is to diversify. Should it produce its own beverages and add these to the menu?

Culture, Religion and Diet

Mohandas (Mahatma) K. Gandhi (1869–1948), the father of India, once said that much can be known about a society by observing how people treat their animals. Indeed, cultural values are very much reflected in the role of animals. Entrepreneurs in Vietnam prosper exporting dogs to butchers and to restaurants in China. Meanwhile, in the district of Chennai, in India, a hundred stray dogs are rounded up each day to be electrocuted with unreliable antique equipment. People are hungry, but it is not considered proper to eat dogs in this country. A sandwich of roasted almonds is more culturally appropriate than meat.

Eating has long been central to the culture of India, as diet is linked to notions of purity and self-control. The Jains (an ascetic religious sect) in India practice *ahimsa*, the absolute prohibition of killing. As such, they are vegetarians. Among high castes, meat is regarded as impure, as it could lead to undesirable lust. In Hindu society, meat is often shunned, especially among unmarried women and elders. Muslims in India eat meat, provided it has been slaughtered according to religious ritual, facing Mecca; however, pork is not allowed in the Muslim diet. Jews, in India, also refrain from pork and all other meats, which are specified as prohibited according to the Bible. A variety of religions, including Bahai, Christianity, Islam, and Judaism, are represented in India, but the Hindu faith is predominant here. Consequently, the slaughtering of cattle can be perceived as sacrilege.

According to Christianity, Mary is the mother of Jesus. Likewise, the cow in India is venerated as the mother of life. The cow provides transportation, power, milk and calves. Oxen are very important in agriculture as they plough fields. They also provide 350 million tons of fertiliser each year. In addition, the amount of dung used for cooking, in India, provides heat equivalent to 35 million tons of coal or 68 million tons of wood.

The regulatory environment reinforces cultural values through government intervention. A bill of rights for cows was written alongside the national constitution. In Chennai, the police searches for sick cattle and encourages these to graze in fields near the police station. Not only are prayers said for cattle that are ill, but government agencies in India even maintain state-funded old age homes for senior cows.

The Environment

In 1977, 90% of India's villages had no safe drinking water, while Coca-Cola had reached every town. Then, distrust of foreign investment led to the departure from India, of major American firms, including Coca-Cola. Others, including IBM, were expelled. Consequently, during the early 1980s, there were few multinationals in India.

In 1986, after an absence of several years, PepsiCo applied to return to India. Eventually, foreign products were allowed to return, provided that they had Indianised brand names, *e.g.,* Hero Honda, Modi Olivetti, Maruti Suzuki. In July 1990, PepsiCo began operations in India, under the name Lehar Pepsi.

Up to the 1990s, India had been greatly influenced by parochial conflicts of caste, religion and region. Cloth was sold by the yard, tea leaves by the kilo, and soap was cut into chunks to be sold by weight. Class mobility was limited, and poverty was widespread. Technological and regulatory changes, however, transformed society. Significant economic reforms raised GDP growth, while the spread of electricity and technology contributed to industrial output.

Major reform came in 1991, when India opened up. Shortly thereafter, Rajan Pillai — a Singapore-based industrialist (of Indian origin) — announced that he would bring Coca-Cola back to India. When Coca-Cola resumed operations in India, it was among the first firms which was not required to use an Indianised name.

After years of restrictive policies, liberalisation opened up India, to imports and to foreign investments. In many industries, foreign technology agreements were granted automatic approval, and no permission was required for hiring foreign technicians. As a member of the Multilateral Investments Guarantee Agency, India would have no restriction on the repatriation of dividends and profits. Across a wide range of industries, India opted to permit up to 51% foreign equity participation, regardless of whether foreign technology was in question and the Foreign Investment Promotion Board was given authority to approve investment beyond 51%. In the case of small-scale units, the ceiling for foreign equity participation was 24%. Also helping new entrants was the reduction of duty on the import of capital goods, from 35% to 25%.

Industrial policy in India was liberalised such that location of an enterprise did not need approval except in the case of highly populated areas. There were further relaxations of policy regulating non-polluting industries, and firms were allowed to generate their own power. Also, India removed its requirement of having a phased manufacturing program. Finally, the controller of capital issues would not longer have control over capital market operations, which instead became guided by an autonomous Securities and Exchange Board of India.

Fiscal policy was also modified. The maximum personal income tax rate (for revenues exceeding 120,000 rupees) had been fixed at 40%. After the tax structure was rationalised and simplified, personal tax rates fell to between 10% and 30%; the corporate tax rate was reduced to 35% for Indian companies and 48% for foreign ones.

India became the world's largest producer of ground-nuts and of tea, the world's second largest producer of fruits, milk, rice, sugar, vegetables, wheat and woven cotton fabrics. Rising literacy along with surging incomes increased the demand for quality. The spread of electricity also created the demand for electric gadgets; among these was the television, a medium used to persuade people to spend whatever money they have. The buying power of the rising middle class, along with the relaxation of government regulations, made the Indian market very attractive for foreign enterprises. Kellogg's was quick to introduce its new product, Basmati Rice Flakes, and has been advertising Kellogg's Frosties (frosted flakes) as a good source of energy.

With liberalisation, Cadbury-Schweppes launched its beverage line in India. The arrival of such giants was a threat to existing bottling plants in India. PepsiCo India Holdings Pvt. Ltd., in Mumbai (formerly Bombay), was allowed to take over Duke's.

Kentucky Fried Chicken, Formerly Owned by PepsiCo

PepsiCo entered India with beverages but soon brought fast food as well. The rise of a new middle class, including 250 million consumers, encouraged PepsiCo to open India's first Kentucky Fried Chicken (KFC), in Bangalore, on June 1, 1995. It was expected that McDonald's would follow. Other American firms expressing interest in India included: AT & T, Black & Decker Corp., Levi Strauss & Co., Mattel Inc., Morgan Stanley & Co., Motorola Inc., Raytheon Co., Sara Lee Corp., Timex Corp., and Walt Disney Co. Even IBM, which had been expelled from India during the 1970s, decided to return to India. The opening of India's first KFC franchise in June 1995 angered thousands of people. The corporation had planned to spend US$40 million in India, opening sixty restaurants there, with an average of 50 employees at each location. However, other issues were considered as having greater impact than that of job creation.

KFC would fatten its chickens on maize, the highest-protein cereal that was also the cheapest source of nutrition for the poor. Those people whose maize was being removed were the ones who could not afford KFC meals.

In 1993, the Karnataka Farmers Association accused multinationals of harming local entrepreneurs, and therefore destroyed the Bangalore offices of the corporate giant, Cargill Seeds. In 1995, the same association claimed that KFC would force small-scale chicken farmers out of business. With 10 million members, this group gained political clout; the association could easily round up 200,000 participants to show solidarity at a single protest. Should American fast food restaurants be concerned?

Indeed, it was argued that KFC would buy chickens from large-scale hatcheries, to the detriment of small-scale farmers. Furthermore, KFC's demand for chicken could affect the demand for chicken feed; grain would be diverted to feed chicken, while peasants would be hungry.

To protect its interests, the Karnataka Farmers Association distributed a leaflet warning of "chemically poisoned meat" which it deemed carcinogenic. Accusations, against KFCs franchise in Bangalore, resulted in government intervention. The health ministry announced that KFC chicken contained excessive quantities of monosodium glutamate (MSG). The KFC outlet then lost its permit.

Despite problems with its Bangalore store, PepsiCo Restaurants International proceeded to open another KFC, this one in Delhi. Here, health inspectors found flies in the kitchen, and the municipal health commissioner ordered that KFC outlet's license be revoked on the grounds of unsanitary conditions.

McDonald's

In 1937, Richard and Maurice McDonald opened a tiny drive-in restaurant east of Pasadena, in California. This was the first McDonald's, and from this new, small business, the two brothers developed food-processing and assembly-line techniques. In 1954, Ray Kroc, a salesman of milkshake mixers at the time, identified an opportunity in this small business; he then negotiated a franchise deal, granting him exclusive rights to franchise McDonald's across the United States. At a time when other franchising companies sold restaurant and ice cream franchises for up to $50,000 for large geographic areas, Mr. Kroc offered franchisees a McDonald's franchise for $950, and a token service fee equal to 1.4% of sales for himself plus a royalty of 0.5% of sales which went to Richard and Maurice McDonald. In 1956, Harry Sonneborn, a partner in Ray Kroc's enterprise, introduced a formula for leasing stores, to be sub-leased to franchisees at a 40% premium. Eventually, McDonald's purchased land for franchisees. Preferring a calmer life, in 1961, Richard and Maurice McDonald sold their shares of this business for $2.7 million.

McDonald's first international venture was in Canada, during 1967. It soon became the country's fast-food industry leader. McDonald's learned that despite the cost savings inherent in standardisation, success is often a function of being able to adapt to an environment. Product lines were constantly evolving, reflecting taste preferences, and potential profitability. In 1980, McDonald's outlets in New York City sold steak sandwiches; however, the product did not prove to be as profitable as others, and it was discontinued. McDonald's introduced lobster sandwiches in New Hampshire, and bagels in Vermont. Some outlets in Canada made available a Quebec specialty called *poutine*, consisting of potatoes covered with gravy and topped with cheese curds.

By the mid-1990s, Cara Operations (the owner of Harvey's and Swiss Chalet) was approaching annual sales of $1 billion Canadian, while McDonald's Canada surpassed $1.6 billion Canadian in sales during 1994. By 1997, McDonald's Canada operated almost 1,000 restaurants in Canada, and had become involved in McDonald's in Russia.

By the late 1990s, there were about 12,000 McDonald's restaurants across the United States, and this was the single most advertised brand in the nation. About 85% of the McDonald's outlets in the United States were franchises, with the McDonald's Corporation receiving a royalty fee based not on profit, but gross sales. Annual advertising and promotion expenditures were $1 billion, and of each three hamburgers prepared in the United States, one was made by McDonald's.

A concern, however, was that domestic growth was on the decline. During the 1970s, the average annual growth rate for the American fast-food industry exceeded 7%. By the 1980s, the annual growth rate of domestic sales had dropped to below 5%; in 1989, for example, McDonald's reported that its sales in the United States grew just 4%. As the American market approached saturation, marketing efforts were shifted toward foreign markets. Soon, McDonald's lost domestic share to competitors such as Burger King (a unit of Grand Metropolitan PLC) and Wendy's International Inc.

McDonald's first Asian investment was a restaurant in Japan opened during 1971. At the time, fast food in this country was either a bowl of noodles or miso soup. The location selected for this new venture was the Ginza, a swinging neighbourhood of Tokyo. McDonald's Co. (Japan) Ltd. introduced a gratin croquet sandwich with a deep-fried patty of macaroni, shrimp and potatoes, but this product failed, and was withdrawn from the Japanese market. Nevertheless, the brand was a success in Japan, and this led to increased competition. The Japanese candy manufacturer Lotte entered the burger business with its Lotteria outlets, serving deep fried salmon burgers with onion sauce. Suntory, Japan's largest distiller of whisky, penetrated with First Kitchen. Morinaga & Co., Japan's leading caramel enterprise, launched its own fast food business, Morinaga Love, featuring a rice burger with grilled rice patties instead of hamburgers. This particular product is filled with grilled squid, seaweed and spicy red cod roe.

Despite success in many key markets, McDonald's also encountered difficulties marketing abroad. In October 1991, a poster illustrating the French celebrity Paul Bocuse was displayed in 66 outlets across the Netherlands; the problem was that it showed him with four other French chefs, examining a batch of dressed chickens, while the caption indicated that the chefs were dreaming of Big Macs. This was interpreted as an insult to French haute cuisine. Then, McDonald's aggravated the situation with a letter of apology, in which it was claimed that the internationally reputed chef was not well known in the Netherlands.

McDonald's Co. (Japan) Ltd. introduced Chicken Tatsuta, Teriyaki Chicken, and the Teriyaki McBurger. With its first mover advantage, McDonald's Co. (Japan) Ltd. kept its lead in Japan. By 1997, it had over 1,000 outlets across that nation, and these sold more food in Japan than any other restaurant company. Burgers were garnished with a fried egg. Beverages included iced coffee and corn soup. Several adaptations were particularly successful overseas. In tropical markets, guava juice was added to the McDonald's product line. In Puerto Rico, McJustas del Sabor became a favourite. In Germany, McDonald's did well selling beer as well as McCroissants. Banana fruit pies became popular in Latin America and McSpaghetti noodles became a favorite in the Philippines. In Thailand, McDonald's introduced the Samurai Pork Burger with sweet sauce. Meanwhile, McDonald's in New Zealand launched the Kiwiburger served with beet root sauce and optional apricot pie. In Malaysia, McDonald's had success with the McRendang and sugar cane juice. In Singapore, where fries came to be served with chili sauce, the Kiasuburger chicken breakfast became a best seller. In Norway, McLaks salmon was introduced. McDonald's also experimented with vegetarian needs. Its first meatless burger was the "Hula Burger," consisting of grilled pineapple with cheese on a bun. This product was a failure, but in the Netherlands, during 1992, McDonald's tried to launch another vegetarian item, the Dutch veggie burger, made of spiced potatoes, peas, carrots and onions. Singapore was among the first markets in which

McDonald's introduced delivery service. Delivery eventually became popular in a variety of other markets, including Egypt.

While KFC had about 10,000 outlets in approximately 80 countries, McDonald's expanded to about 20,000 restaurants, in over 100 countries. The McDonald's outlet in Delhi, the first in India, was a partnership with local entrepreneur Mr. Vikram Bakshi. It opened in late October 1996, substituting the Big Mac with the Maharaja Mac, made from mutton, and offered vegetarian rice-patties flavoured with vegetables and spices.

The Beverage Sector

India is the world's largest producer of tea, and the second largest producer of milk. It is also the second largest producer of fruits and the second largest producer of sugar, giving India the potential of becoming a major producer of juice and/or fruit drinks.

Among the most popular drinks in India is freshly squeezed sugar cane juice. Also, almost everyone enjoys the water inside fresh, green coconuts. Mangoes grow in abundance, and mango juice is common. Several bottlers prepare mango-flavoured drinks, including Mangola and Slice.

Duke & Sons Pvt. Ltd. developed Duke's Mangola, containing water, mango, pulp, sugar, citric acids, permitted class II preservatives and colour. As well, Duke's prepared soda, simply mixing treated water and carbon dioxide. West Bengal became the most popular market for India's own brand-name cola, Thums Up, the generic description of which is "sweetened carbonated beverage." The S. David Soda Water Factory was one of numerous local producers of soft drinks, and for years business was going well.

Liberalisation of the late twentieth century brought major changes. PepsiCo India Holdings Pvt. Ltd., in Mumbai (formerly Bombay), was allowed to take over Duke's. Maximum retail prices (MRPs) continued to be government regulated, but not all retailers respected them. MRP for a 300ml. bottle of Duke's soda was six rupees, and for a 200ml bottle of Duke's Mangola, eight rupees, inclusive of taxes, but excluding the glass container. Coca-Cola's Limca was more expensive than Thums Up, bottled by Prabha Beverages, Pvt. Ltd., in Marthandam.

While Mangola dominated the mango beverage sector in Mumbai, Slice had more extensive distribution channels in Delhi and better brand recognition. Therefore, PepsiCo acquired not only Duke's but also Slice.

PepsiCo also launched Pepsi-Cola, the generic description of which was "sweetened carbonated water."

The Coca-Cola Company's developed interest in India led to the acquisition of Thums Up, with very well developed distribution channels and excellent brand recognition, especially in the northeast of India. The Coca-Cola Company also launched Coke. In Calcutta, Black Diamond Beverage Ltd. became a Coca-Cola bottler. Near Mumbai, Britco Foods Co. Ltd. bottled Coca-Cola products in Pune, an industrial town in Maharastra state.

The Coca-Cola Company benefited from the Thums Up distribution channels, and PepsiCo from those of Duke's and Slice. Cadbury-Schweppes, meanwhile benefited from its own reputation and from the established distribution channels of its confectionery line. There was already strong brand recognition for Cadbury chocolates, as Hindustan Cocoa Products Limited used to make Cadbury chocolates, in what was then Bombay. After liberalisation, Cadbury India Limited produced chocolates in its own three factories. One was in Pune and another in Thane, both in Maharashtra state. Cadbury also had a factory in the village of Gurikha (MP state).

Cadbury Schweppes brought orange-flavoured Crush to India and also ginger ale under the name Canada Dry. Where there was already strong brand loyalty to Cadbury chocolate, Canada Dry and Crush both did well. In Mumbai, a special promotion was held at the Regal movie theatre, where people were eager to have a Cadbury drink with a Cadbury chocolate, during intermission. In Mumbai, Coca-Cola was dwarfed in Cadbury's shadow.

Another player in the soft drinks industry was Rogers & Co. Pvt. Ltd. (64 Mirza Ghalib Marg, Mumbai 400 008). This firm bottled drinks under license from Kickapoo Joy Juice Limited, in Toronto, Canada.

In summary, Cadbury Schweppes brought Canada Dry and Crush to India, and benefited from the fact that Cadbury's was already a well-known brand, as its chocolates were being made by Hindustan Cocoa Products Limited. Also taking advantage of existing distribution channels, the Coca-Cola Company acquired India's own famous cola, Thums Up; PepsiCo India Holdings Pvt. Ltd. took over Duke's Mangola from Duke & Sons Pvt. Ltd. Later, Coca-Cola acquired the soft dink business of Cadbury Schweppes.

Table 5A. Mango Drinks in India

Brand	Producer	Ingredients
Aavin (marketed by Tamil Nadu Co-op Milk Producers' Federation Limited, Chennai)	The Salem District Co-operative Milk producers Union Ltd., Salem	Water, mango pulp, sugar, citric acid, ascorbic acid, colour, flavour
Frooti	Licensee of Parle Agro Ltd., Mumbai	Mango juice drink
Fruitnik	Sivas Beverages, 5/160A Kunathur High Road, Porur, Chennai 600116	Water, mango pulp, sugar, citric acid, permitted colour, added flavour, permitted class II preservatives
Lehar Slice	Pepsico India Holdings Ltd.	Water, mango pulp, sugar, citric acid, permitted colour, class II preservative, added flavour
Maaza	Chennai Bottling Co. Ltd., 423 Poonamalle High Road, Arumbakkam, Chennai 600106	Water, mango pulp, sugar, citric acid, added flavour, permitted class II preservative
Mango Time	Sree Mahalakshimi Food Industries Limited, Kalamassery	Water, mango pulp, sugar, citric acid, permitted class II preservatives, colour, added flavour

Case Study Assignment

Act as consultant to Nirula's and prepare a feasibility study to help decide whether the food provider should manufacture drinks — and if so which — for distribution in its fast food restaurants.

Chapter 6

Indonesia[1]

Introduction

Comprised of 13,667 lush islands, Indonesia is the world's largest archipelago. Its total land area is 1.92 million square kilometres. Entrepreneurs, here, are concentrated in labour-intensive industries where the use of traditional methods result in a competitive edge. Popular sectors include clothing, foodstuffs, footwear, furniture, leather, metal products, pottery and wooden products. Most manufacturing takes place in small-scale establishments.[2]

The Central Bureau of Statistics, in Jakarta, defines small industries as units of production using five or more workers, but less than 20. More traditional are the cottage household industries — units with up to four people, usually family members. Officially, entrepreneurs are required to obtain a basic business permit, *Surat Izin Untuk Perusahaan.* However, there are hidden costs involved, as civil servants often require an abusive bribe before issuing a permit. Therefore, it is common for entrepreneurs not to have one. When officials come around and hassle them, cigarettes and cash are used to avoid fines. Thus, it is easy to function without a permit, but as noted by Parnwell and Turner (1998), without one, it is impossible to obtain institutional credit. Vial (2011) discussed how corruption hinders entrepreneurship in Indonesia.

---

[1] The chapter is based on information obtained from a variety of sources, including: the Department of Communication and Informatics; the Department of Industry and Trade; the Directorate General of Small and Medium Industry; the Investment Co-ordinating Board (BKPM); the Ministry of Commerce; the Ministry of Cooperatives & SMEs; the Ministry of Culture and Tourism; the Ministry of Finance; and Statistics Indonesia. The chapter includes historical material that first appeared in Dana (1999b).

[2] See also Tambunan (1992).

Figure 6.1 No Institutional Credit; photograph by Léo-Paul Dana.

Indonesia has introduced a unique model, a special guidance scheme to assist entrepreneurs in clusters. The state identifies clusters of entrepreneurs in the same economic sector and in the same geographic region. The clusters — *sentras* — are provided with training, facilities and subsidies.

Indonesia is the world's principal supplier of vanilla. Growing vanilla is labour-intensive; plants are fertilised by hand, contributing to the cost. Hence vanilla — when pure — is among the most expensive spices. (Saffron costs more.) In Indonesia, small-scale farmers of vanilla beans co-operate in local farming associations facilitating exports. Their vanilla is used in Ben & Jerry's ice-cream, and sold around the world. 85% percent of Indonesia's vanilla is grown in Bali.

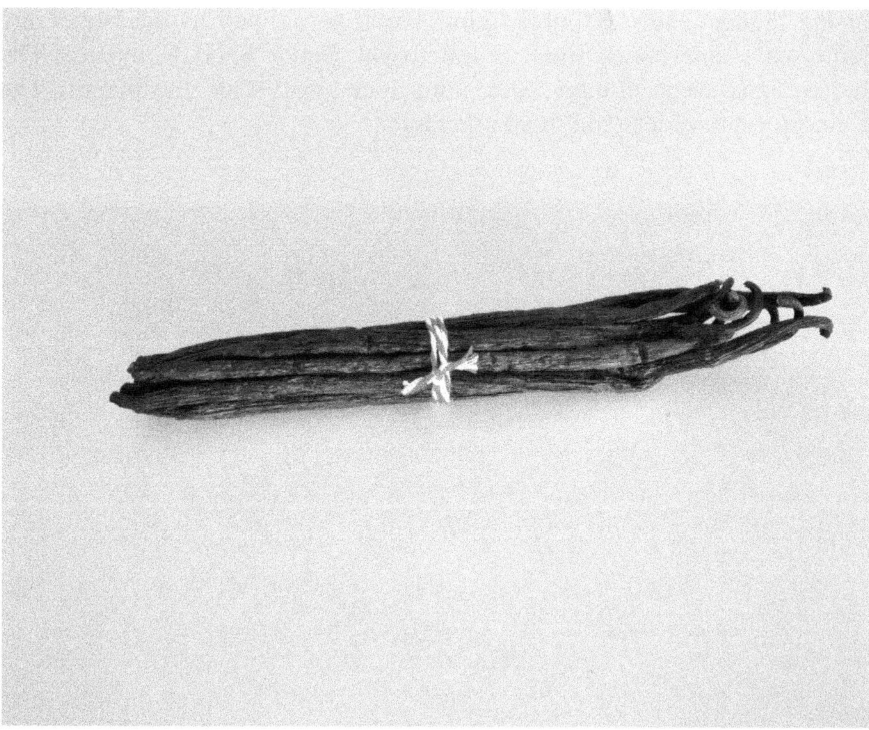

Figure 6.2 Dried Vanilla Fruits; photograph by Léo-Paul Dana.

Historical Overview

About 5,000 years ago, Indians and Malays arrived. Buddhism was brought from India, almost 2,000 years ago. When merchants spread Islam to the region, Hindus who resisted Islam relocated to Bali. During the 15th century, the Portuguese came in search of spices. The Dutch arrived, and subsequently established the Dutch East India Company in 1602. The Dutch created the Netherlands East Indies, which they governed between 1799 and 1942. The Portuguese kept eastern Timor until 1975. In contrast to the British who tried to dissolve the caste system of India, the Dutch opted to develop relations with the Indonesian elite. Descendants of Javanese royalty were invited into the civil service. Under Dutch rule, Indonesia had three classes. Dutchmen were in control of the higher levels of public administration, as well as the banks and large-scale enterprises such as the Royal Dutch Shell Company. The Indonesians were farmers, and some had small-scale businesses. The Chinese were traders and money-lenders.

Figure 6.3 Indigenous Musician; photograph by Léo-Paul Dana.

Figure 6.4 Dutch Architecture in Indonesia; photograph by Léo-Paul Dana.

Prior to the Great Depression, a small number of large-scale merchants prospered. During the 1930s, peasants turned to cash crops. Eventually, the market was saturated with micro-traders, each one making a marginal living.

In 1942, Japan took over Indonesia. In 1944, Japan proclaimed that Indonesia would become independent once the war ended, and independence was formally declared after the Japanese surrendered in 1945. The Dutch attempted to reinstate their government, but the United States threatened to cut off Marshall Plan assistance to the Netherlands, unless the Dutch let go of their former colony (excluding the western portion of Papua New Guinea). Independence was proclaimed on August 17, 1945, and Sukarno became the first president of the republic.

In 1963, Indonesia annexed the western portion of Papua New Guinea. Unlike other Indonesians, the people here are primarily Papuan. A failed coup by communists, in September 1965, was followed by a blood bath. Thousands of Chinese Indonesians were slaughtered in 1966. In 1967, General Soeharto took the place of Sukarno. That year, Indonesia became a founding member of the Association of Southeast Asian Nations (ASEAN). The other founding members were Malaysia, the Philippines, Singapore and Thailand. In 1976, Indonesia annexed formerly Portuguese Timor.

During the 1980s, non-tariff barriers were converted to tariffs, and tariff rates were lowered. Financial services were deregulated. Income tax rates and property taxes were reduced. In 1989, foreign direct investment was freed from most controls. In 1990, $1 bought 1,828 rupiahs (Rp).

A political patronage system, under Soeharto, allowed nepotism and corruption to thrive. Soeharto gave the flour monopoly to his friend Liem Sioe Liong. In partnership with Soeharto, Chinese entrepreneurs controlled 70% of the private sector. The gap between rich and poor widened. Street peddlers were fined Rp 1,000, or imprisoned, for operating at road junctions. In 1992, the collapse of Bank Summa shook confidence in the banking sector. The rupiah tumbled during the financial crisis of 1997. Devaluation led to inflation.

Angered over increases in the prices of milk and rice, in January 1998, Indonesians looted stores reported to be charging excessive prices. Shops owned by Chinese entrepreneurs become the focus of aggression. This happened in several Javanese towns, including Jember, Kragan and Losari. On February 13, in Pamanukan (Java), about 600 people attacked every store owned by Chinese entrepreneurs. The rioters hurled stones at some shops and burnt others down, using cooking oil.

Figure 6.5 The Gap Widened between Rich and Poor; photograph by Léo-Paul Dana.

By March, prices for food staples had risen by as much as 300% in local currency. In April, seven banks were closed down. These were: PT Bank Centris International; PT Bank Deka; PT Bank Hokindo; PT Bank Kredit Asia; PT Bank Pelita; PT Bank Subentra; and PT Bank Surya. In May, the prime lending rate rose from 36% to 45%, and more price increases led to new riots in Bandung (Java) and Medan (Sumatra). On May 12, looters ransacked Jakarta. *Newsweek* reported that 4,940 buildings were damaged. According to Reuters, damage affected 4,168 stores, 383 offices, 24 restaurants, 13 public markets, 12 hotels and nine service stations. Riots, in Solo (Java), prompted 600 ethnic-Chinese families to move away. Many wealthy Indonesians left the country. Tourism in Indonesia dried up.

Following the 80% plunge in the value of the rupiah, many foreign parties were reluctant to honour letters of credit that had been issued in Indonesia. Being flexible and less reliant on formal markets and formal credit, SMEs (with up to 50 workers) were found to have weathered the financial crisis better than was the case among larger firms (Tambunan, 2005).

Figure 6.6 Wealthy Indonesians in Europe with Friends from Overseas; photograph by Léo-Paul Dana.

Soeharto was forced to step down in May 1998, and his vice-president, Dr. Bacharuddin Jusuf Habibie began to lead Indonesia out of the Asian Financial Crisis. Nevertheless, the economy contracted by about 4% in 1998, while inflation approached 80%. In 1999, much attention was shifted to ethnic fighting on eastern Timor, where separatists clashed with federalists. Finally, it was resolved that the 1999 national elections be followed by a referendum on the future of self-rule in Timor. After the crisis, formerly legal tender banknotes were made obsolete. As part of an autonomy package to quell separatism in Aceh, in 2003, Aceh courts were granted the freedom to apply Shariah law. Public canings were hence legalised.

A devastating tragedy in 2004 was a tsunami that caused considerable damage to Indonesia among other places. Mydans (2005) reported that Indonesia received billions of dollars in aid, but that relief efforts were delayed by bureaucratic requirements. An earthquake in 2006 caused yet another setback. Entrepreneurs helped the economy rebound.

Figure 6.7 Indonesia is the World's Largest Producer of Pineapples; photograph by Léo-Paul Dana.

Diversity

The population of Indonesia is quite diverse. On the island of Lombok (east of Bali and west of Sumbawa Island), people practise a unique form of Islam, called *Wektu Telu;* followers retain many animist or spiritualist beliefs. Entrepreneurs from Nusa Tenggara dominate towing services. Further west, entrepreneurs from Tegal, on the island of Java, have a reputation for being in the food business; many own street-side food stalls — known as *warung tegal* or *warteg* — catering to low income people. Even further west, Bataks from North Sumatra are clustered in the sale of oil products and the servicing of vehicles. Madurese entrepreneurs are famous for owning satay stalls.

On the island of Java, a small number of Jews reside in Surabaya. Of Iraqi origin, their community has given rise to many entrepreneurs with international networks spanning the world, with hubs in India, Singapore, North America and Europe.

Across Indonesia, the Chinese minority has been successful in entrepreneurship. Chinese entrepreneurs have dominated distribution networks for food and other essentials. Ethnic Chinese entrepreneurs from Pontianak (West Kalimantan) are traders in building materials.

The Chinese in Indonesia

During the 1800s, the Dutch welcomed Chinese traders in Indonesia, and entered into business partnerships with them. Thus, the success of ethnic-Chinese entrepreneurs in Indonesia dates back to the *Vereenigte Oost-Indische Compagnie* (United East Indies Company), which granted them monopoly leases. Later, the Dutch colonial government did the same, further contributing to the economic success of Chinese entrepreneurs on these islands. Even when the monopoly leases were phased out, at the end of the 19th century, former lease-holders continued trading.

By 1900, there were 227,000 ethnic-Chinese in Java and another 310,000 on other Indonesian islands. They included self-employed artisans, builders, contractors, furniture-makers, manufacturers, money-lenders, repairmen, shippers, shopkeepers, smiths, speculators, suppliers, and tanners; they owned abattoirs, gambling dens, grocery stores, pawnshops, real estate and warehouses.

As explained by Kahin (1952), sharp trading practices used by aggressively competitive Chinese entrepreneurs contributed to the rapid growth of *Sarekat Dagang Islam* after 1909. This propagated anti-Chinese sentiment, and by 1912 anti-Chinese riots were a reality in Surabaya and Surakarta.

The 20th century saw demographic and social changes among the Chinese in Indonesia. Fluent in Dutch, the children of established families strayed away from their family businesses, and drifted toward salaried professions. The more recent immigrants did not integrate into the established community. Many newcomers became peddlers or low-wage labourers. This caused an increasing gap between the existing Indonesian Chinese and new arrivals from China. During the 1920s, however, many Chinese wage-workers became small-scale merchants. By 1930, according to the census of that year, there were 1,230,000 Chinese residing in Indonesia.

Among the Chinese immigrants who arrived in Indonesia, in 1938, was Liem Sioe Liong. During the 1950s, he befriended an army supply officer, who later became President Soeharto. Through his Salim Group, Liem Sioe Liong became Indonesia's most successful entrepreneur, with 300 companies producing cars, cement, chemicals, cooking oil, flour, milk, noodles and steel.

During the rule of Sukarno (1945–1966) anti-Chinese pressure prompted 119,000 ethnic-Chinese people to leave Indonesia. Those who stayed were prohibited from being entrepreneurs in rural areas. The rational was that Indigenous Indonesians should have a chance to be merchants. Under Soeharto, the Chinese were barred from government office and most professions. The lack of alternatives encouraged them to concentrate their efforts in the commercial realm.

During the 1950s, new legislation prevented the Chinese from living in certain towns. This included the locally-born Chinese (Peranakans), as well as ethnic-Chinese immigrants (Totok). The objective was to give a competitive advantage to the Muslim *pribumi* people. Customs regulations also prohibited the import of Chinese medicines and/or printed matter in Chinese characters.

The Soeharto regime followed with a policy favouring the *pribumis*. These people were entitled to favourable credit terms, and they had easy access to permits. Indonesians could acquire permits, and they did. Then, they sold them to Chinese entrepreneurs, with immense mark-ups.

The Chinese community in Indonesia has been very heterogeneous, with differences based on origin and on socio-economic class, as well as on the degree of assimilation. The diversity within this population has prompted some commentators to suggest that these people can hardly be considered one entity (Rigg, 1997). Nevertheless, *pribumi* anti-Chinese sentiment seldom makes distinctions (Turner, 2003b).

Throughout Soeharto's rule, the identities of the Chinese in Indonesia (about 3% of the population) were politically contested. The government erased the diverse cultural identities of the Chinese, placing priority on assimilation (Turner, 2003b).

In June 1998, there were about seven million ethnic-Chinese in Indonesia. This represented 3.5% of the country's population. Yet, ethnic-Chinese entrepreneurs owned 70% of the private sector in Indonesia. In September 1998, ethnic-Chinese entrepreneurs controlled 170 conglomerates in Indonesia as well as 5,000 medium-sized firms and 250,000 small enterprises. According to Yeung (1999), the overseas Chinese controlled 80% of corporate assets in Indonesia in 1999. Although the Chinese in Indonesia adopted Indonesian names, they never fully integrated with the Indigenous population. Half of Indonesia's Chinese are Hokkien.

Culture and Entrepreneurship

Penujak, on the island of Lombok, is home to potters who use the *turun temurun* method of making pottery. Since the 1500s, this skill has been passed on from mother to daughter, using no tools other than a round stone and a wooden paddle.

In Sukhara, a village of 3,000 people, also on Lombok, about 600 families are self-employed weavers. The men grow cotton and the women weave it into cloth, which is sold in larger towns, such as Sweta. Families also grow cloves, coffee, garlic, rice, soya beans and tobacco for personal use.

Indeed, many Indigenous Indonesians are self-employed, inasmuch as they are subsistence farmers. However, market-oriented entrepreneurship is not central to the culture here. In Javanese, the word for trader also signifies "tramp," or "foreigner."

In contrast, the ethnic-Chinese, in Indonesia, have thrived in entrepreneurship. One causal variable may be their culture, but it should also be emphasised that they were given few alternatives, as they were barred from many other occupations open to Indigenous Indonesians. By the same token, Indigenous Indonesians complained that ethnic-Chinese entrepreneurs also created barriers to entry.

As ethnic-Chinese entrepreneurs became increasingly successful in Indonesia, Javanese would-be-entrepreneurs complained that Chinese entrepreneurship was a de-facto barrier to entry, inhibiting the Javanese from becoming self-employed. The Chinese had more experience in business, more capital, better networks, and international contacts.

Public Policy on Entrepreneurship

At the National Level

President Sukarno, who ruled from 1945 to 1966, introduced anti-business policies to Indonesia. The Land Reform Bill of 1960 redistributed property; individuals were limited to 7½ hectares, the equivalent of approximately 19 acres.

Beginning in 1969, Indonesia implemented a series of national development plans, each known by the acronym REPELITA (for *Rencana Pembangunan Lima Tahun*). These typically emphasised development in rural areas. The first two plans focused on agriculture.

In 1973, Indonesia introduced its Small Enterprises Development Programme (SEDP). This was a subsidised credit scheme to help cottage industries and small-scale Indigenous enterprises controlled by *pribumis*. The SEDP was discontinued in January 1990.

REPELITA III (1979–1984) began giving assistance to clusters of similar types of small firms — known as *sentras*. These will be discussed in a separate section.

REPELITA IV established a framework for the development of national industry. Among the plan's objectives was finding solutions for major problems facing small-scale entrepreneurs, in financing, marketing and technical problems. As the price of oil dropped, Indonesia deregulated large sectors of its economy. In October 1988, Indonesia launched important bank reforms, which reduced capital restrictions.

REPELITA V (1989–1994) emphasised entrepreneurship and the development of small industries. The plan called for tripling private sector investment in targeted industries, including agriculture and tourism. The plan focused on small-scale and household industries, especially those outside urban areas. In October 1989, policy changes allowed foreign entrepreneurs to have 100% ownership of an enterprise in the Batam Economic Zone, for a period of five years. Also, private firms were permitted to set-up industrial estates.

In January 1990, the SEDP was replaced by the *Kredit Usaha Kecil* (KUK), an unsubsidised credit scheme. The Directorate General of Small Industry was created (within the Ministry of Industry) with the purpose of financing the new ventures of competent entrepreneurs. The *Kredit Investasikecil* — the government's small-scale investment credit scheme — made it possible for small-scale industries to obtain capital for the purpose of purchasing fixed assets. As well, *Kredit Modal Kerja Permanen* — the permanent working capital credit scheme — allowed firms to receive working capital loans, through banks, at subsidised rates. Also, the (central) Bank of Indonesia started a Small Enterprise Development Project, the purpose of which was to train loan officers and to simplify lending procedures.

During the 1990s, the banking sector was liberalised, but Soeharto asked banks to increase lending to small firms. Until 1992, the seven state banks of Indonesia specialised in different sectors: Bank BNI met the needs of manufacturers and traders; Bank Bumi Daya served plantations; Bank Dagang Negara focused on mining; Bank Exim financed international trade; Bank Pembangunan Indonesia specialised in finance for transport; Bank Rakyat Indonesia financed farmers; and Bank Tabungan Negara mobilised public savings.

In 1992, reforms blurred the distinction between different banks. Indonesia's new Banking Law was passed in February 1992, and in August, Indonesia's seven major state banks became joint stock enterprises. This was a move away from bureaucratic regulations and toward profitability. A problem with this restructuring, however, was that it became expensive for entrepreneurs to borrow capital. Also in 1992, the Directorate General of Small Industry adopted an official policy of promoting entrepreneurs who employed between five and 19 workers. The Directorate General subsequently focused on helping entrepreneurs with financing, production and marketing.

REPELITA VI included the development of small enterprises in 2,200 villages. This plan was discussed in detail by Booth (1994). In 1995, the government passed Small Business Law Number 9. This act led to the National Partnership Programme. Indonesia amended import duties, effective January 1996. On fish, duty rates ranged from 0% to 25%. In 1996, the National Agency for Export Development began reporting to a recently enlarged ministry. The agency included centres for export information, promotion and product development.

REPELITA VII showed a paradigm shift in the country's development as progress, independence, fairness and increased welfare became important key words, along with increased education and industrialisation. The eras of REPELITA VIII (2004–2009) and REPELITA IX (2009–2014) coincided with a period of growth.

Provincial Efforts

The provincial governments and the provincial offices of the (federal) Ministry of Industry jointly implement a Small Industries Development Programme, the *Program Pembinaan dan Pengembangan Industri Kecil*, commonly referred to as BIPIK. Unlike the federal credit programmes, BIPIK provides no capital. Instead, it contributes technical assistance.

Under the wing of BIPIK, the Directorate General of Small Industry got involved in the *Bapak Angkat-Mitra Usaha* (Foster Father Business Partner) linkage scheme, to assist, finance, train and facilitate marketing for entrepreneurs. This involves a large "Foster Father" firm and a small business partner, both entering in a symbiotic, co-operative agreement. Several thousand large firms have signed co-operation agreements with tens of thousands of small business partners across Indonesia.

Provinces also have their own development programmes. The island province of Bali, for instance, has carefully formulated economic and social objectives, which bridge the gap between village life and commerce. Emphasis is on agriculture and small-scale industries, as well as tourism. In addition to vanilla, farmers here also produce cashew nuts, cinnamon, cocoa, coffee and nutmeg. In addition, women in Bali raise pigs, which are exported live to Singapore. As well, Bali is a regional exporting centre for canned tuna fish. Although Indonesia exports tin, a commercial beef-canning facility closed when it could not obtain tin-plate for its cans.

Figure 6.8 Nutmeg; photograph by Léo-Paul Dana.

Figure 6.9 Emphasis on Service at Hotel in Bali; photograph by Léo-Paul Dana.

Figure 6.10 Indonesia also Caters to Backpackers; photograph by Léo-Paul Dana.

International Entrepreneurship

Indonesia has relaxed restrictions on foreign direct investment, allowing a foreign entrepreneur 100% ownership of a firm in the industrial and services sectors. The Capital Investment Co-ordinating Board — locally known as BKPM — oversees such enterprises. Restrictions are published in the Investment Negative List — locally called the DNI — listing businesses for which foreign ownership is restricted. Approved entrepreneurs may be entitled to exemption from import duties and to postponement of Value Added Tax (VAT), in addition to unrestricted international movement of funds.

Non-Governmental Assistance to Entrepreneurs

In Indonesia, not only the state, but also large firms have programmes to assist entrepreneurs. A motivating factor is that once assisted, entrepreneurs often become subcontractors, suppliers and/or distributors for the assisting firm. This results in sophisticated vertical integration.

In 1980, PT Astra International established the Dharma Bhakti Astra Foundation (YDBA) to demonstrate the firm's commitment to the Small to Medium Scale Enterprise and Co-operative Reinforcement Programme. The foundation's mission is to assist entrepreneurs in production techniques, processes, financing, management, and marketing. The YDBA began providing on-the-job training for entrepreneurs, and many of these became sub-contractors for PT Astra International. Until the Asian Financial Crisis, 243 foundation-assisted firms were subcontractors, while 224 served as suppliers and vendors for multinationals.

Other non-governmental organisations, which assist entrepreneurship in Indonesia, include the Association for the Promotion of Small Enterprises and the Indonesian Chamber of Commerce and Industry. In addition, the Institute of Management Education and Development provides training for entrepreneurs.

Sentras

Sentras are clusters of similar small-scale enterprises in the same line of business and in geographical proximity of one another. These clusters exist in the rural areas of each province, and also in some urban centres, including Bandung, Jakarta, Semarang and Surabaya. The clusters are based on comparative advantage.

The first clusters occurred naturally. These included the producers of batik in Java and weavers of cloth on several islands. Other clusters were created by government initiatives.

Tambunan (2005) identified different types of clusters in Indonesia:

(i) The first involves low productivity and wages, usually in the context of micro-enterprises. This is the most common in Indonesia, indicating that the process of clustering in this country is still at an infant stage. This type of cluster displays characteristics of the informal sector; the levels of productivity and wages are lower than those of clusters dominated by formal SMEs. Tambunan wrote, "many producers are illiterate (2005, p. 143)." Producers rely on middlemen for sales;

(ii) Active clusters involve better technology and result in successful penetration of domestic and export markets;
(iii) Dynamic networks have extensive international trade networks. The clusters exhibit internal heterogeneity; and
(iv) The modern or advanced cluster is complex in structure, with a high degree of inter-firm co-operation. Networking includes banks and universities.

Sentras facilitate the state's task of providing assistance to entrepreneurs. Machinery and technical support — unaffordable by any one firm — are made available for common use, within a *sentra*. In some cases, participating firms also form *kopinkras* — small-scale craft co-operatives — to facilitate procurement of inputs and access to credit; these also strengthen the marketing programmes of smaller firms.

Such networking and co-operation between entrepreneurs has enhanced performance, and competitiveness. Also, the cluster approach has been cost-effective. From the government's perspective, clusters facilitate logistics of assistance, by the state and by state-owned firms such as the electric utility company, PLN.

Clusters of traditional craftsmen include silversmiths in Sumatra and copper specialists in Java. Clusters of wood carvers exist in Bali. Other clusters group together entrepreneurs in the chemical, food, footwear, leather and textile industries.

Sentras encourage co-operation among different firms in the same industry. Clustering may also facilitate marketing. The geographical proximity of firms — within a cluster — simplifies sub-contracting to firms that require huge quantities of goods.

Toward the Future

When, in 1998, the flight of capital coincided with the exodus of ethnic-Chinese entrepreneurs, this led to economic and social chaos. Chinese entrepreneurs had controlled important distribution channels in Indonesia and these took time to be replaced. Government efforts were needed, in order to create a new class of *pribumi* entrepreneurs. In 1999, populist decision-makers were giving loans based on economic need, rather than on entrepreneurship potential. The return on capital would be low. Critics accused such incidents as attempts to buy votes.

Old-style entrepreneurs in Indonesia usually had two or three sets of accounting books: one for personal use, another for shareholders, and yet another for tax purposes. The new generation includes MBA graduates more open to a Western management style. However, it is very likely that corruption will survive into the future. Corruption, common in business and in government, is a reason for which people aspire to be civil servants. Parnwell and Turner (1998) and Turner (2003a) reported that individuals may pay Rp 5 million to obtain such a job, and then spend a large part of their career trying to obtain bribes to make their money back.

Entrepreneurship in Indonesia is in transition. Each year, the Capital Investment Co-ordinating Board (BKPM) publishes a priority list, which targets areas for growth. Entrepreneurs, in desired sectors, may qualify for incentives. The Bank of Indonesia oversees the implementation of credit facilitation to entrepreneurs. The Directorate-General of Small-Scale Industry contributes technical assistance. The Ministry of Manpower operates an entrepreneurship-training programme, and the National Agency for Export Development assists entrepreneurs to sell overseas. Yet, many would-be entrepreneurs are not aware of the incentives. Another concern is that despite Indonesia's secular constitution, "Nearly 30 local governments have introduced Shariah laws or Shariah-inspired legislation.... To many, the new laws represent stealthy movement toward excessive intrusion of Islam into Indonesia's political process (Perlez, 2006, p. 2)."

In 2012, real GDP growth in Indonesia was 6.2%. Indonesia was shining with global demand, for its resources, while the nation enjoyed a domestic consumer boom. That year a current account surplus yielded to a deficit. In 2013, inflation increased, growth slowed down and investors expressed concerns, as did entrepreneurs.

Almilia, Diptyana, Budisusetyo and Nita (2013) focused on managerial practices, showing that SMEs in East Java have problems with management, human resources, marketing and strategy implementation. Torri (2013) explored internationalisation from Indonesia and sheds light on the challenges met.

Case Study: Kelowna Flightcraft

Kelowna Flightcraft was founded in 1970 by entrepreneurs Barry Lapointe and Jim Rogers. A few years earlier, while studying at Yale University, Frederick W. Smith, conceived of the idea to begin an air cargo company. He was a Memphis native whose father made his fortune thanks to a bus company he established.

To fulfil a school requirement, Fred authored a paper describing the concept of a freight-only airline that would fly all packages to one central point, where they would then be distributed and flown out again to their respective destinations. His proposed operations would occur overnight when airports were less crowded, and with the proper logistics, the packages would reach their destination by the next day. Whether it was the novelty of his idea, that his professor was a staunch supporter of the current system of airfreight, or that it was written in one night and turned in late, the first presentation of Smith's grand idea earned him a mere 'C'. However, his idea was about more than a creative term paper, as he watched how the technological base of the United States was changing. More companies were becoming involved in the production of mass produced technology, such as computers, and Fred was convinced that his air cargo plan would help control their inventory costs. Overnight delivery from a single distribution centre to anywhere in the United States could satisfy customers' needs without a company needing to duplicate investment in inventory to be stored in regional warehouses. He even considered the Federal Reserve Banks a potential customer, with the vast quantities of cheques that had to be shipped to all parts of the country every day.

The key to Fred Smith's company would be its ability to service a large segment of the business community from the very beginning, and the key to the required level of service was cash. He went to Chicago and New York, confident that he would be returning with the funds necessary to start his venture. Progress turned out to be slower than he anticipated, but he was relentless and through his technical knowledge of the airfreight industry he was finally able to find an enthusiastic backer in New Court Securities. This Manhattan-based, Rothschild-backed bank contributed around $5 million in capital to his start-up. New Court's support encouraged others to jump on Fred Smith's bandwagon. Five other institutions, including General Dynamics and Citicorp Venture Capital, Ltd., decided to commit funds. Smith eventually returned to

Memphis with $72 million. This was the largest venture-capital start-up deal in American business history.

Federal Express thus began its operations in April 1973, at which time it introduced a fully integrated door-to-door overnight delivery, small package express service. Fred defined the business as time-definite transportation and distribution throughout the world. The firm introduced the hub-and-spoke system of route structures, which was later adopted by passenger airlines. Federal Express carried computer components and later documents and packages. Until 1977 Federal Express used a fleet of Falcon 20 twinjets. Then, the Cargo Reform Act allowed the firm to purchase larger planes.

In 1977 the U.S. government deregulated the airfreight industry and the industry changed dramatically. Airfreight companies were able to acquire their own aircraft to create a privatised industry for the express air delivery service. Large-scale overnight deliveries soon became the heart of the airfreight industry. This system, commonly called the hub-and-spoke system, is characterised by all packages being shipped to a central distribution centre then resorted and distributed to their destinations across the country.

During the 1980s Fred decided to take his company global and Federal Express expanded to Europe. In 1988 financier Saul Steinberg (who owned 16.5% of Tiger International) approached Federal Express and offered to sell Tiger International's Flying Tigers cargo airlines. At the time, Federal Express served only five airports outside the United States: Brussels, London, Montreal, Tokyo and Toronto. In 1989 Smith's Federal Express paid $895 million for Tiger International.

An important competitor at the time was Emery Worldwide. In contrast to other firms that focused on documents or the small package market, Emery Worldwide's primary target market was identified as the business-to-business commercial shipper. In 1989 Emery Worldwide was acquired by Consolidated Freightways (CF) and its operations merged with those of CF AirFreight. In 1991 Emery president, W. Roger Curry, oversaw a major restructuring. The firm opted to move away from envelope services, and this enabled it to downsize its personnel by 2,000 employees and to reduce its ground fleet by 1,800 vehicles.

In 1992 Federal Express received publicity when Cessna ran an ad about Federal Express's use of big, tough and reliable aircraft: the Cessna Grand Caravan. This type of airplane can haul 340 cubic feet of cargo up to 1,000 nautical miles at speeds of up to 180 knots. With an optional cargo pool, the Caravan's capacity is increased to 451 cubic feet. Federal Express reportedly had over 200 Cessna Grand Caravans. Yet that same year Federal Express reported its first loss of $147 million. Experts suggested that this was a result of growing too fast. Nevertheless, in 1993 Federal Express expanded operations to 180 countries, up from 127 in 1992. A new corporate image was established in 1994 with an abbreviated company name—FedEx. The company obtained permission to work in China in 1995 through an acquisition from Evergreen International Airlines. Under this authority, Federal Express became the only U.S. based, all-cargo carrier with aviation rights to the world's most heavily populated nation. The firm soon gave jobs to over 6,000 people and FedEx deliveries became a reality in more than 200 cities in China.

Case Study Assignment

As Indonesia's economy expanded, this country also had a growing appetite for air express service. Mohammed recognised this opportunity and with his family fortune he has the capital to set up a national cargo airline. However, he is tempted to operate as a contractor for a multinational with whom coordination could increase profitability. One option is for him to approach FedEx, among others:

- *DHL Worldwide Express (DHL):* Unlike other U.S. based express firms, DHL started with a very international outlook. During the 1970s DHL worked with maritime shippers along the Pacific Rim. DHL expanded by chartering flights and subcontracting to other firms. In addition, it developed its own route network with a hub in Cincinnati.
- *TNT Express Worldwide (TNT)*: The Australian firm TNT established itself as a provider of worldwide door-to-door express service, with world headquarters in Amsterdam and another head office in Florida. It opted to specialise in same-day service.
- *United Parcel Service (UPS):* Based in Louisville, Kentucky, UPS launched its air service in 1953. For its first couple of decades it owned no aircraft. Instead, it leased space in commercial aircraft. In 1981 it bought its first airplanes — a fleet of seven Boeing 727s, operated by a contractor. 1990 UPS revenues reached $13.6 billion;

this was more than the entire express industry had earned in 1987. UPS came to own and operate the world's largest privately-owned package distribution and courier system.

As a consultant, advise Mohammed on establishing an air express service across Indonesia.

Figure 6.11 A Reliable Aircraft Used by Kelowna Flightcraft in North America is the Convair 580; photograph by Léo-Paul Dana.

Chapter 7

Japan[1]

Introduction

Japan is an archipelago with thousands of islands, covering about 378,000 square kilometres. *The Economist* reported that the self-employed, and their unpaid family workers, account for nearly a third of the labour force in Japan; this corresponds to Japan having more entrepreneurs per capita than any other big industrial economy. The flagship of entrepreneurship, here, is the sector of small and medium enterprises. Of all enterprises in Japan, only 1% is considered to be large. Over 80% of Japan's farms plant rice annually.

An old proverb teaches, "When seeking a shelter, look for a big tree." Rather than compete with large firms, entrepreneurs in Japan co-operate with them, serving as suppliers and assemblers, in an intricate relationship revolving around cultural beliefs. Japan has an ancient and intricate cultural tradition, founded on legends, myths and rituals.

---

[1] This chapter is based on information obtained from a variety of sources, including: the Association for the Promotion of Traditional Craft Industries; the Central Federation of Societies of Commerce and Industry; the Institute of Small Business Research and Business Administration at the Osaka University of Economics; the Japan Chamber of Commerce and Industry; the Japan Federation of Smaller Enterprise Organisations; the Ministry of Economy, Trade and Industry; the Ministry of Foreign Affairs (MOFA); the National Association for Subcontracting Enterprises Promotion; the National Small Business Information Promotion Centre; the Organisation for Small & Medium Enterprises and Regional Innovation; the Small and Medium Enterprise Agency; and the Traditional Craft Industry Committee. Travel to Japan was provided by Kansai University and the University of Pittsburgh. The chapter includes historical material that first appeared in Dana (1999b).

Figure 7.1 Land is Used Efficiently; photograph by Léo-Paul Dana

Figure 7.2 Harvest; photograph by Léo-Paul Dana

Figure 7.3 Maxell, TDK and Terumo are Important Japanese Firms; photograph by Léo-Paul Dana.

Figure 7.4 SMEs are very Visible; photograph by Léo-Paul Dana.

Figure 7.5 Industrial Units; photograph by Léo-Paul Dana.

Japan's Small and Medium Enterprise Basic Law defines SMEs such that a firm may qualify according to various criteria. Included is a service enterprise with up to 100 employees and up to 50 million yen in capital; or a retail operation with up to 50 employees and up to 50 million yen in capital; or a wholesaler with up to 100 employees and up to 100 million yen in capital; or a manufacturer or other enterprise, with up to 300 employees and 300 million yen in capital. Small enterprises are defined as those with 20 or fewer employees; in commerce and in the service sector, a firm must not have more than five employees in order to qualify as being small. In the mould industry, a firm with 100 employees is considered to be a major producer.

Central to the Japanese belief system are the concepts of mutual obligation, indebtedness, hard work, self-sacrifice and loyalty, all of which reinforce the very important notion of harmony for the common good. In Japan, the individual is conscious of belonging to a group, and enterprises also tend to form associations. The concepts of obligation, indebtedness and loyalty contribute to the unity and success within each partnership, and to the harmony among groups.

Historical Overview

External influences were often responsible for major changes in Japan. Until the 9th century, the Japanese archipelago was home to a gathering society who fished and hunted for subsistence. Approximately in the 3rd century, the Yayoi era started, and people cultivated rice. The art of farming was introduced from the mainland. Metal tools, such as ploughshares, arrived from inland by way of the Korean Peninsula, and the development of agriculture led to community life. Hence, villages were settled. Eventually, with the collapse of the Han dynasty in China, a huge wave of migration was observed all over the archipelago. The 7th century was typically characterised by the whole range of movements that took place. As the number of Chinese refugees increased, there was a wave of people moving down the Korean Peninsula and up to those that are now considered the Japanese islands.

As movements of people, together with mixes, borrowings and exchanges, increased all through the archipelago and as writing and the Buddhist religion were introduced, inequalities became accentuated and some began to enjoy much more power than did others. Out of this situation emerged the Yamato court, which seemed the most powerful because of its close ties with the Korean court. The latter, in turn, had the closest links with the powerful lineage that ruled China from 618 to 907 — the T'angs. Thus, as time went on, a trend toward private land ownership, by nobility links to the Yamato court, became increasingly accentuated, especially during the Heian Period. The year 894 AD marked the beginning of Japan's cultural independence. In 940, the Naritasan Shinshoji Temple was founded by the monk Kancho-sojo; it is the heart of the Shijan sect of Buddhism.

Between 1185 and 1868, Japan continued to have an emperor but the ruling power of the land was the shogun, the head of the samurai. During the 14th century, a civil war was fought over two lines of emperors. In 1467, the destruction of Kyoto — the capital of Japan, at the time — was an important turning point in history. During the Azuchi-Momoyama Period, from 1573 to 1603, manufacturing and commerce were greatly encouraged, and international trade flourished. (Table 7.1 provides a chronology of Japan.) A concern, however, was that contact with foreigners introduced Christianity and Western influence to Japan, beginning around 1600. In response to this, the principal characteristic of the Edo Period (1603 to 1868) was a severe policy of seclusion.

Historical Periods		Years
Ancient or Early Japan	Nara	710–794
	Heian	794–1185
Medieval Japan	Kamakura	1185–1333
	Kenmu Restoration	1333–1336
	Muromachi	1336–1573
	Azuchi-Momoyama	1573–1603
Early Modern Japan	Edo	1603–1868
Modern Japan	Meiji	1868–1912
	Taishô	1912–1926
	Shôwa	1926–1989
	Heisei	1989–date

Table 7.1 Historical Periods in Japan.

The Japanese were divided, according to the Confucian model, into distinct social classes: (i) samurai, including bureaucrats as well as warriors; (ii) farmers, a class comprised of entrepreneurs who owned their own land as well as peasants who did not; (iii) craftsmen; and (iv) merchants. (There were also outcasts known as Eta or Hinin.) This, coupled with efficient government personified by the shogunate, maintained harmony in Japan. In an effort to end a period of war, the Tokugawa leaders came up with the Confucius-inspired *Baku-han* policies that divided the empire into various little groups called *han*. The fact that all of these autonomous regions reported directly to the shogun resulted in a total lack of lateral contacts between various *hans*. This totalitarian top-down political system led to the isolation of the archipelago from other countries, because of bureaucratic law.

It is important to realise that the insulation of the shogunate did not imply ignorance of what was going on in the rest of the world. Rather, information was tightly controlled. For instance, while a group of people was sent abroad to study Dutch medicine, Christian missionaries were crucified because they represented a threat. Consequently, contact with the outside world was to be avoided — in order to limit European impact and influence — and was officially restricted to the port of Nagasaki, where a limited amount of trade was permitted.

Japan's self-imposed isolation ended when US Navy Commodore Perry penetrated Tokyo Bay on July 8, 1853, ending Japan's 250 years of seclusion, and asking for the opening up of Japan to trade with Westerners.

Japan was faced with the dilemma of how to form a modern nation in order to not surrender to colonialism. In 1868, power was returned from the shogun to the emperor; this was referred to as the Meiji Restoration. The end of a policy of seclusion, coupled with the Meiji Restoration, led to rapid industrialisation.

Japan opted to invest heavily in infrastructure and in the establishment of pilot industrial plants in various sectors, including bricks, cement, glass, machine tools, military needs and mining. In order to avoid being engulfed by industrialised powers of the West, Japan would need to master the fundamentals of Occidental economics. The Japanese government hired several prominent Jews to help modernise Japan.

Thus, the 1860s were characterised by the "opening of Japan" as various revolutions to dismantle the shogunate and its overarching power structure took place. Afterwards, during the first decade of the Meiji era, the doctrine of *bunmei kaika* (civilisation and enlightenment) prevailed. This was characterised by a collective effort to eradicate the past and to modernise, in order to "look" Western. Tokyo was rebuilt by the end of the 1870s. Japanese adopted Western fashions, read Shakespeare and Tolstoy. At the heart of all this was a firm, optimistic belief that enlightenment, science and modernisation would bring solutions. Japan adopted standardised mass production along and modified economic models in order to incorporate Japanese cultural values. The motto was *wakon yosai*, which is roughly translated as "Japanese spirit and Western knowledge." The *sai* is more than knowledge; it also incorporates skills and wisdom.

The 1880s arrived with a financial crisis, to which the government reacted by privatising some industries. In 1884, the Ministry of Agriculture and Commerce promulgated the Trade Association Regulations, the purpose of which was two-fold: to protect traditional industries and to prevent the mass-production of poor quality goods. In 1897, the government passed the Law on the Trade Association Dealing with Major Export Products, establishing an association of exporters. However, three years later, this law was repealed, and replaced by the broader Law Regarding the Trade Association Dealing with Major Products. This new law shifted the focus of policy from exporters to manufacturers and marketers of domestic products.

The co-operative association system was launched in 1900, with the Industry Co-operatives Law. In 1904, Japan imposed a tariff on rice imports. In 1914, the Japanese Commerce and Industry Association was established. An account of Japan at the time appears in Scidmore (1914). In 1920, Japan had only thirty large firms in the machinery sector. In contrast, there were 6,450 firms with between five and 30 employees. There was a large gap between the large and the small firms. The preponderance of small, low-precision, engineering firms gave Japan a reputation of being backward in the machinery industry. In 1927, the Law on the Chamber of Commerce and Industry was passed. The Japan Chamber of Commerce and Industry was established in 1928. Castle (1932) and Griffis (1933) described Tokyo and Japan, respectively, during the early 1930s. In 1931, Japan enacted the Industrial Co-operatives Law and in 1932, the Commercial Co-operatives Law legalised the commercial co-operative system. The year 1934 saw the introduction of the Unfair Competition Prevention Law. Patric described his experience in Japan, "Often I saw cans and packages whose shape, color, and familiar American labels made me think of home. But always, though almost identical with an American in appearance, it turned out to be an imitation (1936, p. 479)."

During the 1930s, a petition was collected from people protesting the establishment of department store branches and the spread of department stores in city-centres. As a result, in 1936, the Retail Industry Improvement Investigation Committee resolved "Matters Regarding the Relationship between Department Stores and Smaller Retailers." This led to the Department Store Law, in 1937. The Commercial Retail Store Law followed in 1938. In 1942, the cabinet announced a policy to improve the retail industry.

Respecting a Samurai maxim from the Bushido code of ethics — "Even a hunter is not allowed to kill a bird who comes to him for refuge" — Japan was a haven for thousands of Jews during World War II (WWII). By 1941, Kobe was home to 2,000 Jews. Among the prominent Jewish entrepreneurs of Kobe was real estate magnate David Sassoon. As noted by Sanghavi, "After World War II … the majority of retailers were on a small scale, serving local markets (2002, p. 270)." The Fair Trade Commission was established in 1947. The Small and Medium Enterprise Agency and the Small and Medium Enterprise League of Japan were both established in 1948, as the National Federation Headquarters established the Committee on Promotion Measures for Small and Medium Industries.

In 1949, the yen was fixed at 360¥ per dollar and the Small and Medium Enterprise Agency launched a monthly journal entitled, *Information on Small and Medium Enterprises*. The following year the agency launched a semi-monthly newsletter. In 1952, the Small and Medium Enterprise League of Japan became the Small Business Associations League of Japan. In 1956, the Small and Medium Enterprise Promotion Council was established.

The Small and Medium Enterprise Basic Policy Council was established in 1962. In 1963, the Institute of Small Business Research was created, at the Osaka University of Economics. Also in 1963, production began on the original Shinkansen bullet train, which began operating in 1964. In 1967, the Small Business Promotion Corporation was launched. In 1971, McDonald's expanded its franchise operation to Japan. In 1981, the Small and Medium Enterprise Agency established the Small and Medium Enterprises' Overseas Investment Advisory Programme to provide advice for entrepreneurs expanding overseas.

Figure 7.6 Modern Retail Sector; photograph by Léo-Paul Dana.

In 1985, the Plaza Accord led to a 50% revaluation of the yen against the dollar. Rather than increase American exports, this action spurred Japan's export performance. In 1988, Japan's per capita GNP exceeded that of the United States for the first time. In 1987, the Kyoto Research Park was established as the first private incubation facility in Japan. Kamei and Dana (2010) demonstrated that this park plays an important role.

By the early 1990s, the so-called bubble economy had burst. Very low interest rates helped the economy recover in 1996. In 1997, Japan raised its consumption tax. Household consumption decreased. Unemployment rose from 3.5% in 1997 to 4.3% in 1998 — the highest since such data was first compiled in 1953. Real GDP growth declined in the fiscal year ending 1998. This was the first incident of negative growth since 1994.

The economy entered a period of recovery in 2002. The number of bankruptcies in Japan fell, in 2004, to 13,697 — the lowest figure since 1981.[2] With the financial crisis of 2008 and the 2011 Great East Japan Earthquake, the economy suffered again but in 2013, recovery was evident. In 2014, the consumption tax rate increased from 5% to 8% (it is set to increase to 10% in 2015).

The Influence of Japanese Culture

Since the Edo Period, wholesalers have held an important position in Japan, and this nation still has four times more wholesalers per retailer than is the case in the United States. While the United States has 1.9 million retailers, Japan, with roughly half the population, has 1.7 million retailers. The average product, in Japan, passes through up to five layers of distribution — more than double that in the United States. Americans may perceive this as inefficient, but for the Japanese, the maintenance of such established relationships is very important.

[2] Small and Medium Enterprise Agency, Ministry of Economy, Trade and Industry (2005).

Given that Japan is, geographically, a small island nation covered largely by rugged mountains, most of the population live in an area occupying a fraction of the country. The result is densely populated cities and high real estate prices therein. Consequently, storekeepers save much rent by keeping their shops small. However, such small shops have limited storage space. Similarly, Japanese homes have small kitchens with limited storage space for fresh foods. Therefore, Japanese consumers shop for food on a daily basis. This contributes to high turnover in small neighbourhood shops. To avoid daily stock-outs, these small shops rely on small-scale wholesalers who make frequent deliveries, each involving a small load. Each small-scale wholesaler, in turn, relies on other wholesalers, and the global picture is one of a multi-tiered distribution system, which emerged as a result of complex cultural, political and physical factors.

Figure 7.7 Bonsai Trees; photograph by Léo-Paul Dana.

In 1974, liberalisation strengthened this pattern, with the Large Store Law, stating that no retail outlet larger than 500 square metres may be built without special permission. This barrier to entry helped maintain the status quo, and the complex network of marketing channel survives, with its implicit code of elaborate interpersonal obligations.

Among Japanese cultural obligations is gift-giving. This interaction can increase harmony, and facilitate business transactions. Knowing what is appropriate for every occasion can lessen somewhat embarrassing moments and actually enhance business and personal relationships.

Shinato, Kamei and Dana (1993) suggested that the traditional cultural climate is not necessarily favourable for entrepreneurs. This may be linked to a tendency to have a lack of entrepreneurship.

Figure 7.8 Fishing Vessel; photograph by Léo-Paul Dana.

Public Policy on Entrepreneurship

Japan has long been interested in its entrepreneurs. In 1930, the Temporary Industrial Council issued a report on public policy for small and medium industries. The League of Small and Medium Commerce and Industry of Japan was established in 1932. Given the then current economic depression, a relief fund was set-up, in the context of a Financial Relief Programme for Small and Medium Commercial and Industrial Enterprises.

In 1938, the Ministry of Commerce and Industry set up its Committee on Unemployment Relief Measures for Small and Medium Commerce and Industries. Also that year, the ministry established basic policies regarding entrepreneurs, and announced the Plan for Small Industrial Enterprises to Co-operate in Performing Shared Activities.

In 1940, the cabinet established Measures for Small and Medium Commerce and Industries. Later that year, the Ministry of Commerce and Industry circulated a document, *Guidance and Counselling to Help Small and Medium Commerce and Industries with Each Other*. As well, the cabinet announced a new economic system in which entrepreneurs were to flourish and streamline themselves voluntarily.

In 1942, the Planning Agency established the Reorganisation Committee for Small and Medium Commerce and Industries. The cabinet announced the Policy Regarding the Improvement of Small and Medium Industries.

After WWII, Division 1 of the Economy Stabilisation Headquarters created the Committee on Measures for Small and Medium Industries. In 1947, new measures prohibited private monopolies and unfair trading. The government established guidelines for small and medium enterprises assistance.

In 1948, the Small and Medium Enterprise Agency Establishment Law was passed. Also that year, the state established guidelines for small and medium enterprises. Meanwhile, the Finance Restoration Committee established procedures for using funds for the financial reconstruction of small and medium enterprises.

In 1952, regulations were established to govern the registration of consultants to entrepreneurs. In 1954, the state created a subsidy programme for the acquisition of modern equipment. This was regulated by the Guidelines Concerning the Granting of Subsidies for Constructing Common Facilities for Small and Medium Enterprise Co-operative Associations.

In 1955, the Small and Medium Enterprise Stabilisation Law was revised, as was the Law Regarding Co-operative Associations of Small and Medium Enterprises. Also, the state established a programme for the granting of subsidies to encourage small and medium enterprises to produce goods for export. A minimum wage law was enacted in 1959.

In 1963, the Small and Medium Enterprise Basic Law created the Small and Medium Enterprise Agency, to safeguard the interests of this sector. In 1964, revisions to the Small Business Association Law imposed restrictions on the advancement of large-scale enterprises into the sectors dominated by small and medium enterprises. In 1967, the Organisation of Small and Medium Enterprise Assistance Law was revised, thereby establishing the joint-business co-operatives system.

In 1970, the government enacted the Law on the Promotion of Subcontracting Small and Medium Enterprise. During the following years, many existing laws were amended. The Small and Medium Enterprise Basic Law was revised in 1973 and again in 1983. In 1993, the state enacted the Law Regarding the Assistance for Small and Medium Enterprises by Societies of Commerce and Industry and the Chamber of Commerce. In 1995, Japan passed the Special Law on Facilitating the Creative Business Activities of the Small and Medium-Sized Enterprise.

Although entrepreneurship in Japan may have acquired Western knowledge, it has retained some Japanese spirit, including cultural and traditional values such as the sense of obligation, indebtedness and loyalty within business alliances. Public policies help perpetuate this pattern, and across industries, small businesses in Japan are usually linked to a network of one kind or another. The new Small and Medium Enterprises Basic Law promotes business innovation, as well as training programmes. Kamei and Dana (2012) examined policy in a changing Japan.

Toward the Future

Since WWII, a few small-scale engineering firms in Japan grew into multinationals. These include Honda and Sony. However, these very large firms were exceptions. The majority of Japanese enterprises specialised in niche activities. For many, the niche was to serve as subcontractor for major enterprises. This complementarity between small and large firms, coupled with a cultural system of harmony, has enhanced efficiency.

By associating with large firms, small firms can often help large ones to prosper, while the latter give entrepreneurs a livelihood. Cultural values helped propagate the inter-firm linkages. Dana (1998b) described the business alliances in Japan: the diversified group *keiretsu* (see Lasserre and Schütte, 1995); the *sanchi* (a group of small firms in a similar line of business); the *kyodo-kumiai* (a co-operative of small businesses); and the *shita uke gyosha* (subcontractors) of the *shita-uke seido* (subcontract system). Such systems can serve as de-facto trade barriers, because loyalty within a network makes it harder for outsiders to penetrate. In difficult economic times, however, financial constraints may strain relationships within alliances.

During the early 21st century, 70,000 Japanese firms were closing every year because directors could not find successors (Kamei and Dana, 2012). For the future, the Ministry of Economy, Trade and Industry is committed to providing support for start-ups; for SMEs entering new activities; for the development and use of human resources at SMEs; for revitalisation of SMEs; and for the revitalisation of shopping districts, including city centres.

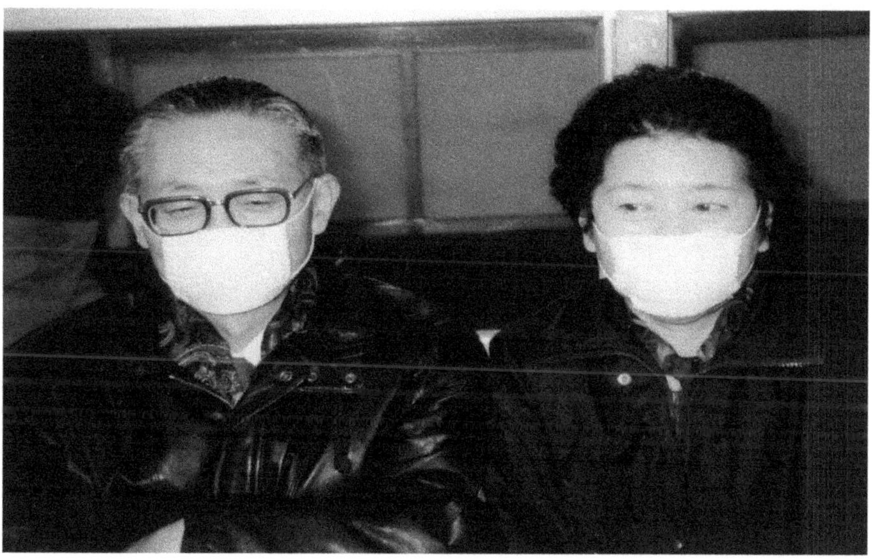

Figure 7.9 Protective Masks in City Centre; photograph by Léo-Paul Dana.

Figure 7.10 Beyond the Cities; photograph by Léo-Paul Dana.

Case Study: Kyoko at Tokyo Disneyland

> Japanese visitors to Tokyo Disneyland are enjoying their own Japanese dream, not the American dream.
>
> — Professor Masako Notoji, Tokyo

Having grown up in Canada, Kyoko returned to her birthplace in Japan. A notice, at a Tokyo hotel, read that "it is forbidden to steal hotel towels please.... If you are not a person to do such thing please not to read." At another hotel the sign read: "You are invited to take advantage of the chambermaid." The Kinki Nippon Tourist Company, a major tourist agency in Japan, had attempted to penetrate anglophone markets, but a problem was that the firm's name led people to inquire about unusual sex-oriented tours. Meanwhile, Salem's "Salem-Feeling Free" had been translated in Japanese as "Smoking Salem makes your mind free and empty."

Kyoko had been educated in English and would avoid making such errors. She felt that given her fluency in English, French and Japanese, while being familiar with Japanese culture and American values, she could become a successful entrepreneur in Japan. She wanted to set up and manage a new hotel, or to sell jewellery, or to launch a sushi restaurant — possibly at Tokyo Disneyland. She would not have any language problems but she would welcome advice for her business plan.

Disney

Mr. Walter Disney was greatly impressed by Tivoli Gardens, a tourist attraction in Copenhagen. This prompted him to create his own version and in 1955, he opened Disneyland, in Anaheim, California. Years later, its success led to the opening of Disneyworld, near Orlando, Florida. Miami-based Eastern Air Lines became the "official" carrier of Disneyworld.

Figure 7.11 Tokyo Disneyland; photograph by Léo-Paul Dana.

The success of the Disney attractions in America led to the creation of Tokyo Disneyland. This would be Disney's first foreign park, and a concern was that Disney had no experience in cold weather. Decision-makers at the Walt Disney Co. let a local enterprise build Tokyo Disneyland. In 1983, the new park opened. The Japanese economy was especially strong at this time. The local company, which owned Tokyo Disneyland, paid royalties to the Walt Disney Co. Both profits and stock values shot up. In 1984, the Walt Disney Co. had revenues of $1 billion. Tokyo Disneyland was a virtual replica of the American original — except that Mainstreet USA was replaced by the World Bazaar, and Frontierland was renamed Westernland. The Main Street House was hosted by Nippon Oil Company Ltd. Other hosts are listed in Table 7A.

Table 7A Hosts at Tokyo Disneyland

Feature	Host
Baby Centre	Meiji Milk Products Co., Ltd.
Shipping Service	Nippon Express Co., Ltd.
Strollers & Wheelchairs	The Dai-Ichi Mutual Life Insurance Co.
Camera Centre	Fuji Photo Film Co., Ltd.
The Toy Kingdom (shop)	Tomy Company, Inc.
New Century Clock Shop	Hattori Seiko Co., Ltd.
Eastside Cafe (restaurant)	Yamazaki Baking Co., Ltd.
Centre Street Coffeehouse	Ueshima Coffee Co., Ltd.
Pastry Palace	Juchheim's Co., Ltd.
Refreshment Corner	Coca-Cola (Japan) Co., Ltd.
Citrus House (restaurant)	Sunkist Growers, Inc.
Pirates of the Caribbean	Kirin Brewery Co., Ltd.
The Enchanted Tiki Room	New Japan Securities Co., Ltd.
Café Orléans	Nisshin Flour Milling Co., Ltd.
Polynesian Terrace Restaurant	Kikkoman Corporation
Country Bear Theatre	House Food Industrial Co., Ltd.
Diamond Horseshoe Revue	Prima Meat Packers, Ltd.
Mark Twain Riverboat	Nippon Suisan Kaisha, Ltd.
The Mickey Mouse Revue	Kodansha Publishers, Ltd.
It's a Small Road (cruise)	Sogo Co., Ltd.
Meet the World (carousel)	Matsushita Electronic Industrial
Captain EO (3-D film)	JCB Co., Ltd.
Star Jets	Japan Airlines

The success of Tokyo Disneyland may be said to have encouraged the launch of yet another Disney theme park, this time somewhere in Europe. In December 1985, France was selected over Spain. In contrast to the terms of the Japanese venture, the Walt Disney Co. acquired equity in the French Disney enterprise, which was to be known as EuroDisney SCA. This investment, however, also meant more risk for the parent company.

EuroDisney opened in April 1992, but lost almost $1 billion during the 1992–1993 fiscal year. To increase appeal, EuroDisney dropped its ban on beer and wine, in June 1993. Nevertheless, by November, stocks were down to $7, and EuroDisney announced losses exceeding $900,000,000. The Walt Disney Co. called on banks to restructure debt, and chairman Michael Eisner suggested that EuroDisney should be closed down. To help the park survive, the Walt Disney Co. agreed to waive its management fees and royalties. (The name of EuroDisney has since been changed to Disneyland Paris.) During 1993, Tokyo Disneyland enjoyed more visitors than did Disneyland (California) and Disneyworld (Florida) put together.

Figure 7.12 Sushi; photograph by Léo-Paul Dana.

Case Study Assignment

Be a consultant for Kyoko and help her decide what to do and how.

Chapter 8

Korea[1]

Introduction

The Republic of Korea — popularly known as South Korea — shares the Korean Peninsula with the Democratic People's Republic of Korea (North Korea). The two Koreas are separated by the Demilitarised Zone (DMZ), a four kilometre-wide strip at the 38th parallel. Prior to the 1945 division of Korea, industry was concentrated in the north, and agriculture in the south. During the three and a half decades during which the Japanese occupied Korea, they built factories, railroads and hydroelectric plants in the north of the country. In the territory that eventually became known as South Korea, the principal industries were farming and fishing. Given its abundant coal and iron reserves, North Korea was expected to prosper more than its counterpart to the south (Hwang, 1993).

Until the financial crisis of the late 20th century, South Korea prospered with a growth-oriented model. Although President Roh Moo-hyun pledged to nurture economic conditions favourable to enterprise, the 21st century ushered in discussion of a "drastic shift in industrial structure (Yang, 2005, p. 12)." In 2005, "the number of people preparing to look for jobs in May hit a record high (Soh-jung, 2005, p. 5). Meanwhile, the government decided to relocate 176 public organisations out of Seoul,[2] in an attempt to promote development in the provinces (So-young and Hae-in, 2005).

---

[1] This chapter is based on information obtained from a variety of sources, including: the Bank of Korea; the Federation of Korean Industries; the Korea Development Institute; the Ministry of Strategy and Finance; and the Ministry of Trade, Industry and Energy. Travel to Korea was provided by Air Canada. The chapter includes historical material that first appeared in Dana (1999b).

[2] During the Japanese colonial period, which lasted until 1945, Seoul was referred to as Keijo (Deering, 1933).

Figure 8.1 Seoul; photograph by Léo-Paul Dana.

Historical Overview

Korea was first unified during the 7th century, and the nation prospered under Buddhist culture.[3] The Yi dynasty, started by General Yi Song-gye in 1392, ruled Korea until Japan abolished the Korean monarchy in 1910. Under the Yi dynasty, Korea maintained a tributary relationship with China. There was little market activity in Korea. Until the 18th century, monopoly rights protected Korean merchants.

In 1876, Japan made Korea accept a one-sided commercial treaty. China and others did the same. Investment flowed to Korea, from Britain, France, Germany, Russia and the United States, but Japanese entrepreneurs dominated the business realm in Korea. As foreign traders controlled the Korean economy, the Yi dynasty instituted reforms, but these were not enough, and in 1894 Korean peasants revolted. Military intervention suppressed the revolt, but this led to substantial Japanese military presence in Korea. Following its victory in the Sino-Japanese War (1894–1895) and the Russo-Japanese War (1905), Japan annexed Korea in 1910 and the Japanese yen replaced the Korean barter system. Japan separated the monarchy from the state, codified civil law, outlawed discrimination against commoners and monetised the economic system. The colonisers appropriated 40% of Korea's area, monopolised natural resources, and took control of finances and public services. The educational system was designed to assimilate the Koreans as lower elements in Japanese society. Japanese firms discriminated against Korean employees, and Korean entrepreneurs were unable to compete with Japanese entrepreneurs. This prompted two million Koreans to revolt in 1919. Nevertheless, the harsh military rule obligated the Korean people to produce more and more rice for the Japanese, and to serve as a market for goods manufactured in Japan. New technologies were introduced as the Japanese invested in irrigation. While the Japanese were countering a rice shortage in their archipelago, Korean farmers starved to death because their entire rice harvest was shipped to the colonising country. Eventually, Japan moved from an "agriculture first" policy to one of manufacturing in Korea. The Japanese owned virtually all large-scale firms in Korea, while Koreans had some smaller factories. The number of Japanese companies increased from 109 in 1911, to 1,237 in 1929. In contrast, Korean entrepreneurs owned 27 firms in 1911, and 361 in 1929.

---

[3] For a discussion, of Buddhism in Korea, see Curzon-of-Kedleston (1924).

Japan implemented a policy to eradicate Korean national identity. The Koreans were forbidden to speak their language and Korean families were forced to replace Korean names with Japanese names. Japan censored the press, and despoiled Korea's resources.

Beginning in 1930, Japan focused on preparing for war. That year, almost one quarter of Korean factory products went to Japan. Northern Korea was used as a manufacturing base for Japan, while the south provided fish and agricultural produce.

Following the Manchurian Incident (1931–1937), the Japanese decided to industrialise Korea in order to fully take advantage of its mineral resources in the north and of its rice supply. The Japanese needed to build factories, hydroelectric plants and railroads. They needed capital (90% of which came from Japanese conglomerates known as *zaibatsu*), technology (100% of which came from *zaibatsu*), and labour (100% of which was provided by poorly paid Korean workers). Consequently, the ratio of light to heavy goods in Korea (which was 80:20 in 1930) became 50:50 during World War II (WWII). By 1940, half of Korean factory products went to Japan. This process resulted in the growth of small and medium scale capitalists, the increase of skilled male workers, migration, urbanisation, and the loss of the black and white nationalist outlook which had characterised the Korean people ever since the arrival of the Japanese.

At the end of WWII, Soviet forces took control of northern Korea, while American troops occupied the south. In August 1948, the Republic of Korea (South Korea) was proclaimed. To the north of the 38th parallel, the Soviets created the Democratic People's Republic of Korea (North Korea).

In 1950, North Korea invaded the south, with the aspiration of creating a united communist Korea. An armistice was signed in 1953. In 1963, Park Chung Hee became the president of South Korea. His policy was to develop the economy of his country. The next section shall examine his policy for economic development and its impact on entrepreneurship in the Republic of Korea.

Public Policy

From 1953 to 1961, South Korea received about two-thirds of its total investment in the form of rehabilitation aid from the United States. These investments were used to implement an import substitution policy.

A military coup in 1961 initiated a policy of rapid industrialisation. As South Korea accelerated its industrialisation, legislation was introduced to protect entrepreneurs and to help them be productive contributors to the economy. In 1961, the Small and Medium Industry Bank Act designated a financial institution — the Industrial Bank of Korea — to make loans only to small-scale entrepreneurs. Similarly, the Kukmin Bank was mandated to give loans only to enterprises with fewer than 200 employees.

In 1962, when South Korea adopted its first Economic Development Plan (1962–1966), per capita GNP was $82. President Park Chung Hee subsequently created a command economy with wages and interest rates at his order. With the objective of maximising growth and export volume, he set wages low and subsidised interest rates.

Several economic development plans helped the president guide the economy. The Second Five-Year Plan (1967–1971) and Third Five-Year Plan (1972–1976) allowed him to encourage exports rather than import substitution. The won was devalued, and financial support was channelled to high performers. Given that market demand interest rates may cause a heavy debt burden on entrepreneurs, and hence decrease the pace of new venture formation while increasing the bankruptcy rate, selected firms in South Korea were granted subsidised interest rates well below the market-clearing point. The low cost of borrowing allowed for the development of capital-intensive methods of production over labour-intensive ones, and the excess supply of labour kept wages low, a competitive advantage for exporting. Thus, instead of helping entrepreneurs at large, President Park Chung Hee specifically used his control over bank credit to channel subsidised loans to export-oriented borrowers. These few exporters soon grew into the debt-based mega-conglomerates known as *chaebols* — literally "financial cliques." Small-scale entrepreneurs were squeezed out of many markets, resulting in numerous monopolies and oligopolies.

The economic effects, of South Korea's Vietnam venture during the late 1960s and early 1970s, went far beyond the simple acquisition of foreign exchange. Many South Korean firms, including Hanjin and Hyundai, got their first big economic boost from the Vietnam War (known in Vietnam as the American War). Korean firms became contractors for the United States army in South Vietnam and later made use of their Vietnamese contacts and experience to expand into the international construction business, most notably in the Middle East. Between 1974 and 1979, South Korea's top 10 *chaebols* took home nearly $22 billion in Middle East construction sales, of which Hyundai's share alone was over $6 billion.

In 1974, the Credit Guarantee Funds Act provided guarantees for liabilities of entrepreneurs. In 1975, the Sub-Contracting System Promotion Act promoted co-operation between large firms and smaller ones. The Fourth Five-Year Plan (1977–1981) perpetuated a tight credit policy. Consequently, the national economy of South Korea was based on rapid industrialisation of only very few non-integrated industries — heavy industry and chemicals — for the purpose of increasing exports. Hence, the economy was dominated by a small number of highly diversified mega-conglomerates, resulting in various problems.

South Korean industry was largely dependent on foreign suppliers for raw materials and light industry components as well as for machinery and replacement parts which also had to be imported, a drain on the country's financial resources. Therefore, much capital had to be raised in the form of foreign loans, causing a further burden — that of debt service.

As national policy favoured the *chaebols,* these flourished while small business remained small. Although the factories of *chaebols* were efficient, their offices tended to be less so, as considerable time was consumed in meetings as well as bureaucracy. A further problem with *chaebol* administration was the highly hierarchical structure, which makes a manager feel very subordinate to an immediate superior, often causing an employee to serve a superior personally instead of concentrating on innovation.

The Small and Medium Industries Promotion Corporation Act, in 1980, provided financial support, technical assistance and managerial consultancy to entrepreneurs. The following year, the Procurement Facilitating Act specified the conditions of government procurements from entrepreneurs. This allowed smaller enterprises to sell to the state, collectively, via co-operatives.

In 1983, the Policy to Support Promising Small and Medium-scale Enterprises provided low interest loans, technical training and management consulting to promising small and medium enterprises. In 1984, the Mutual Assistance Fund Act provided special loans to entrepreneurs. In 1988, the Production Research Institute Act created an institute to assist entrepreneurs with technology transfers and product development.

Figure 8.2 SMEs; photograph by Léo-Paul Dana.

Prior to the labour unrest of 1989, wages were very low, a factory worker earning as little as the equivalent of roughly $50 for a 72-hour week. Wages were subsequently raised substantially. Salaries were 45% higher in 1989 than in 1987, and those in automotive industry climbed 80% from 1986 to 1989 — contributing to price increases, which were already high due to the lack of competition in many monopolistic and oligopolistic markets. Rationalisation, which followed, led to increased unemployment. In 1989, the government made available credit guarantee funds for technology development among entrepreneurs. Also that year, several commercial banks were permitted to provide services exclusively to entrepreneurs. Five *chaebols* were producing more than 50% of Korea's GNP. In consideration of this fact, a government priority during the 1990s was to build up small and medium-sized firms and to encourage the development of innovative entrepreneurs, with programmes such as capital assistance including low cost loans for new ventures and R&D incentives to facilitate innovation.

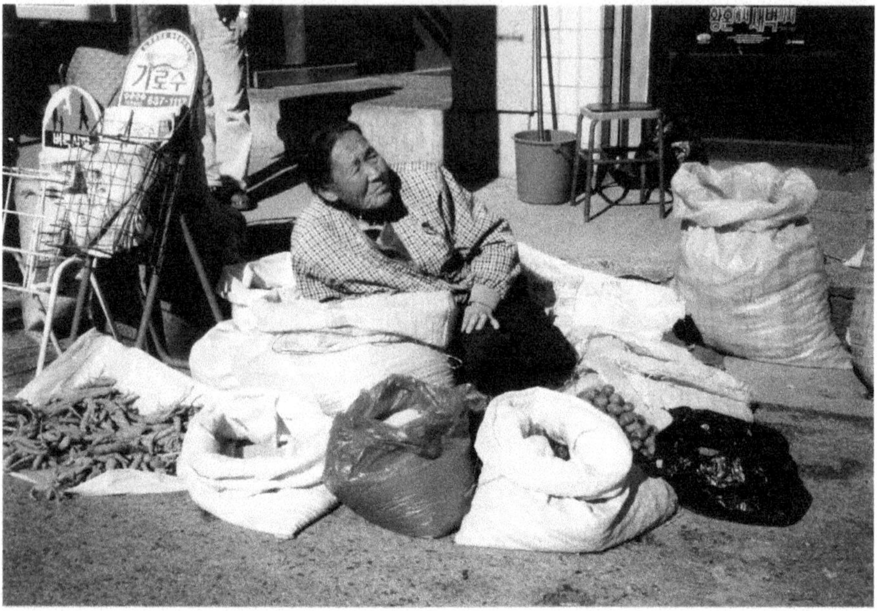

Figure 8.3 Self-employed Petti-vendor; photograph by Léo-Paul Dana.

Government initiatives were designed to encourage: a general trading company system and the provision of fiscal or commercial advantages; commitment by the constitution to foster small business; special support for small exporters; direct and indirect financial assistance for small business; commitment by banks to make 35% of their loans to smaller firms; tax concessions for new ventures, particularly those with innovative ideas or using competitive technologies; and facilitation of foreign investment.

In 1993, the government issued a new Five-Year Plan, calling for deregulation and reduced government intervention in the economy. Tariffs were reduced. Many restrictions on the import of capital goods were eliminated. A special depreciation allowance was introduced for fixed assets. High-tech entrepreneurs were allowed to import capital goods duty-free, and their firms were granted a five-year exemption on corporate income tax. Registration qualifications for trading enterprises were abolished effective 1997. Lee (1998) gave an overview of small Korean firms during the 1990s.

Figure 8.4 Self-employed Cobbler; photograph by Léo-Paul Dana.

In 1998, the government established the Corporate Restructuring Fund, with a value of $1.2 billion, half of which was provided by the Korean Development Bank, and the other half by a consortium of banks, insurance companies and investment houses. Seventy percent of the fund was earmarked for established small and medium firms, especially those focusing on high technology and exports. The top five *chaebols* were banned from borrowing from the fund. Yet, public policy initiatives to promote SMEs have had little success in this country where *chaebols* remain prominent.

During the early years of the 21st century, Korea implemented policy initiatives for the long-term planning of research and innovation. This is discussed by Lee and Kwun (2003).

Figure 8.5 Itinerant Vendor; photograph by Léo-Paul Dana.

Pre-Crisis Trends

Development of a Domestic Component Industry

The *chaebols* traditionally imported raw materials and components. The development of one million SMEs diversified in various sectors, including manufacturing, trading, service, transportation, and construction as well as mining, led to increased trade between *chaebols* and small firms providing components. Gradually, foreign suppliers were replaced by small local firms.

Productivity and Exports

Until the Asian Financial Crisis, small manufacturers consistently increased their production at a rate higher than that of large manufacturers. Productivity in South Korea's manufacturing sector improved by an average of 11% per year, while productivity among smaller firms — in the same sector — increased by an annual average of 14%.

The general trading company systems, as initiated by the government, significantly contributed to export volume by small firms. Product and market diversification became prime objectives of the trading companies, resulting not only in short-term profit but also in long-term growth. Small firms began to export labour-intensive light-industry goods, which South Korea previously did not export. Their production also developed component industries within South Korea, thus helping domestic growth and further helping exports indirectly.

Figure 8.6 Self-employed Vendor at Food Stall; photograph by Léo-Paul Dana.

Figure 8.7 More Sophisticated Sushi Establishment; photograph by Léo-Paul Dana.

The Crisis and Beyond

The post-1993 financial liberalisation in South Korea encouraged entrepreneurs to obtain short-term loans. Some borrowers opted to borrow abroad. In 1996, the country qualified for admission to the Organisation of Economic Corporation and Development (OECD). However, problems soon emerged. Although *chaebols* had an average debt-equity ratio of 400%, the economy was still healthy in 1997. Growth rate was 5.5%, inflation was stable at 4.4% and unemployment at 2%. A foreign exchange crisis, however, led to an economic crisis. Korea's meltdown, in November 1997, led the government to seek an International Monetary Fund (IMF) package. The following month, Korea signed a $58 billion IMF bailout. Financially-fragile entrepreneurs faced the domino effects of bankruptcies.

Before the crisis, Korea's economic sector was stable with *chaebols* dominating the economy. Since 1998, there have been high fluctuations in business conditions, considerable financial restructuring and an increasing influence of foreign enterprises. Up to the crisis, owners tended to be active managers, and seniority was paramount. More recently, chief executive officers have gained importance, as have ability and outcome.

Figure 8.8 Hyundai is among the *Chaebols*; photograph by Léo-Paul Dana.

In the social sector, low levels unemployment before the crisis, and high levels of saving, have given way to rising unemployment, in turn causing growing gaps between the rich and the poor. Lee (2003) pointed out that the crisis laid down favourable conditions for enabling employers to introduce performance-based personnel systems. In 2005, the Anti-Corruption Act was amended henceforth including indirect corruption. Park Geun-hye became President of Korea in 2013. In her inaugural address she shared her vision for creating a second miracle by means of a creative economy.

Toward the Future

The South Korean policy approach, subsidising credit to selected export-oriented firms, resulted in a command economy dominated by *chaebols*. From 1961 to 1967, the government supported *chaebols*, and these generated full employment. *Chaebols* could produce mediocre products in a protected environment and Korean consumers bought their products. Then, tariff reductions made South Korea increasingly open to competition from abroad.

The opening of the economy, coupled with the Asian Financial Crisis, necessitated changes. As the highly diversified *chaebols* were being trimmed, cost reduction measures released skilled personnel with entrepreneurial potential. Product restructuring gave rise to new opportunities for emerging entrepreneurs. Thus, the restructuring of *chaebol* portfolios provided opportunities for entrepreneurship. However, in 1998, 1,000 Korean entrepreneurs were going bankrupt every month. Documents at the Bank of Korea showed that 18 large companies and 5,221 smaller ones declared bankruptcy during the first five months of 1998, compared with 10 and 2,197 during the same period in 1997. Some communities experienced reverse industrialisation, as entrepreneurs gave up industrial production, in favour of agriculture. Nevertheless, the economy rebounded.

In 2009, South Korea commisioned the icebreaker RV *Araon,* which now explores Antarctica. (RV is the ship refix for research vessels.)

In July 2011, a free trade agreement came into effect bewween the European Union and Korea. In 2012, real GDP growth in Korea was 2%.

Figure 8.9 Korean Icebreaker RV *Araon*; photograph by Léo-Paul Dana.

Figure 8.10 Young and Old Moving to the Future; photograph by Léo-Paul Dana.

Case Study: Voluntourism

The EarthWatch Institute recruits volunteers who pay to work on data collection relevant to manatees, with the purpose of increasing the chances of this species' survival.

The manatee is a large, ancient species, weighing two tons, and up to four metres long. It is a descendent of a species which vanished 60 million years ago, and its closest land relative is the elephant. Like its cousin, the manatee is gentle and moves slowly. It is also herbivorous, slow breeding, social and playful. The manatee has elephantine-like skin and an elephant-like face. Its eyes are innocent eyes but without a trunk. Unlike the elephant, the manatee has flippers with nails and a flat tail used when swimming.

Manatees are also known as sea cows, and they are sometimes called the last mermaids; they may very well be the last, as their slow speed puts them high on the list of endangered species. They are not hunted for sport nor culled for profit. Nor are they pests. However, they are often victims of boat traffic accidents in the coastal waters of Florida.

Speed limits have been imposed; however, these are seldom observed. Like pedestrians in a world of motor cars, manatees see danger approaching them, but they move too slowly to dodge the traffic; they get injured by boat hulls and by propellers. Three-quarters of the scars found on survivors are on the upper back, indicating that the victims were attempting to move away. In 1992, there were about 2,000 manatees in Florida, and a million motor boats. Since 1993, EarthWatch has sent paying volunteers who, at Sarasota's Mote Marine Laboratory, observe the manatees' habitat, study feeding patterns and record the births of manatee calves. The volunteers also research interaction with motor boats and charting the scars resulting from accidents. Almost 200 deaths occur each year. When a mother manatee is killed by a boat, its young often die too.

Case Study Assignment

It is EarthWatch belief that the world should be made aware of the situation and that individuals should be encouraged to respect speed limits. Volunteers are needed, and these require the stamina to wait many hours on a boat, under the summer sun, spotting manatees. Help a local entrepreneur set up a travel agency in Korea, recruiting volunteer tourists.

Chapter 9

Laos[1]

Introduction

The Lao People's Democratic Republic (Laos) is one of the least developed and poorest countries in Southeast Asia. Perazic wrote: "Once a great kingdom, 'the Land of the Million Elephants and the White Parasol' faces its struggle for survival (1960, p. 46)." The landlocked country, enclosing 236,800 square kilometres, nestled between Cambodia, China, Myanmar, Thailand and Vietnam is among the least urbanised in Asia. The official calendar here is that of the Lao Buddhist era; the year 2015 corresponds to 2653 in the Lao calendar, and 2558 in the Thai calendar.

Figure 9.1 Vientiane Airport; photograph by Léo-Paul Dana.

---

[1] This chapter is based on information obtained from a variety of sources, including: the Ministry of Foreign Affairs; the Ministry of Industry and Handicraft; and the National Small and Medium-Sized Enterprise Office (SMEPDO). The chapter includes historical material that first appeared in Dana (1995b; 1997c; 1999b; 2002).

Figure 9.2 Among the Least Urbanised; photograph by Léo-Paul Dana.

Traditionally, business activities in Laos have not been associated with high social status. Cultural values, stemming from religious beliefs, emphasised, instead, the elimination of desire. Commerce, on the other hand, is perceived as a means to satisfy desire. Social forces thus discouraged enterprise, and trade has usually been the role of those with inferior social standing. Where Lao men refrained from doing business, women often succeed (Dana, 1997c). Yet, the communist take-over further discouraged entrepreneurial spirit. As a result, Lao society is generally non-entrepreneurial. The Chinese community is very active in the entrepreneurship sector. Large corporations in Thailand, each earn more than the value of all the goods and services produced in all of Laos.

O'Driscoll, Holmes and Kirkpatrick (2001) reported a black market in Laos, larger than the formal economy. The popularity of the parallel economy is no surprise, considering the low initial role of legitimate private enterprise, coupled with a high degree of liberalisation, and hindered by the lack of macro-stability in the absence of a sufficiently developed legal framework.

Lao people appear to have much social capital, but this does not promote entrepreneurship unless supportive cultural capital is in place. This aligns with findings of Light and Dana (2013).

Figure 9.3 Not Lacking in Social Capital; photograph by Léo-Paul Dana.

Figure 9.4 Entrepreneurship Sector; photograph by Léo-Paul Dana.

Figure 9.5 Vientiane is Home to Embassies; photograph by Léo-Paul Dana.

Historical Overview

The Lao people are thought to have arrived from China during the 8th century. During the 1200s, Kublai Khan led the Mongols to seize power in China. This prompted further migration to the region, which would later become Laos. During the following century, a Khmer empire was established here. It was known as *Lan Xang* — literally "Million Elephants." The Lao people organised themselves into Lao principalities.

During the 19th century, France persuaded one of the leaders to accept a French protectorate, as insurance against conquest by China or Siam. France then united all of the Lao principalities into one country. Thus came to be the name Laos, which is the plural of Lao.

France used Laos as a buffer between French Vietnam and British Burma. The French imposed a Vietnamese-staffed civil service in Laos, but they did not contribute to the protectorate. When the Japanese occupied French Indochina in 1941, the Lao people obtained more autonomy than they had experienced under French protection. Following World War II (WWII), France tried to take back Laos; in 1949 the latter was declared an independent associate state of the French Union. The United Nations recognised Laos as a separate country, and in 1953 France allowed Laos to become a monarchy.

Figure 9.6 French Language Still Important; photograph by Léo-Paul Dana.

In 1954, communists occupied areas of two Lao provinces, namely Phong Saly and Sam Neua. In 1959, King Savang Vatthana became monarch of the Lao kingdom. By 1960, the communist-led *Pathet Lao* (Lao People's Party) forces made advances, and during a three-day period in December that year, Vientiane was ruled by four successive governments (White, 1961a).

In 1962, the Royal Lao Government and the State of Israel embarked on a joint experimental farm, along the Mekong River. Known as the Vientiane Pilot Project, this project provided farmers with seed, fertiliser, insecticide and even irrigation. The objective was to transform subsistence farmers into market-oriented entrepreneurs. Participants prospered and by 1968, 250 families participated in the project (White, 1968).

In December 1975, the Lao Patriotic Front — the political arm of the *Pathet Lao* — abolished the monarchy and created a communist entity (see Brown, Zasloff and Staar, 1986), the Lao People's Democratic Republic. All Christian seminaries were closed that year. Zasloff and Unger (1990) presented a detailed account of Laos following the revolution.

When the Lao People Revolutionary Party took control of the Lao People's Democratic Republic, in 1975, it implemented a policy of accelerated socialisation. Harsh policies shunned entrepreneurship and co-operatives replaced private initiatives. Former royalists were sent to re-education camps where they were forced to accept communism. In 1977, Laos and Vietnam signed a treaty of friendship and co-operation.

Figure 9.7 Communist Era Architecture; photograph by Léo-Paul Dana.

A Radical Model of Transition: The New Economic Mechanism

In 1987, Laos implemented its New Economic Mechanism — a radical shift in public policy. This recognised market forces as legitimate, and began liberalising the centralised economy. The first national election took place in 1989. Inflation reached 76% that year. In 1990, the state launched a drive to attract foreign investment, privatise state enterprises, develop import-substitution industries and promote exports. In 1991, a new constitution ushered in further economic reforms. New laws were subsequently introduced, governing property, labour and foreign investment. Laos signed treaties of friendship and co-operation with Thailand in 1991, with Cambodia in 1992, with China in 1994, and with Myanmar in 1994.

In April 1994, Laos and Vietnam signed an agreement on goods in transit, which allowed these commodities to be transported across either Laos or Vietnam, on the way to the other. The following month, Laos introduced a liberal law governing investments. This streamlined foreign investment regulations and tax structures. Legislation included tax holidays, a 1% import duty on capital goods associated with production, and a flat-rate corporate tax of 20%. This was to lead to a major influx of foreign capital to create joint ventures, as well as 100% foreign-owned investments in commerce, industry and services. Furthermore, the government committed itself to expedite the business application process. Japanese and Taiwanese investors expressed considerable interest. Until 1996, Laotians needed permission to change residences; then, this requirement was done away with.

In 1997, Laos joined ASEAN. In 2000, GDP per capita was a mere $272 and half the nation's budget came from foreign aid. In March 2001, Laotian and Thai officials initialled an agreement to build a second bridge to link the two countries; the geographic position of Laos could help it become an important assembly and trans-shipment centre.

The Traditional Belief System

W. Robert Moore, Chief of Foreign Editorial Staff at *National Geographic*, wrote about Vientiane, the capital of Laos, "Biggest buildings in town, except for a few government offices are the Buddhist temples (1954, p. 666)." Even today, Theravada monasteries, known as wats, dominate every town in Laos; almost every house, shop and office has a private temple. It is even common for boats, cruising along the Mekong River, to dock for the crew to jump ashore, light incense and pray. The Lao wats are architecturally distinct from monasteries elsewhere in Asia. In Laos, wats have large terraces, and flare symbols on the roofs. Religious beliefs are very important in this country, and Laotians are noticeably influenced by folk tales, superstitions, and traditional animist beliefs — in addition to the ancient beliefs of the national religion, Theravada Buddhism. An article in the August 28, 1992 issue of *Asiaweek* explained that it is commonly believed that the Mekong River gets "hungry" for human souls, without which the annual rains will not arrive:

> ... a little girl (was) swept away by the current while picnicking with her family on a sandbank. Her mother and father made no attempt to save her. Two foreigners snatched the child from the swift water after a desperate effort. The parents were fearful because the river had been thwarted in claiming the child (p. 63).

Figure 9.8 Belief in Religion is High; photograph by Léo-Paul Dana.

Theravada monks are highly influential in Lao society. They are consulted on virtually all matters, thereby playing a role in a diversity of spheres, ranging from private life to government policy. They have traditionally had a great impact on the educational system; it used to be that the only schools were in wats.

Central to the belief system in Laos is the ultimate goal to extinguish unsatisfied desires. Its doctrine focuses on aspects of existence, including *dukkha* (suffering from unsatisfied desire), and *anicca* (impermanence). Assuming that unsatisfied desires cause suffering, suffering can be eliminated if its cause — desire — is eliminated. A respectable person, according to this ideology, should not work towards the satisfaction of materialistic desires, but should rather strive to eliminate the desire itself. A monk is specifically prohibited by the religion, from tilling fields or raising animals. Lao folk tales reinforce the belief that a male monk should not labour for material wealth; yet, the same folklore conditions women to accept a heavy burden in exchange for honour, protection and security.

Figure 9.9 Rice is Important; photograph by Léo-Paul Dana.

Numerous Lao families who farm during the wet season become self-employed gold-diggers during the dry season. The prospectors camp along the Mekong River, especially in the region of Luang Prabang, the former royal capital, discovered by Henri Mouhot in 1861. The women do the heaviest work, digging for dirt and panning it in wooden trays. The men weigh the gold, up to one gram per day. The *Far Eastern Economic Review* quoted a London newspaper as saying that "Lao rice farmers have a reputation in this dynamic region for lying down, closing their eyes and listening to their crops grow in fertile paddy fields (1994, p. 60)." Indeed, entrepreneurial spirit is not very prevalent in the traditional Lao belief system. Dana (1995b) addressed this issue in detail.

Figure 9.10 Along the Mekong River; photograph by Léo-Paul Dana.

Pluralism

Laos has a diversity of ethnic minorities with a variety of beliefs, attitudes and traditions. White reported: "There's a Thai Dam...They sacrifice dogs to the spirits. They beat them to death before they roast them, so that the meat will be tender. And here's a Kha Koui. They never wash...(1961a, p. 260)."

According to government sources, ethnic minorities in Laos include: Lan Tene; Meo Khao; Meo Lay; Mouseudam; Mouseudeng; and Mien, formally known as Yao. In addition, Laos is home to eight kinds of Kais, and to seven types of Thais. There are also the Hmong people, referred to by the Chinese as *Miao* — literally meaning barbarians; these are the subject of Garrett (1974).

In all, there are 68 recognised ethnic groups in Laos. White (1987) grouped these into three broad segments: the highlanders, known as Lao Theung; the mountain tribes, called Lao Soung; and the valley dwellers, referred to as Lao Lum. According to United Nations sources, the Lao Lum people comprise 60% of the country's population; these people are involved in government, as well as wet-rice agriculture. The Lao Theung people are concentrated in slash-and-burn subsistence agriculture, and they have less contact with consumer culture and the monetised economy. The Lao Soung people are cut off from any legal sector of the monetised economy; some are involved in the smuggling of gems or narcotics.

Given the traditional belief system of Laos, the business sector in this country consists largely of people who are not ethnic Laotians. A significant Chinese minority is prominent in small-scale enterprise. This community consists primarily of people — most of whom are Teochews — who are descendants of migrants from southern China. Vientiane is home to at least 2,500 Chinese entrepreneurs, and these people own a disproportionate percentage of restaurants, movie theatres, hotels, repair shops and jewellery shops in this capital city.

Muslim men are also very active in the small business sector of Laos. Individuals from India and Pakistan are especially active in the garment industry. In addition, Thai and Australian entrepreneurs have created numerous new ventures in Laos. Unlike the Chinese and the Muslims who reside in this country permanently, the Thais and Australians in Laos tend to be sojourners.

Entrepreneurship

Whereas American involvement in Lao business tends to be in the form of large business, Thai investments tend to be in the medium-size category, as are Australian ventures. Even more involved in small business are French entrepreneurs.

One problem encountered by entrepreneurs in the manufacturing sector is the poor infrastructure. Given the generally inadequate conditions of the roads — often flooded during the rainy season — and the lack of a railway, a quarter of all traffic in Laos uses the Mekong River. People and buffalo stand side by side, on boats or barges, for hours. Sometimes, cargo gets damaged. A gift from the people of Australia, the $30 million Friendship Bridge across the Mekong River between Laos and Thailand was opened in 1994.

As for the Lao people, 85% are involved in agricultural sectors. Crops include coffee, corn, rice, tea, tobacco, vegetables and wheat. Given that three fifths of the GNP comes from agricultural output, the government has instituted reforms providing incentives to farmers. The plan introduced preferential tax policies for agriculturalists, and increased investment in the sector, especially in irrigation. The plan also raised the prices of produce, and linked remuneration with output. Yet, although annual per capita rice output in Laos is 350 kilogrammes, some provinces still experience occasional rice shortages.

Many farming communities are migratory; they deforest land for a crop, and then move elsewhere. There is a constant breeze of smoke and ashes over the Mekong River. Opium is an important crop, of which Laos produces about 300 tonnes annually.

Toward the Future

Reforms have increased the autonomy of firms, and the state no longer has the monopoly on supply, purchasing and marketing. Yet, O'Driscoll, Holmes and Kirkpatrick (2001) reported that Laos, with its average tariff exceeding 19%, had less economic freedom than any of its neighbours. Furthermore, enterprise is largely limited to women and minorities, as local culture does not encourage it. The local shortage of skilled labour limits manufacturing. The shortage of educated individuals limits the service sector.

Figure 9.11 A Generation of the Future; photograph by Léo-Paul Dana.

Case Study: Madame Vongpackdy Sithonh

As the hot season was giving way to the rainy season, important decisions had to be made, but only after opportunities were evaluated. As well as having a 23-year-old son living with her and her husband, Madame Sithonh had another son and two daughters studying in Vientiane, less than one kilometre from Thailand. All had agreed to meet together the coming weekend. Their international opportunities were to be discussed.

Born in a small village in the Vientiane province of Laos, Vongpackdy Sithonh went to study in Vientiane prefecture. She obtained her *brevet* diploma from the Lycée Vientiane, in 1966. Mastering French, English and Thai, in addition to her native Lao tongue, she worked as a typist and later as a secretary, for an American in Laos.

In 1974, Ms. Sithonh got married. Meanwhile, the war in Indochina had heated up, and as the United States was preparing to withdraw from Vietnam, Vongpackdy lost her job when her boss returned to America. Time would come for Madame Sithonh to create her own job, and one for her husband since, the traditional belief system in Laos kept most Lao males away from entrepreneurship.

Lao folk music was still very popular, and men were encouraged to pray and play music, rather than work as entrepreneurs. Their self-employment was largely limited to hunting, fishing and making utensils by hand.

Figure 9.12 Not An Entrepreneur; photograph by Léo-Paul Dana.

Lao women, in contrast, are often self-employed, although these tend to be informal, marginal earners. Some are street vendors and others have shops. Since the 1987 liberalisation of economic restrictions, many women have obtained stalls at expanding markets. Some sell rats and spiny anteaters at the Ban Thalat market of Vientiane. At the Ban Thong Khan Kham market of Vientiane, other women sell charcoal-broiled duck eggs along with bear paws and snakes.

Some Lao women also operate food establishments. The national dish involves taking glutinous rice with one's fingers, and dipping it in spices. Fancier restaurants also have forks and spoons, but knives are rare. Food tends to be quite fresh, as it is often purchased after the clients make their order. Service is therefore rather slow.

Lao women were also involved in black market money exchange, trading Lao kip for dollars. Although these entrepreneurs offered the convenience of being able to change money after banking hours, their exchange rates were slightly lower than official bank rates, quite a contrast with the situation elsewhere.

Madame Sithonh inherited her father's house in the city of Vientiane; however, rather than live in it, she leased it to cousins. She chose to reside in the outskirts of Bolek. There, she raised two sons and two daughters.

Bolek is a small town 35 km from the nation's capital. Located in the fertile Mekong River Valley, the area is ideal for growing rice. Most Bolek people derive their livelihood from rice. The poor gather frogs in rice fields, and sell them in town.

Separating rice seeds from the husks is a very laborious and time-consuming task when done manually. Yet, machines can do the job very efficiently. Surprisingly, until 1991, there was no rice processing machine in Bolek. This prompted Madame Sithonh to import one from Thailand. A dog called Vilie would guard the machine at night.

Madame Sithonh decided that she would not charge anybody for using her machine. She would simply keep the husks for use as animal feed. Her rice-processing machine soon became very popular, working some nights as late as 10 p.m. In addition to having her eldest son working with her full-time, Madame Sithonh hired an assistant. As a side-line business, Madame Sithonh raised pigs, and the cost of feeding them was nil.

With rental income from her inheritance, Madame Sithonh acquired a diesel truck, to transport rice. Her husband operated the truck; its capacity was 150 bags.

Madame Sithonh's truck might be used to export her pigs to Thailand; rather than return empty, it might be feasible to bring Thai-made products to Laos. The Lao Soft Drink Co. was bottling Pepsi, 7-Up and Mirinda in Vientiane, but Coca-Cola, Sprite and Fanta had to be imported into Laos, as were Chiclets, toothpaste and numerous other consumer goods. Madame Sithonh had an entrepreneurial spirit, but she was not sure whether to, nor how to, expand internationally.

Case Study Assignment

As a small business consultant, provide Madame Sithonh with advice.

Figure 9.13 Madame Sitonh; photograph by Léo-Paul Dana.

Chapter 10

Malaysia[1]

Introduction

Located between Indonesia, Singapore and Thailand, Malaysia occupies 332,633 square kilometres. It covers the Malay Peninsula and it shares the island of Borneo with Brunei Darussalam and Indonesia.

Under colonial rule, the British encouraged Malays to work the land, while the Chinese dominated entrepreneurship in Malaya. Since independence, efforts have tried to change this, by formulating an ethnic-based policy in Malaysia. Schaper and Volery (2004) described specific programmes aimed to help Indigenous entrepreneurs in this country. Nevertheless, ethnic-Chinese entrepreneurs own most firms in Malaysia.

In 2012, real GDP growth in Malaysia was 5.6%, but Ahmad and Xavier (2012) found that the number of early-stage entrepreneurial activities in Malaysia was lagging; the obstacles that they identified in Malaysia were inadequate financial support, bureaucracy and inconsistency of government policies, lack of entrepreneurial education at tertiary level and inadequacy of entrepreneurial training. Zainol (2013) focused on Bumiputra family firms in Malaysia and concluded that in Malay firms, the relationship between personality traits, cultural background and government aided programmes with firm performance were not mediated by entrepreneurial orientation.

---

[1] This chapter is based on information obtained from a variety of sources, including: the Central Bank of Malaysia; the Labuan Financial Services Authority; the Malaysian Industrial Development Authority; the Ministry of Finance; and the Ministry of International Trade and Industry. Travel to Malaysia and within Malaysia was provided by the Malaysian Entrepreneurship Development Centre (MEDEC) at the MARA University of Technology. The chapter includes historical material that first appeared in Dana (1999b).

Figure 10.1 Variety of Languages; photograph by Léo-Paul Dana.

Historical Overview

Ancient remains suggest that the original Malays came from south-western China, via Indochina. These people were invaded by the Sumatran ancestors of today's Malays. In 1402, Prince Parameswara of Sumatra founded Malacca, on the west coast of the Malay Peninsula. In 1405, Emperor Yung-Yo, of the Ming dynasty created favourable relations between China and Malacca. Chinese traders came to the Malay Peninsula and this attracted merchants from distant places. Malacca thrived as a port-of-call for entrepreneurs from China, India, and Arab lands. The trading centre was home to Bugis, Chettiar, Chinese, Gujerati, Javanese, Mon and Tagalog Muslim entrepreneurs who prospered in the entrepôt trade. In Malacca, cloves and pepper were exchanged for western textiles. Some entrepreneurs on the Malay Peninsula dealt in minerals, rice and teak in addition to cloves and pepper. In time, these traders developed a sophisticated network, which included entrepreneurs in Burma and Sumatra.

Portugal used Goa, as a base from which to set off to Malaya. In 1511, the Portuguese conquered Malacca, but the Dutch defeated them, in 1641. The Dutch introduced monopolistic practices and disrupted the traditional commercial patterns of local entrepreneurs. The Mons abandoned their long distance trade routes. The Indigenous trading networks collapsed, and by 1681 Malay entrepreneurs gave up their trade with China, India, Japan, Persia, the Philippines, Siam and Vietnam. The Dutch imposed a 20% duty on Chulia entrepreneurs, but the Chulias kept their lead in the textile trade.

In 1786, in exchange for British protection from raiders and pirates, the Sultan of Kedah granted to the East India Company, a virtually uninhabited island off of the west coast of the Malay Peninsula. It was here, on Prince of Wales Island (Penang) that Georgetown, the first of the British Straits Settlements was established. Its founder was the British captain, Francis Light, whose son later founded Adelaide, Australia, which eventually became a sister city to Georgetown. European entrepreneurs set up spice plantations on the island, but growth was constrained due to a labour shortage. In addition to handling rubber and tin from the Malay Peninsula, Penang became "an important coal- and water-supply station for merchant and war vessels (Simpich, 1926, p. 243)." In contrast to Penang, that had a policy of free trade, the Portuguese and the Dutch had monopolistic intentions. In 1795, Malacca was given to the British.

In 1824, the Anglo-Dutch Treaty gave Bencoolen (a British post) and the rest of Indonesia to the Dutch, while the British were allowed to control Malaya and Singapore. In 1826, the British formalised the entity that they named the Straits Settlements, under the jurisdiction of the British East India Company, in Calcutta. The British East India Company controlled the Straits Settlements until the demise of the company, in 1858. The settlements then came under the control of the India Office, in London. In 1867, they were transferred to the Colonial Office, as the Straits Settlements became a Crown Colony. At the time, the Straits Settlements consisted of Penang, Malacca and Singapore. In 1874, the Islands of the Dindings were added to the colony. For the convenience of the British, the Cocos Keeling Islands were attached in 1886, followed by Christmas Island in 1900 and Labuan, off the coast of Borneo, in 1906. For administrative purposes, the colony was divided into four settlements: Singapore (including the Island of Singapore, the Cocos Islands and Christmas Island); Penang, including the Island of Penang, Province Wellesley, and the Territory and Islands of the Dindings; Malacca; and Labuan.

Figure 10.2 Remnant of Dutch Presence; photograph by Léo-Paul Dana.

Figure 10.3 British Architecture in Penang; photograph by Léo-Paul Dana.

Small-scale rubber production gained popularity in the early 20th century, as there were virtually no barriers to entry. The industry required minimal capital and this was readily available. According to Drabble (1973), by 1921, 37% of the total rubber acreage in Malaya belonged to small-scale entrepreneurs. This corresponded to one-eighth of the total world production of rubber. Simpich wrote, "three-fourths of all our rubber comes out of Malaya (1926, p. 235)." However, many Malay entrepreneurs lost their plantations to Chettiar money-lenders from southern India. This led to the Smallholdings Restriction of Sale Enactment, in 1931.

The Straits Settlements were dismantled in 1946, just months after the Japanese surrender. Also in 1946, the British territories on Borneo were re-organised such that North Borneo (Sabah) and Sarawak became two separate colonies. That same year, the British also forged the Malayan Union, consisting of Malacca and Penang, along with the nine existing Malay states. The union was dissolved in 1948 when the states of the Malay Peninsula formed the Federation of Malaya, which became independent in 1957. Having lost its status of free port, Penang's importance as a trade centre declined during the 1960s.

Figure 10.4 Small Business in Penang; photograph by Léo-Paul Dana.

In 1963, Malaya joined Sabah, Sarawak, and Singapore to create a new kingdom, Malaysia. Tension escalated between the ethnic-Chinese and the Malays. In 1965, Singapore was separated from the union. Chinese people in Malaysia became the victims of racial riots.

Pluralism

Most Chinese immigrants to Malaya did not come as entrepreneurs. During the 19th century, labourers left China to work in the mines of Malaya. Their passage was usually sponsored by an entrepreneur, who became entitled to be their exclusive employer for a period of one year. When they docked in Malaya, the newcomers were taken by armed guards, to their place of employment and locked up at night. The employees were virtual prisoners, until they had paid back their debt.

Figure 10.5 Chinese Ghost Festival; photograph by Léo-Paul Dana.

Secret societies were principal organisations of Chinese immigrants. Chinese entrepreneurs — *towkays* — were the leaders of these societies and they controlled their employees through these societies. The dominant society in Kuala Lumpur was the Hai San, led by Hakka entrepreneurs. Hokkien entrepreneurs developed an important rice network, importing rice from Burma and elsewhere, milling it in Malaya and exporting it to Hong Kong and beyond. According to the *Straits Settlements Trade Commission's Report,* rice imports to Penang reached 213,648 tonnes in 1918.

Figure 10.6 The Indian Minority is Important in Malaysia; photograph by Léo-Paul Dana.

Chinese entrepreneurs own much small-scale industry in Malaysia. Expansion is not common, and many firms remain sole proprietorships. The Hokkiens are the largest group of Chinese in Malaysia (one-third of the Chinese population). The prominent Chinese dialect federation — the Federation of Hokkien Associations of Malaysia — developed its own business arm, with investments in China as well as in Malaysia.

The Evolution of Public Policy

The British colonial administration, in Malaya, encouraged a marked division of economic roles, along ethnic lines. Indians were given jobs in plantations, at the post office and in the police service. While rural Malays remained peasants and urban Malays were offered employment in the public sector, many Chinese people became entrepreneurs. Income gaps were significant. Even after independence, the Chinese continued to dominate the economic realm and this caused racial friction.

With the objective of fighting poverty among Indigenous Malays, the People's Trustee Council — known by its acronym, MARA — was established in 1966. Its role was to promote Indigenous entrepreneurship; it identified opportunities for Malay *bumiputras* — literally "sons of the soil" — to become entrepreneurs. Throughout the 1960s, Malaysian policy encouraged diversified, import substitution.

Following the ethnic riots of 1969, the government opted to create a policy that would achieve more economic parity between *bumiputras* and ethnic minorities. In 1970, *bumiputras* owned 2.6% of the corporate structure in Malaysia. The government's goal was for *bumiputras* to control 30.0% of the nation's capital within 20 years. The reality remained below target for decades.

In 1971, the New Economic Policy was launched, to fight poverty and to achieve more ethnic parity. *Bumiputras* were granted special privileges to help them purchase land, obtain business permits, and improve their economic situation.

The Second Malaysian Five-Year Plan (1971–1975) was designed to create a generation of Malay entrepreneurs. It specified that the objective of entrepreneurship training, in Malaysia, was "to foster the emergence of a full-fledged Malay entrepreneurial community, within one generation." The Ministry of Trade and Industry *Bumiputra* Participation Division was created to assist the Indigenous Malays in particular, and the Export Trade Centre came to assist *bumiputras* to identify opportunities for entrepreneurship.

In 1975, the Industrial Co-ordination Act made it mandatory for all manufacturing establishments with a registered capital above 100,000 ringgit to be authorised by the Ministry of Industry. The threshold was subsequently raised to 250,000 ringgit.

The Institute Teknologi MARA (ITM), in 1975, established the Malaysian Entrepreneurship Development Centre (MEDEC), to help develop *bumiputra* entrepreneurship. The National Productivity Centre prepared a management-training package, in conjunction with MEDEC and the National Economic Research Development Association. In 1977, MEDEC launched a three-month long, part-time, Entrepreneurship Development Programme (EDP), and in 1981 a full-time programme was introduced. The focus of the EDP was to help potential entrepreneurs, with new venture start-ups. This included a 5-day Achievement Motivation Training (AMT) component, the purpose of which was to overcome the frequent complaint that *bumiputras* suffered because of their attitude.

The Fourth Malaysian Five-Year Plan (1981–1985) provided 318 million ringgit to various agencies responsible for promoting entrepreneurship. This included the Agricultural Bank of Malaysia, and the Development Bank of Malaysia.

The Central Bank of Malaysia set a maximum lending rate on loans to *bumiputras*. In addition, the Credit Guarantee Corporation introduced a credit guarantee scheme.

In 1985, small-scale entrepreneurs, in the manufacturing sector, were exempted from the requirement of applying for a manufacturing permit from the Malaysian Industrial Development Authority. To qualify for the exemption, entrepreneurs were not allowed to have more than 49 full-time employees. As well, equity was restricted to below one million ringgit.

While the Malaysia Industrial Development Berhad introduced assistance to entrepreneurs at large, the Ministry of Finance's New Investment Fund of Malaysia was created, to give priority to export-oriented projects. In addition, the state laid down specific guidelines for banks to allocate a specific proportion of their loans to small-scale entrepreneurs.

In 1986, Malaysia launched its Industrial Master Plan, emphasising the need for local firms to internationalise. In 1988, there were 28,335 manufacturers in Malaysia, of which 92.6% were small or medium industries (SMIs)[2] and four-fifths of the SMIs had a capitalisation of less than 50,000 ringgit. In consideration of this bi-modal distribution of very large and very small manufacturers, the state intervened to assist SMIs. This was done with the co-operation of the Malaysian External Trade Development Corporation; the Malaysian Industrial Development

[2] In Malaysia, an SMI is defined as a manufacturing company with equity not exceeding 2.5 million ringgit.

Authority; the Ministry of Human Resources; the Ministry of Science, Technology and Environment; and the Prime Minister's Support Department.

Figure 10.7 Wealthy Capital City of Kuala Lumpur; photograph by Léo-Paul Dana.

Figure 10.8 Less Wealthy Countryside; photograph by Léo-Paul Dana.

Figure 10.9 Bumiputra Retailing; photograph by Léo-Paul Dana.

The year 1990 saw the introduction of an offshore infrastructure in the Federal Territory of Labuan. This included the Offshore Banking Act, the Offshore Companies Act and the Offshore Insurance Act. As Labuan became an international, offshore financial centre, foreign entrepreneurs paid only 3% tax, or a flat fee. During the Sixth Malaysian Five-Year Plan (1991–1995), private investment in Malaysia increased by an average of 16.6% per annum. In 1992, the Malaysian Technology Development Corporation Sdn Bhd was incorporated, as a joint venture between government and industry, to increase technology-based entrepreneurship in Malaysia. The institution operates as a venture capital company, and identifies entrepreneurs whose ventures can become high-tech companies.

In May 1996, the Seventh Malaysian Five-Year Plan (1996–2000) emphasised the importance of having an export orientation in the increasingly liberal world trade environment. Also in 1996, the Labuan Offshore Financial Services Authority was established. Until 1998, the law required at least 30% of every company in Malaysia to be owned by *bumiputras*. To cope with this requirement, ethnic-Chinese Malaysians used *bumiputras* to register companies and to pose as majority shareholders, but without powers. Thus, *bumiputras* owned the majority of a firm (on paper), while Chinese partners kept control.

This was called the Ali-Baba system, Ali referring to *bumiputras* and Baba to the Chinese. In general, the Chinese disliked the *bumiputra* policy, which they described as a political instrument to limit their entrepreneurial activity. Yet, in some cases, Chinese entrepreneurs benefited by appointing influential *bumiputras* to their firms.

Figure 10.10 Silent Partners; photograph by Léo-Paul Dana.

During the Asian Financial Crisis of 1998, *bumiputra* entrepreneurs faced financial difficulties. The government consequently relaxed its *bumiputra* equity ownership restriction, allowing non-Malays to provide unlimited capital to some firms. Since then, ethnic-Chinese Malaysians have been allowed to own up to 100% of a local company. Since August 1998, all new manufacturing projects have been free from equity requirements. Entrepreneurs who qualify for "pioneer status" have been entitled to a five-year exemption from income tax. In September 1998, Malaysia pegged its currency at a rate of 3.80 ringgit to the dollar. The currency wasw unpegged in 2005. The Ninth Malaysian Plan (2006–2010) encouraged the development of value-added manufacturing. In 2013, the dollar was trading at 3.27 ringgit.

Figure 10.11 Passenger Transport; photograph by Léo-Paul Dana.

Figure 10.12 Transporting Goods; photograph by Léo-Paul Dana.

Figure 10.13 Micro-enterprise; photograph by Léo-Paul Dana.

Figure 10.14 Coffee Factory; photograph by Léo-Paul Dana.

Toward the Future

When the 1998 Asian Financial Crisis affected enterprises belonging to *bumiputra* entrepreneurs, Malaysia allowed Chinese and foreign entrepreneurs to inject more capital into ailing enterprises. Such relaxation of equity restrictions allowed Chinese entrepreneurs to buy into enterprises at low, crisis-time prices. This will enable Chinese entrepreneurs to gain greater control of the economy than in the past. However, according to the Selangor Federation of Chinese Guilds and

Associations, half of all entrepreneurs in Malaysia wind up their enterprise by the third year of operations.

The objective behind entrepreneurship promotion in Malaysia has been to redress economic differences between *bumiputras* and other ethnic groups in the country. Abdullah Ahmad Badawi, who became prime minister of Malaysia in October 2003, introduced the concept of *Islam Hadari*. As discussed in Badawi (2006), this includes the principle of balanced and comprehensive economic development.

Gadar and Yunus (2009) and Ong and Ismail (2011) focused on gender issue of entrepreneurship in Malaysia. It is likely the future will see more women entrepreneurs.

Case Study: Paul Smith

"We have between four and ten companies coming in here every week with their corporate credit cards, buying a whole lot of stuff to take to Hong Kong or wherever to copy," said Mr. Paul Smith, the chairman of Paul Smith Ltd. The blatant theft of ideas was irritating.

Mr. Paul Smith was born in 1946, in Nottingham, where he met a lecturer, Pauline Denyer, a powerful individual who became his girlfriend. Paul was working as a shop assistant at the time, and Pauline suggested that he should have his own shop. In 1970, Paul opened his first boutique, on Nottingham's Byard Lane. Although Paul neither used an artist's pencil, nor sketched a design for himself, Pauline gave him the inspiration to start designing and the self-confidence to launch his own brand of fashionwear.

In 1997, Paul was living in London's Holland Park. Pauline was still his girlfriend, three decades after their first meeting. While competitors copied one another, Paul kept relying on his creativity.

Harvard University's Frederick T. Knickerbocker postulated in 1973, that enterprises imitated each other in order to reduce the risk of being different. In contrast, Paul Smith believed in being different.

First he conceives an original style or concept, but unlike other designers, he does not do the actual design. Instead, he verbalises his design to convert the words into clothes. Mr. Smith believes that design can be the differentiating feature influencing the consumer's buyer behavior.

The Paul Smith collection is a blend of conservative Britishness with a tad of eccentric. The result is a line that is classic, yet creatively unique.The shops are also original and colourful. They radiate a smell of coffee. The music is relatively soft.

In London, England, Paul Smith has a boutique for women at 40 Floral Street; next door, at 41 and 42 Floral Street, is the men's shop, while Paul Smith for Children is at number 43, around the corner from the Covent Garden Underground tube (urban transit) station.

In 1982, Paul Smith expanded his enterprise to include Japan. This was a major step, given the vast differences between English and Japanese cultural values; the lack of sensitivity to such details caused numerous other foreign entrepreneurs to fail in Japan.

Since 1982, Paul Smith has returned to Asia many times. Paul Smith Ltd. has evolved into a world network, including a shop in Malaysia.

Case Study Assignment

As a consultant, design a strategy to help entrepreneur Paul Smith expand across Malaysia.

Figure 10.15 Paul Smith Shop in Covent Garden; photograph by Léo-Paul Dana.

Chapter 11

Myanmar[1]

Introduction

Myanmar — formerly the Union of Burma and among the most prosperous economies of Asia — covers 678,500 square kilometres, bounded by Bangladesh, China, India, Laos, Thailand, the Bay of Bengal and the Andaman Sea. In approximately 1295, Marco Polo described the wonders of Burma with astonishment (Moore, 1963). Kipling (1890) said of Burma, that it was quite unlike any land. Garrett used the words "virtually unknown to the outside world (1971, p.343)." Hodgson summarised Burma as the "most reclusive country of mainland Southeast Asia (1984, p.90)." Swerdlow described Myanmar as "the secretive nation (1995, p.73)." Hirsh and Moreau called it "East Asia's last frontier (1995, p.10)."

Hagen noted, "the Burmese level of living was higher than that of India or China (1962, p. 436)." Until the 1950s, Burma was the world's foremost rice exporter. After an era of socialism, a market-oriented model was introduced in 1988. Since then, many of Myanmar's social indicators — including the literacy rate, and the doctor:population ratio — have compared favourably with those of its richer neighbours (Thein, 1996). Yet — although the country is generously endowed with hardwood forests, oil, precious gems, silver and other minerals — its people have not prospered. Bah and Cooper (2012) discuss constraints to growth of small firms in Myanmar.

---

[1] This chapter is based on information obtained from a variety of sources, including: the Ministry of Agriculture and Irrigation; the Ministry of Co-operatives; the Ministry of Commerce; the Ministry of Finance and Revenue; the Ministry of Industry; the Ministry of Information; the Ministry of National Planning and Economic Development; the Ministry of Rail Transportation; the Myanmar Timber Enterprise; the Federation of Chamber of Commerce and Industry; and the University for the Development of the National Races of the Union. The chapter includes historical material that first appeared in Dana (2002).

Figure 11.1 Processing Rice; photograph by Léo-Paul Dana.

Historical Overview

The Pyu — a people who used the Sanskrit script and observed Buddhism with some elements of Hinduism — are the earliest people known to have flourished in this region. They were defeated by ancestors of today's Burmese. Based in Pagan,[2] King Anawrahta — founder of the Pagan dynasty — ruled from 1044 to 1077, and it is under his rule that Buddhism spread across his unified kingdom.

In 1287, the Mongols — under the leadership of Kublai Khan — arrived from China and destroyed the empire of the Pagan dynasty. The region was then ruled in the form of small states, dominated by three ethnic groups — the Burmese,[3] the Mons,[4] and the Shans.[5] This was so until the 16th century, when King Bayinnaung created a second Burmese empire. In 1752, King Alaungpaya established a third empire, which lasted until the arrival of the English. Traders from England arrived in the 17th century. Border troubles between Burma and British India led to war, which lasted from 1824 to 1826, when the British annexed the Burmese provinces of Arakan and Tenasserim. Following a second war, between 1852 and 1854, the British occupied Lower Burma. During a third war, in 1885, the British took over Upper Burma, making the former Kingdom of Burma a province of British India. While the Tibeto-Burmans and the Thai-Shans became British subjects, the Red Karens retained their special citizenship, in accordance with a treaty signed in 1875 (Christian, 1943). During the 1890s, Burma became an important exporter of oil.

The Young Men's Buddhist Association, established in 1902, promoted the independence of Burma, as did Buddhist monks during the 1920s. A peasant uprising, in 1931, also put pressure on the British. The India Act of 1935 became effective in 1937, separating Burma from India. Outram and Fane (1940) gave an account of pre-war Burma. Swerdlow (1995) noted that Burma's annual rice exports exceeded three million tonnes, making the nation the number one exporter of rice in the world. Christian elaborated, "Burma is one of the few countries in Asia that have a considerable exportable surplus of food (1942, p. 3)."

---

[2] See Roberts (1931).

[3] The Burmese were in control of Upper Burma since the 9th century.

[4] The Mons had come from the east, taking control of Lower Burma.

[5] Hagen (1962) traced the origins of the Shans to the Yünnan plateau of south-eastern China.

In December 1941, the Japanese invaded Burma, and by early 1942, the British withdrew. Burma had been an important base for Allied help to China, and the Japanese occupation of Burma was tragic for China, as the Burma Road was closed (Christian, 1943).

In 1943, Japan declared the independence of Burma, and set up a pro-Japanese government. After a long struggle (Arnold, 1944), Allied troops defeated the Japanese in 1945. On October 17, 1947, a treaty signed in London established the independence of Burma, and the Union of Burma came into existence on January 4, 1948 — a day of good omens, according to Burmese astrologers. The Karens[6] — a largely Baptist Christian minority with Chinese origins — waged war against the new government. Civil war lasted until 1952.

On March 2, 1962, General Ne Win pushed aside Burma's only elected prime minister and introduced military rule, along with the "Burmese way to Socialism," a blend of Buddhism, central planning and isolationism. Also in 1962, English was banned as "representative of a degenerate and decadent culture (Maung, 1991, p. 222)." The Burma Socialist Programme Party became the only legal political party. Banks were nationalised, along with the transportation system, wholesale trade, retail trade, and foreign-owned companies. This led to a progressive breakdown of the formal firm-type sector of the economy. The state-controlled planned sector engulfed the national economy. The lack of foreign capital and technology resulted in limited growth during the 1960s.

In 1974, the Union of Burma became a single-party socialist state, and the one-party constitution renamed the country the Socialist Republic of the Union of Burma. The government confirmed its commitment to self-reliance, state control, isolation, and strict neutrality. In 1979, Burma isolated itself even from the movement of nations professing non-alignment. Steinberg (1982) gave a comprehensive socio-political account of the era.

From 1986 to 1988, declining trade contributed to severe economic recession. Per capita income tumbled while inflation escalated. The author observed that between 1986 and 1987, military personnel quadrupled the price of petrol they were selling in the parallel economy.

---

[6] For a detailed discussion of the Karens, as researched by anthropologist Peter Kunstadter, see Kunstadter (1972).

By 1987, Burma was designated by the United Nations as one of the least-developed nations in the world. Per capita income — which had been $670 in 1960 — fell to $190 in 1987, according to World Bank figures. In September 1987, people aspiring class mobility lost faith in their currency when the government invalidated all notes of 25, 35 and 75 kyat.[7] Falling living standards, coupled with political frustration, contributed to widespread riots during the first half of 1988. Although 77-year old Ne Win, Chairman of the Burma Socialist Programme Party, resigned in July 1988, his party remained in power (*Herald Tribune*, 1988). In August 1988, tens of thousands of demonstrators toppled the dictatorship. In the absence of an entrepreneurial class, a new leadership arose from the military.

Figure 11.2 Avoiding Escalating Price of Fuel; photograph by Léo-Paul Dana.

Following a *coup d'état*, on September 18, 1988, the State Law and Order Restoration Council took control of the country, and adopted a market-oriented policy, officially discarding central planning. On June

[7] The unit of currency, spelled kyat, is pronounced "chat."

19, 1989 the government changed the English version of the country's name to the Union of Myanmar. During the early 1990s, about 6% of the GDP was accounted for by the manufacturing sector. Exports were encouraged, to obtain foreign exchange, but this resulted to local shortages, pushing domestic prices up. The mid-1990s met rampant inflation. A *pyi* — the local unit of weight equal to two kilogrammes — of rice that cost 11.72 kyat in 1991, was worth 41.11 kyat in 1993, and 60 kyat in 1996.[8]

In April 1997, the United States enacted economic sanctions against new investments Myanmar. A few weeks later, on July 23, 1997, Myanmar joined the Association of Southeast Asian Nations (ASEAN). As Asia entered its financial crisis, the market rate of Myanmar's currency tumbled in July 1997 and the dollar traded at more than 300 kyat. Meanwhile, the official exchange rate stood at about six kyat per dollar. In March 1998, new import restrictions were imposed. In 1999, approvals for foreign direct investment fell by 96%. Annual inflation during the 1990s averaged 27.13%.

Toward Centrally Planned Transition

Colonial policy, in Burma, is said to have obstructed the development of local entrepreneurship. "Burmese enterprise was discouraged…the manufacture of mechanical lighters was made illegal, lest it should prejudice the revenue from a tax newly imposed on matches (Furnivall, 1956, p. 166-167)." The colonial government gave preferential treatment to those it favoured, including the British India Steamship Navigation Company, the British Overseas Airways Corporation (BOAC), the Burma Match Co. Ltd., and the Bombay Burmah Trading Corporation, Ltd. (Furnivall, 1957; Macaulay, 1934). Kyi (1970) also examined the impact of Westerners on the evolution of an Indigenous entrepreneurial class.

Nevertheless, there appears to have been an entrepreneurial spirit, despite colonial policy. "Contrary to the widely accepted assumption that European and Indian immigrants monopolized entrepreneurial roles in Lower Burma, the Burmese displayed considerable entrepreneurship in J. A. Schumpeter's sense that they put into effect new combinations in the

---

[8] In 1996, $1 was worth 5.75 kyat at the official exchange rate, or 125 kyat in the black market.

means of production and credit (Adas, 1974, p. 210)." In particular, Burmese entrepreneurs were successful in the motion picture industry (Christian, 1943; Sein, 1950), printing (Swe, 1972), and rice milling (Hla, 1975). Burmese financiers were prosperous moneylenders (Wai, 1955), as were the Chettiars, who traced their origins to southern India. As well, Christian (1942) and Steinberg (1982) both pointed out that the Burmese were successful middlemen in the rice business. This is noteworthy, because elsewhere in the region it was the Chinese who dominated the middleman occupations.

Post-independence Burma — committed to self-reliance, state control, and isolation — adopted an economic policy that conformed to the import substitution model. In line with this model, the means to national economic development was to produce locally, thereby reducing the need for imports. This approach necessitated the existence of high tariffs, quotas and other regulatory mechanisms to discourage importation of goods. Rather than encourage specialisation in sectors of competitive advantage, this resulted in over-diversification. The model allowed the creation of a highly protected, low quality, high cost, and inefficient industrial sector. Furthermore, exports were biased against, due to a typically overvalued official currency exchange rate.

As Ne Win resigned, in late 1988, the Burmese Socialist Programme Party discussed proposals to reform the economy such that the "state would retain monopoly in commodities, broadcasting, the oil industry and gems and jade mining, but private enterprise would be allowed in transport, all kinds of industry and services, fishing, publishing and trade (*Herald Tribune*, 1988, p. 2)."

It was the State Law and Order Restoration Council that initiated a centrally-planned market-oriented model, in 1988. Private enterprise was resumed that year. The Foreign Investment Law, enacted in November 1988, allowed foreign investment manufacturing, tourism and transportation. Other important reforms included the State-owned Enterprises Law of 1989.

The 1965 Law for the Establishment of a Socialist Economic System was revoked in March 1989. In 1990, further liberalisation measures were introduced to promote a market economy. As well, the Commercial Tax Law was introduced in 1990. The agricultural sector was stimulated by the reduction of controls and regulations relating to the cultivation, milling, storage, transport, and marketing of agricultural products. Records at the Planning Department of the Ministry of National Planning and Economic Development report that the economy grew by 3.7% and 2.8%, during the 1989–1990 and 1990–1991 periods respectively.

The Short-term Plan (1992–1996) had as objective to pursue an export drive and to achieve an average annual growth rate of 5.1%. Efforts were made to increase savings and to channel these savings into productive investments. According to San Khup, Director-General of the Planning Department of the Ministry of National Planning and Economic Development, actual growth rates — of 9.7% the first year, 5.9% the second year, and 6.8% the third year — were higher than projected (Khup, 1996). It may be argued, however, that these figures are distorted by the fact that inflation is underestimated.

During 1994 and 1995, government emphasis was focused on foreign investment and trade. Certain price controls were phased out, as were subsidies. Taxes were streamlined, banking was restructured, and international business was facilitated. The capital city was revitalised.

The Foreign Investment Law welcomed capital into Myanmar. Foreign-owned enterprises were permitted, as were joint ventures with local enterprises. The law provided income tax holidays and further tax relief for exporters. It guaranteed repatriation of profits and stated that investments would not be nationalised. Private traders arrived from Singapore, South Korea and Thailand. Yet, a difficulty that remained was the inability of the state to mobilise domestic capital for investment. Another problem was the exchange constraint; although this encouraged barter, it limited trade.

In April 1995, the Rangoon City Development Committee made international news, by announcing the ban of the sale of betel in the nation's capital. This chewable nut, a mild stimulant that grows on areca palm trees, had been integral to the social and medicinal history in this country. Street-corner betel stands had provided employment for hundreds of people in Rangoon. In March 1998, new import restrictions were imposed, and this led to a boom in the parallel economy.

Myanmar's economic objectives of the 1990s included the development of agriculture as the base sector of the economy and the evolution of the market-oriented economic system. Yet, it was clearly specified that the initiative to shape the national economy must be kept in the "hands of the State and the national peoples."

Figure 11.3 Scene in Yangon — Formerly Rangoon; photograph by Léo-Paul Dana.

The Bazaar

Christian described bazaars in Burma, "Rubies, spinels, garnets…are bought and sold in open market…next to a bazaar selling potatoes, garlic, and Chinese radishes (1943, pp. 501–502)."

Typical of the bazaar, shops are clustered according to products or services sold. Jewellery shops stand adjacent to other jewellery shops; each offers jade and fresh water pearls along with gold earrings and rings sold by weight. Likewise fruit-sellers are clustered with other fruit-sellers. There are bananas and coconuts in abundance. Some vendors sell only tomatoes, while others specialise only in onions. Garlic is sold alongside ginger. Straw baskets contain different varieties of dry seeds. Rice comes in many varieties and different grades; some is damaged from poorly maintained husking machines. Cleaning, sorting and packing rice is for some women a social activity. Citrus fruits are not far from the tea specialist. A man is bargaining with a pharmacist as to the fair price of antibiotics. Ampicillin and tetracycline are available, as is penicillin solution for injection. None of these require a prescription.

Figure 11.4 Umbrella Repairman; photograph by Léo-Paul Dana.

Food is plentiful. Palmyra palms are sold along with fresh apples, carrots, cauliflowers, coffee beans, cucumbers, grapes, jackfruits, lotus fruits, mangoes, mangosteins, papayas, peanuts, plums, strawberries, sugarcane and sunflower seeds. There are also dried fruits, and baked goods. As well, one finds pineapple jam, and mango jam, along with glass bottles of beverages. Lemon-barley is a favourite, as is green-coloured cream soda.

Beasts of burden — cattle and water-buffalo — watch as chickens, ducks, goats, hogs, quail and sheep are sold alive. Lined up in a row, children are selling dry fish carefully laid out on the pavement. Lizards and stray dogs — friendly toward people, but at times territorial amongst themselves — scrounge for scraps. As the animals sense the oncoming storm, merchants act fast to pack up. Shoppers put their groceries on their head and make their way carefully to the waiting oxcart. The wind can be violent and bicycles can be sent flying. After the storm, the umbrella repairmen will have more business.

As is the case with traditional merchandise, modern items are also clustered. Perhaps most notable are the moneychangers, who use identical exchange rates. They trade currency as a commodity. Nobody has any competitive advantage. There is no product differentiation. The author observed several moneychangers clustered together: Ein Phyusi; 704; Bonton; Win; Yuzana; Crown; Forex; Gonshein Myint; User Friendly Stag; and May Flower. Although it is seemingly not possible to differentiate among them, each has own, loyal clientele. The focus here is not merely on transactions, but on the relationship between buyers and sellers.

Handicrafts

In 1857, King Mindon moved his capital to Mandalay and its Zegyo Bazaar became a principal distribution centre for beans, betel nuts, citrus fruit, cotton, nuts, onions, rice, tobacco, and wheat. The town prospered and artisans made it the handicraft centre of Myanmar.

Among the crafts developed in Mandalay is *shwe saing* — the making of gold leaf. This is occupation is concentrated in the Myatpa Yat Quarter, and found nowhere else in Myanmar (May, 1996). The skills are propagated from father to son, and non-family members are kept away from this occupation. The making of gold leaf is thus restricted to few families. Rather than compete with one another, about forty entrepreneurs join forces to produce and sell gold leaf in a symbiotic manner. The co-ordination of activities, among the firms, facilitates an otherwise complicated process of production and marketing.

Figure 11.5 Scene in Mandalay; photograph by Léo-Paul Dana.

The first stage involves melting gold blocks; five households are involved in this initial phase of production, each with three or four skilled employees, and 30 households — each with about two-dozen workers are involved in the later stages of production. The molten gold is poured into a conical vessel, producing finger-shaped bullions. Rollers flatten these bullions, which are subsequently beaten by skilled craftsmen resulting in thin sheets of gold, referred to as *shwe-let* — literally "golden fingers." Each sheet — about 2½ centimetres wide and over one metre long — takes about 4½ hours to flatten. These are then sent to another household for further processing. The gold is further cut up, into pieces about 2½ cm by 5mm. These are placed between *shwekhat setku* — sheets of bamboo paper made for the purpose of producing gold leaf. The artisans then wrap layers of this in deer-hide, and the gold is beaten again, to become film-thin. Once this is done, the strips of gold are joined with one another, to form quadrangles — each about 25 square centimetres. The final product is stored in *shwehlaung setku*, a paper made in Amarapura, from straw. Much of the gold leaf is used by religious people, to gild pagodas and images of Buddha. As is the production of gold leaf, stone carving is also a hereditary occupation. This activity is clustered in the Kyauk Sit Tan Yat Quarter of Mandalay.

As is the case with the production of gold leaf, this industry is also intertwined with Buddhism and much of the carving — in marble and in wood[9] — involves making images of Buddha.

Images of Buddha are also cast in bronze, and bronze casting is important in Myanmar. In Amarapura is an area called the Bronze Village, where bronze casting works are clustered. Bronze and copperware are often produced by trained silversmiths who are lacking silver, a scarce metal in Myanmar. Silversmiths are clustered in Ywataung, not far from Sagaing.

Silver and gold are used to make embroidery in Myanmar. In contrast to gold leaf, which is produced for consumption by local people, embroidery — containing gold and silver thread — is used to make tapestries, fabrics and cushion covers, for sale to tourists visiting Myanmar.

Another craft that thrives in Mandalay is silk weaving. Silk — mostly imported from China — is spun into thread, which is boiled in dyes to get coloured. It takes about ten days to weave a metre of cloth. Firms active in this industry are clustered east of the royal palace, in a neighbourhood of Mandalay called Nan Shay.

Covert Economic Activity

According to sources at the United Nations Office for Drug Control and Crime Prevention (UNODCCP), Myanmar is the source of 23.4% of the 4,653 tonnes of opium produced around the world each year. It is from these opium poppies that heroin is made. The wholesale price per kilogramme of heroin, in New York, is $80,000, according to sources at *The Economist*, and at 40% purity, the retail price is $290,000. Production is inexpensive, and the profit margin is immense. Its profitability makes it hard to control, because the hefty contribution margins make it easy to bribe poorly paid law enforcement officials.

Pluralism

According to the Ministry of Information, there are 135 national groups in Myanmar, with the Bamar being the majority; these different

[9] Puppets are also carved in wood.

ethnicities are classified according to distinct ethno-linguistic groups. While the majority of the people are Tibeto-Burman, the country is also home to Mon-Khmers, and Thai-Shans, as well as Karen people. The Tibeto-Burmans speak a Sino-Tibetan language, as do the Karens. In contrast, the language of the Mon-Khmers belongs to the Austro-Asiatic family, while the Thai-Shans comprise one of the Thai groups.

In addition, there are Chinese and Indian minorities in Myanmar. It was the British who encouraged the immigration of Indians to Burma. Some became moneylenders, and others were given government positions. By the 1930s, the immigrant Indian community in British Burma numbered 600,000, amounting to less than 10% of the population; yet these people held over half the government jobs.

Ethnic consciousness is notable. Dunung noted, "Burmese having Westernized attitudes are looked down upon. The Burmese also consider themselves to be superior to Indians, Chinese, and Eurasians (1995, p. 528)."

Elephant Labour

Smith described the elephant as a supermachine in Burma's logging industry, and argued, "Efforts have been made to make machinery do elephants' work in the forest, but without success. Machines cannot think (1930, p. 256)." Although machinery has improved, elephants are still very useful today, and their working life is 50 years.

Myanmar is home to as many as 6,000 wild elephants, and up to 7,000[10] domesticated ones (Gray, 2001). The Myanmar Timber Enterprise — which has a monopoly on teak extraction — employs 2,700 elephants. These are very useful in areas where vehicles cannot penetrate without causing major ecological damage. A 30-year cycle is used to harvest teak, and only trees of a designated girth are felled within a given area. Given this selection process, trained elephants do a neater job than would be possible if machinery was used.

An elephant starts school at the age of three. Students can learn one command every two days. Classes alternate with recess for bathing and resting. Once on the job, a bull elephant can work five to eight hours per

[10] This is a significant number, given that there is a total of 15,000 Asian elephants in captivity (Chadwick, 2005).

day, depending on the temperature. The animals use their husks, forehead and trunks to literally push tonnes of logs at a time.

Figure 11.6 Horses are also Useful; photograph by Léo-Paul Dana.

Toward the Future

Since 1988, steps have been taken to liberalise the agriculture sector, legalise trans-border trade, and encourage foreign investment. Firms in Myanmar are involved in agricultural processing, light manufacturing, and the production of footwear, pharmaceuticals and textiles. Their export markets include China, India, Singapore and Thailand. Yet, as reported by Speece and Sann (1998), managers complain about labour shortages and the lack of loyalty among employees. Many local enterprises operate at the subsistence level. A tourist is being shaven for the price of a coconut. Nearby, a micro-scale merchant sells flashlights and lighters. Another vendor is weighing nails. A woman walks by on her way to the station; she has prepared food to sell to passengers on the train.

Figuree 11.7 Impromptu Stall; photograph by Léo-Paul Dana.

At a pagoda, a woman sells sparrows to worshippers who will free them for good luck. As soon as they are let loose, she catches them again, as her inventory is fixed. Meanwhile, the parallel economy is thriving with consumer goods and pirated intellectual property. A merchant sells photocopies of George Orwell's 1930 book *Burmese Days*. A Ronald McDonald look-alike promotes Mac Burger, serving MacHam, MacChicken, and MacBurgers. A client takes out his "Solem" cigarettes from a pack that looks like that of Salem. An ambulant vendor heads for a bus on which she hopes to sell quail eggs.

While the government has focused on improving agricultural output, thus increasing the production of land, Myanmar remains among the less developed countries. Yet, the extent of absolute poverty is limited due to the abundance of inexpensive food and other essentials.

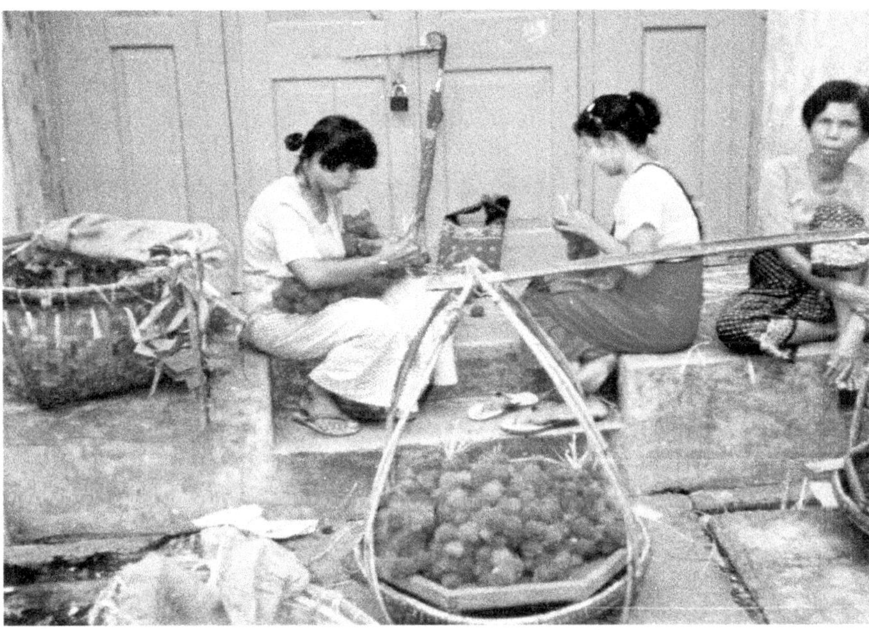

Figure 11.8 Inexpensive Food; photograph by Léo-Paul Dana.

Case Study: Hibiscus for Export

The many uses of hibiscus include making tea. According to Nevade, Lokapure and Kalyane (2011) hibiscus extract is be effective in protecting skin from excess solar radiation. China and India produce large quantities of hibiscus. Although several varieties of hibiscus growing in Myanmar, it is not among the country's major exports. Thiri likes hibiscus and is interested in launching a new venture to grow, process and export hibiscus. She is looking for ideas.

Tea

Tea was first used as a medicine. In moderation, it calms nerves; however, in excess, it causes agitation, insomnia and indigestion. The tea leaf contains theine, similar to caffeine in that it stimulates the heart and the brain. It also contains a slightly poisonous substance called tannin which increases its presence in a drink directly proportionally to the amount of time the leaves are left to steep. Generally, tea leaves should be left a maximum of five minutes.

The Chinese and Japanese tend to drink it plain, while the English and Irish add milk and sugar to a generally strong and dark brew. In Russia, sugar and lemon is added to the drink which is presented in glasses rather than in cups. In Tibet and in Central Asia, it is common to add salt and rancid butter to tea. North Americans use tea bags rather than leaves.

The United Kingdom is the world's largest buyer of tea. An average of ten pounds of tea is sold to each person per year. That can be interpreted that most drink between 1,500 and 2,000 cups of tea per year. Surprisingly, this drink has only been popular in Europe for 300 years. It is the national drink of several countries including Australia, China, Japan, Russia, and New Zealand.

Orange pekoe is made from the smallest leaf of the plant, and pekoe, from the second leaf. Pekoe-souchong and souchong come from the third and forth leaf, respectively, and the largest, or fifth leaf makes Congon tea. The flavour of each will depend on the preparation.

Scented teas (*i.e.,* camomile, jasmine, mint...) are created by drying the leaves with flowers. Sometimes, the blossoms are sifted out. Fermented leaves are used to make oolong tea, as are the leaves used to make black tea. The latter are covered and kept warm for longer in order to loose their color, thus changing the flavour.

While hibiscus tea is very popular in some markets, it is less well-known in others. Egypt is a major producer and consumer of the product. The plant is cultivated in Upper Egypt, especially in the areas of Luxor and Aswan, located in the southern part of the country near the border of Sudan. Its flowering top is boiled for approximately 30 minutes. The product is then drained and the fluid is diluted with water, until it reaches the desired concentration. It resembles cherry juice in colour and has a rich, flowery taste which is quite thirst quenching. Sugar may be added and the beverage can be enjoyed hot or cold.

Not only is this hibiscus tea an appetizer, but it also has medicinal effects, as it is an anti-flatulent, thus providing a relief from gas and bloating. Hibiscus tea also contains chemicals of the alkaloid group which act as an anti-spasmodic agent. Furthermore, there are unverified claims that this plant controls blood level cholesterol and lowers high blood pressure. The hibiscus flowers were traditionally sold in mesh or cloth bags. In modern times, plastic bags are used, containing flowers in bulk. Tea is also sold in pre-packaged single serving bags.

Case Study Assignment

As a consultant, help Thiri prepare a business plan.

Figure 11.9 Hibiscus; photograph by Léo-Paul Dana.

Chapter 12

Nepal[1]

Introduction

Formerly a kingdom, Nepal covers 147,181 square kilometres, landlocked between China and India. (It abolished its 240-year-old monarchy in 2008.) Nepal has always been independent. Nepal time is five hours and 45 minutes ahead of GMT, *i.e.*, 15 minutes ahead of Indian standard time. Nepalese people belong to two distinct groups, namely the Indo-Aryans and the Tibeto-Burman Mongoloids. Nepali is written in Devanagari script. As noted by Rosenbloom and K.C. (2005), Nepal is the only country in the world to officially declare itself a Hindu state. Christian missions are permitted but conversions prohibited.

Rosenbloom and K.C. noted that Nepal is often overlooked, "Numerous examples exist of Nepal's 'invisibility' in the academic and professional business/management literature (2005, p. 69)." Indeed, there is relatively little literature available about entrepreneurship in this country. Rosenbloom and K.C. elaborated, "Consistent with an economy that is agriculturally based, Nepal has a low unemployment rate (2005, p. 70)." As the economy shifts away from a dependence on agriculture, entrepreneurship and small business is being promoted via a variety of schemes.

Ngudup, Chen, and Lin (2005) described Nepal as an underdeveloped country. Most people here are subsistence farmers (see Henker, 1999). Roth noted, "In Nepal, 7 percent of girls are wed before they turn 10 (2006, p. 26)." Pandey (2009) noted that electrification was awarded as a political favour.

---

[1] This chapter is based on information obtained from a variety of sources, including: the Federation of Nepal Cottage and Small Industries; the Industrial Enterprise Development Institute; the Ministry of Commerce and Supplies; the Ministry of Finance; the Ministry of Industry; and the Trade and Export Promotion Centre.

Nepal is where the model of the Small Business Promotion Project was developed. Its success prompted the German Agency for Technical Cooperation to market this model internationally, using the brand name Creation of Enterprises, Formation of Entrepreneurs. This model has since been implemented in over 70 countries.

Figure 12.1 Nepali Styles; photograph by Léo-Paul Dana.

Figure 12.2 Subsistence Farming; photograph by Léo-Paul Dana.

Historical Overview

Ancient Nepal was composed of small principalities. In 1769, these were unified into one nation, by King Prithivi Narayan Shah, who lived from 1722 to 1775. Prior to 1846, Nepal was ruled by a hereditary king. Beginning in 1846 and until 1951, the kingdom was ruled by hereditary prime ministers, members of the Rana family. Chetwode (1935) provided an account of Nepal at the time. In 1951, the monarchy was restored under King Tribhuvan, after whom Kathmandu's airport is named. Tribhuvan's son Mahendra succeeded him in 1955.

Following the 1959 rebellion in Tibet, 10,000 Tibetans migrated to Nepal; a discussion appears in Chadwick (1987). In April 1961, Nepal's 15 feudal chieftainships were integrated into the kingdom. The Customs Act was enacted in 1962. The royal constitution was implemented on December 16, 1962, and the national flag was officially adopted. King Mahendra was succeeded by his son Birendra in 1972. That same year, the Handicraft Association of Nepal was formed as a non-profit organisation. Its purpose is to improve the productivity of the member artisans and to promote their handicrafts in various foreign markets.

In 1990, Nepal became a constitutional monarchy. In 1992, the Federation of Nepalese Chambers of Commerce and Industry became actively involved in SME promotion. In 1993, the Ministry of Industry reorganised its Department of Cottage and Small Industries. The Cottage and Small Industry Development Board was established that year. In January 1994, the Nepal Stock Exchange began trading in Kathmandu. In 1996, Nepal's Information Technology Park was placed under the umbrella of the Industrial Enterprise Development Institute. The objective of developing the park was to create favourable environment by providing basic infrastructure to attract entrepreneurs. In 2001, two of Nepal's leading banks were declared insolvent (Rosenbloom and K.C., 2005). Although infrastructure was improved and taxation reformed, Khatiwada (2002) suggested that banking reform was urgently needed.

Nepalese artisans linked up with European buyers at Kathmandu's 11th Handicraft Fair in 2013. The fairs aim to develop stronger understanding, in Europe, of Nepalese micro-enterprises and their products.

Figure 12.3 Terraced Agriculture; photograph by Léo-Paul Dana.

Figure 12.4 Kathmandu; photograph by Léo-Paul Dana.

Economic Policy

Nepal's first economic development plan was launched in 1956, known as the First Five-Year Plan (1956–1961). The Export and Import Control Act was introduced in 1957.

Hagen (1960) suggested that the cheese industry was a path to prosperity in Nepal. Following his suggestion, the government of Nepal, with the help of Swiss experts and the United Nations Food and Agriculture Organisation, established the nation's first cheese factory, in the Lanting Valley. The success of the first stone factory led to the construction of three others, ultimately boosting exports to India.

The Second Plan (1962–1965) focused on infrastructure development and on institutional reform. The Federation of Nepalese Chambers of Commerce and Industry was established in 1965. The Third Plan (1965–1970) emphasised infrastructure development in order to accelerate the pace of economic development.

Agriculture and transport were central to the Fourth Plan (1970–1975). Introduced in 1971, the New Education System Plan attempted to establish vocational education in every secondary school throughout Nepal. The Trade Promotion Centre was also established in 1971.

Liberalisation of the financial sector began in 1984 (see Rothenberger, 1999). An offshoot of the Economic Promotion Unit of the Nepal-German Bhaktapur Development Project, the Small Business Promotion Project was initiated in 1984. It was assisted by the German Agency for Technical Cooperation. In 1989, the Project was brought under the Ministry of Industry. The objective of the Small Business Promotion Project was to contribute to the economic and social development of Nepal. Specifically, the Small Business Promotion Project offered training and consulting for entrepreneurs, as a means to attaining poverty alleviation. It is a decentralised organisation with several branches; its approach has been to co-operate with people and empower them to make decisions for their enterprises. Core programmes of the Small Business Promotion Project have included: (i) New Business Creation; (ii) Small Business Consultancy; (iii) Services to Institutions; (iv) Planning and Business Information; and (v) the Complementary Credit Scheme.

The New Business Creation programme developed knowledge, skills and motivation among prospective entrepreneurs. Business schemes were then presented to fellow participants for constructive criticism and to the banking community. It is estimated that this programme led to the creation of about 1,000 jobs annually. The Small Business Consultancy focused largely on assisting newly established small-scale industries with promotional activities. The programme offered technical consultancy, in addition to accounting, marketing and production management expertise. The Services to Institutions programme involved co-operation with organisations, in the implementation of effective income-generation and entrepreneurship programmes for various target groups. This included the training of rural trainers in methods of income generation. The Planning and Business Information office made available a well-stocked library and provided information to other programmes of the Small Business Promotion Project. This included technical consultants who visit clients on a cost sharing basis. The Complementary Credit Scheme maintained a revolving fund for credits to entrepreneurs. The fund was administered by the Agricultural Development Bank of Nepal. Loans were secured with collateral from entrepreneurs.

Participants of training programmes were required to pay a non-refundable deposit, which was forfeited if they failed to complete the training. The experience of the Small Business Promotion Project suggested that: (i) only clients who possess observable potential should receive assistance; (ii) a target group must be identified before services are designed, as opposed to designing a service and then seeking a target group; (iii) the only services that should be delivered are those which can be adequately managed with available resources; (iv) transparency benefits all parties; (v) services must last a limited time, as entrepreneurs must eventually be able to operate without assistance from a programme; and (vi) services should be cost-effective.

In 1995, the Small Business Promotion Project was transformed into the Industrial Enterprise Development Centre. The following year, this was institutionalised as the Industrial Enterprise Development Institute. With branch offices across Nepal, this institute is actively involved in training the trainers of SME programmes.

The Seventh Plan (1985–1990) emphasised industrial and commercial sectors. This plan encouraged the private sector to take lead role in the promotion of industries, in order to accelerate import substitution and export promotion. In 1989, the National Science and Technology Policy was enacted to create a favourable climate for scholars, scientists and entrepreneurs to work together.

The Industrial Policy of 1992 stressed privatisation, market oriented pricing, determining wages on the basis of productivity and protecting industries through custom duties. The Labour Act of 1992 established the framework governing employers; small-scale enterprises were made exempt from obligation of this act. The Eighth Plan (1992–1997) was implemented beginning in July 1992; its objective was to promote import substitution and improve cottage and small-scale industries using locally available resources to meet internal demand. The plan highlighted sustainable economic growth, poverty alleviation, rural development, regional balance, and the promotion of cottage industries. The plan included: (i) development of import substituting and export promoting industries; (ii) giving priority to private participation; (iii) emphasis on the development and expansion of cottage and small-scale and agro-based industries; (iv) institutional arrangements to familiarise cottage and small-scale industries with market, technology, and skills; and (v) strengthening existing financial institutions and establishing new ones to assist cottage and small-scale industries.

The Ninth Plan (1998–2002) aimed to train people in order to develop, expand and integrate necessary technical and support services required for cottage and small industries; rural entrepreneurship development programmes were created to encourage the establishment of industries in rural areas. In 1999 the National Policy on Technical Education and Vocational Training recognised the need for a nation-wide coordinated effort to develop human resources such as to enable people to get employment or become self-employed, and thus contribute to economic development.

Nepal's 10th Plan (2002–2007) focused on poverty reduction. The 11th plan (2007–2011) was the last five-year plan, followed by shorter ones. The 13th Plan covered the fiscal year 2013–2014 to fiscal year 2015–2016.

Figure 12.5 Rural Beggar; photograph by Léo-Paul Dana.

Figure 12.6 Learning from an Elder; photograph by Léo-Paul Dana.

Toward the Future

In order for entrepreneurs to benefit from clustering, the government has set up several industrial districts. The Industrial Enterprises Development Institution has established a technology park.

Nepal plans to limit the role of its public sector, such that the role of the state simply be that of serving as a catalyst to expand the role of the private sector. As well, the taxation system is to be simplified. Nevertheless, factors hindering entrepreneurship include corruption, deficiencies of the infrastructure, a weak base of human resources, and inadequate awareness of entrepreneurs.

Figure 12.7 Advancing into the Future; photograph by Léo-Paul Dana.

Case Study: Advertising in the Himalayas

PepsiCo has had tremendous success licensing and distributing its soft drink products around the world. It even succeeded in distributing its Pepsi-Cola brand in Nepal through a local SME, a bottler by the name of Swastik Aerated Products. However, distribution was sometimes a problem, due to poor road maintenance and the fact that Nepal has one of the highest elevations in the world. When the fleet of trucks could not make it, porters had to carry the product on their backs. The cold weather in the mountains was also a factor hindering transport.

Ad campaigns must reflect the nation's level of development as well as media and cultural factors. A big uncertainty is the labour force, as many people see no point in working hard. Another issue is the market environment, *i.e.,* how to create a demand in Nepal which only has a small upper class and is mostly populated by Indians and Tibetans who often are satisfied with basic necessities. Tourism, increasing steadily from year to year, would be a possible market segment. There is doubt, however, as to whether or not Swastik will be able to sell the annual target of 14,400,000 bottles.

Nepal, landlocked between China and India, is the birthplace of Buddha. It is one of the poorest countries in the world, facing typical problems of developing nations: overpopulation, pollution, and deforestation.

The north is inhabited by Tibetan-speaking Mongols while the south is home to Indo-Aryan people. Nepal has 35 distinct ethnic groups and castes. There are 22 major languages, and non-verbal communication is very important in this high-context society. Half of the population does not understand the official national language, Nepali.

Nepal is a right-hand side society, as the left-hand side is the "toilet hand," and it is naturally considered quite impolite to use it when eating. Furthermore, Hindus consider food contaminated or polluted once it has been touched by Westerners who are casteless.

Nepal's economy is largely agrarian. 90% of its population is dependent on agriculture. The most cultivable land is in the Tarai, which covers 15% of the land mass and houses 40% of the nation's population. The Tarai is also Nepal's industrial centre due to its proximity to India. Swastik's plant is located here in the Tarai. Despite this region's relative prosperity, most people — including the heads of households — cannot read. Typically, the Nepalese get married between the ages of 10 and 12 years old.

Thus, Nepal has a number of characteristics which set it apart from other countries, and that makes advertising in Nepal a unique challenge. This includes a low literacy rate (one out of three men can read and one out of ten women); the use of many different languages; the low income of most Nepalese; the very young age distribution; the lack of television coverage; and the popularity of radios and of attending the movies.

Pepsi-Cola

Pepsi-Cola was created during the summer of 1898, in the small American town of New Bern, North Carolina. Its inventor was Mr. Coleb D. Bradham, a Jewish pharmacist, who was mixing African kola nuts with herbs, in search of a relief from gastro-intestinal discomfort such as dyspepsia and peptic ulcers. The attempt to cure dyspepsia with kola nuts led to the name Pepsi-Cola.

At the time, Bradham was not looking to compete with Coca-Cola, which had been launched in Atlanta during 1886. Yet Pepsi-Cola's later owner, Mr. Charles Guth, developed an aggressive penetration strategy to face Coca-Cola. Although Pepsi-Cola went bankrupt three times, it finally got its breakthrough during the Depression of the 1930s, when Guth offered twice as much Pepsi-Cola for half the price of Coca-Cola.

The Coca-Cola Company accused Pepsi-Cola of copyright infringement over the use of the word "cola." The former even claimed that it succeeded in eliminating competitors by means of lawsuits; however, it was soon discovered that Cleo Cola, a producer in a town called Orange, New Jersey, had been paid to close down.

Pepsi-Cola expanded into the Canadian market in 1906. It finally entered the Soviet Union in the mid-1970s and China during the 1980s. In various markets, Pepsi-Cola is positioned differently as it is at different stages of its product life cycle. In time, Pepsi-Cola expanded to 148 nations. Nepal would become country 149. As Pepsi-Cola was being introduced in Nepal, it was at a growth stage in Europe, and approaching maturity in North America.

The bottling plant in Nepal, was a huge red building between Kathmandu and the medieval town of Sano Thimi. It was scheduled to produce 96,000 250ml bottles of Pepsi-Cola each day. The plant also bottled Mirinda, an orange-flavoured soft drink comparable to Coca-Cola's Fanta Orange.

Whereas international expansion in the soft drink industry is complex, the local bottler system facilitates matters. Major concentrate producers sell to local bottlers who add sweetener and water, and who then bottle and distribute the final product. Thus, franchising allows PepsiCo to enter a foreign country relatively rapidly, while keeping a certain degree of control over the production. In this case, PepsiCo (the parent company), gives the right to Swastik (the franchisee) to partly produce, bottle and sell its product.

Franchising calls for a great degree of standardisation for international recognition. Even if the franchisee knows the market better, PepsiCo should closely monitor the business operations of Swastik in order to keep a high international standard in Nepal.

In exchange for contractual obligations, bottlers are usually given exclusive rights to specific geographic territories. The production of another cola by Swastik would be deemed to be a conflict of interest; nevertheless, Swastik would be allowed to continue production of beer and of orange-flavoured soda. Pepsi-Cola would benefit from Swastik's developed market channels.

Distribution is key in the beverage industry. Given the specific terrain of Nepal, the logistics of transportation is a difficult aspect of marketing. The road networks are undeveloped, and in the mountainous regions, walking is the primary mode of transport. To get to these areas, where a considerable number of people live, goods must be transported on the backs of porters. Therefore, it is important to strike a working relationship with these porters who carry up filled bottles of soft drinks and carry back down the empty bottles. Thus, each firm focuses on its respective core competence. Swastik is in charge of bottling and distribution, while PepsiCo brings technical expertise and a marketing budget.

Although such an arrangement decreases PepsiCo's risk and investment, it also has drawbacks:

1. PepsiCo lacks management control over beverage production (quality and/or otherwise);

2. mistrust may transpire between the two companies, should certain conflicts not be resolved; and

3. the local company can get involved with other products that are incompatible with the brands and image of Pepsi-Cola.

Thus, the choice of a bottler is important, especially when entering a market that is very foreign. The bottler should be experienced in beverage production in the country. In the case of Nepal, PepsiCo chose a bottler owned by a notable family experienced in beverage production. Especially in the Asian context, powerful families make a difference.

Swastik Aerated Products was owned by the notable business family of Madanial Chiranjiiai. Its sister company also produced soft drinks, namely Lemu and Aqua. With technical assistance from Germany, the plant also produces Star Beer. The machinery required for the production of Pepsi-Cola was imported from the federal republic.

PepsiCo had been the first company to use a jingle in radio advertising and has always used innovative advertising techniques. Swastik's chairman, Mr. C.L. Agarwal, anticipated an enormous multimedia campaign on Nepal TV. He also had plans to use other mediums such as Radio Nepal, newspaper publication, stickers, banners, signs, etc.

Although Mr. Agarwal spoke of an enormous multimedia campaign, much is *press publicity* as opposed to *paid advertising*. Generally, advertising expenditures are lower, in nations with low personal income, than in the West.

The Coca-Cola Company and PepsiCo are both famous for their standardised product and for their *pattern advertising*. Despite globalisation of markets, some *environments* may demand considerable *adaptation*. It should be stressed that in Nepal: (i) most of the target market is illiterate and per capita newspaper circulation is low; (ii) Radio Nepal operates 13 hours daily and lower income markets may be reached via radio advertising as many shopkeepers let their radios be heard in the streets such that even those who cannot afford a radio will hear it; (iii) cinema advertising is useful, given the fact that attendance is relatively high; and (iv) it is only the upper class which can afford a television, and television ownership is low relative to the population base. Also, the use of multiple languages and regional dialects complicates the task of communicating a mass appeal to the Nepalese people, and requires firms to use creative strategies to reach the people in an efficient and economical way.

Case Study Assignment

Set up a marketing consultancy or advertising agency in Nepal and attempt to get the account of Swastik.

Chapter 13

The Philippines[1]

Introduction

The Republic of the Philippines (named after King Philip II of Spain) is an archipelago of over 7,000 islands, with a total land-mass of almost 300,000 square kilometres. While the Filipino tongue is Tagalog-based, English is the language commonly used in commerce, making this the world's third largest English-speaking country (although not all are conversant in English).

Numerous studies have investigated entrepreneurship in the Philippines. Moser discussed "sidewalk entrepreneurs (1977, p. 361)." Sharma (1979) found that entrepreneurs in the Philippines were independent and highly motivated to take risks, with a great desire to maximise their potential. The same study also asserted that the "Filipino entrepreneur is college educated and hails from a business-oriented family (p. 223)." El-Namaki (1988) reported a declining level of small business self-employment in the Philippines. According to Swierczek and Jatusripatak (1994), who examined cultural features of entrepreneurship in the Philippines, entrepreneurs in this country appear to have had greater advantages than elsewhere in Southeast Asia; the authors described their sample as technically skilled, innovative and opportunistic. Chen (1997) focused on small scale retailers in the Philippines. Ruane (2007) studied entrepreneurship development with a focus on motivations.

---

[1] This chapter is based on information obtained from a variety of sources, including: the Department of Labour and Employment; the Department of Trade and Industry; the Institute for Small-Scale Industries; the Philippine Chamber of Commerce and Industry; the Philippine Institute for Development Studies; and the Small Enterprise Research and Development Foundation, in Quezon City. Travel to the Philippines was provided by the Philippine Small and Medium Business Development Foundation. The chapter includes historical material that first appeared in Dana (1999b).

Figure 13.1 Raised for Subsistence; photograph by Léo-Paul Dana.

While the ethnic-Chinese here have been very active in small business development, Indigenous Filipinos have tended to exhibit a lesser incidence of entrepreneurship. Since the 1980s, several measures have been taken to broaden the appeal of enterprise and to assist Filipino entrepreneurs. Despite efforts to promote and to finance business ventures, several constraints have hindered small enterprise development in the Philippines. Furthermore, the nation encountered fiscal problems during the 21st century.

Historical Overview

The first Westerner to discover this archipelago was Ferdinand Magellan, in 1521. The islands were already thriving with commerce, as Arab, Chinese and Indian merchants had come to trade here. King Philip II of Spain took interest in the area, and sent later expeditions.

Figure 13.2 Fresh Pineapple for Export; photograph by Léo-Paul Dana.

The Spanish introduced the pineapple — a native of South America — to the Philippines. In time, the Philippines became one of the world's leading pineapple producers. Over three centuries of Spanish rule came to an end in 1898, when independence was declared. In 1900, the United States took control, followed by the Japanese in 1942. The Americans returned during World War II (WWII), and a second republic was created in 1946. Ferdinand Marcos acquired power in 1965 and declared martial law in 1972. He was ousted in 1986, when Corazon Aquino (widow of his assassinated opponent) took over. One of her major plans was to implement the Comprehensive Agrarian Reform Programme, which was meant to redistribute vast holdings from the elite to the rural poor; however, this programme was less successful than she had planned. Meanwhile, local entrepreneurs lobbied aggressively for an increase in protective trade barriers. Mrs. Aquino survived seven attempted coups and a struggle with the New People's Army, the aim of which was a communist take-over. In 1992, Fidel Ramos succeeded her with a platform to create jobs, revitalise the economy, reduce debt and fight corruption.

Figure 13.3 Dole is a Big Player in the Philippines; photograph by Léo-Paul Dana.

Affected by the Asian Financial Crisis of 1998, growth slowed down and unemployment rose. The government lifted exchange controls and reformed the tariff structure. In May 1998, the central bank reduced the reserve requirement for banks, from 10% to 8%. This led to the lowering of the prime lending rate. By June, one could obtain a loan for 16% (compared to 30%, six months earlier).

When Joseph Estrada became president, on June 30, 1998, he promised to continue market reforms. Nevertheless, as the effects of the Asian Financial Crisis affected the economy, the jobless rate rose to its highest level in seven years and the budget deficit continued to grow. In time came recovery. In 2012, real GDP growth in the Philippines was 6.6%.

Pluralism

The population of the Philippines is heavily concentrated (more than 50%) on Luzon and Mindanao, the two largest islands. The Indigenous Filipinos are of Malayo-Polynesian origin. The Chinese minority is an important one. About one million people in the Philippines have some Chinese ancestry and they tend to be quite visible in the realm of business. During the late 20th century, *The Economist*[2] reported that although less than 1% of the population in the Philippines was of pure Chinese descent, firms owned by ethnic-Chinese accounted for two-thirds of the 67 biggest commercial outfits. The same essay added that the Chinese dominated the small business sector to an even greater degree.

Although Spain was very successful in its efforts to convert the Filipinos to Christianity, it failed in its attempt to displace the economic prominence of Chinese entrepreneurs in the Philippines. The Spanish restricted the Chinese and often threatened violence. Between 1603 and 1762, there were constant massacres of Chinese people in the Philippines. Yet, Chinese entrepreneurs continued to thrive in commerce and they mastered the Spanish language. A new class emerged — multilingual Chinese entrepreneurs.

Descendants of marriages between Christianised Chinese men and Indigenous Filipinas resulted in Christian Chinese-mestizos. Both the Spanish Church and the authorities gave greater privileges to these people than to pure (non-Christian) Chinese. As a class, the Christian Chinese-mestizos were considered higher than the Chinese. Their descendants are quite different than the Peranakans in Malaysia, in the sense that the Chinese-mestizos identify themselves as Christians rather than Chinese.

During the 1700s, the largest landholdings in the Philippines were those of Christian religious orders. Wealthy Chinese entrepreneurs subsequently purchased estates from the clergy, and time widened the gap between the per capita income of economic elites and that of the masses. Among wealthy Chinese parents, a priority was to provide their young with educational opportunities beyond those available to the masses. The emerging educated class of elites acquired the name *ilustrados*, Spanish for "those who are enlightened."

The 19th century brought a new wave of immigrants from China's Fujian Province. These also prospered in commerce, and in money-lending as well as in agriculture. However, they had a lower social standing than the more educated, established Chinese.

The ethnic-Chinese in the Philippines comprise 2% of the population; yet, they control more than half of market capitalisation.

[2] "The Overseas Chinese," July 18, 1992, p. 21.

Most of them (85%) are Hokkien. It is perhaps on the island of Cebu that one best sees Chinese entrepreneurship in the Philippines. Most of the entrepreneurs on this island are ethnic-Chinese and real economic growth, here, is consistently higher than is the national average.

Figure 13.4 Duck is Popular among Chinese People in the Philippines; photograph by Léo-Paul Dana.

Facilitating Entrepreneurship

Considerable effort has focused on broadening the appeal of entrepreneurship, and entrepreneurs in the Philippines have long been assisted by foreign donors as well as by local sources. In 1974, the Canadian International Development Agency (CIDA) sponsored the Cagayon Valley Co-operative Development Programme, to develop farmers' co-operatives in the Philippines. In 1978, the same agency launched the Industrial Co-operation Programme (ICP) which soon became involved in matching Filipino entrepreneurs with counterparts overseas. In 1981, another CIDA project was designed to assist small-scale Filipino fishermen. Additional Canadian funds were allocated to help micro-enterprises and small business development. During the late 1980s, CIDA planned an Enterprise Development Project geared to cottage industries as well as to micro-enterprises and small businesses. Another project of CIDA is the Philippine Development Assistance Programme (PDAP), funded by the National Initiatives Programme — of the federal government of Canada — but implemented by a non-governmental organisation. In order to maximise the input of the PDAP fund, small-scale projects were given priority, with the aim of helping self-employed tenant farmers, and fishermen among others. The initial success of the initiative led to its later enlargement.

The international organisation, Approtech Asia — based in the Philippines and financially supported by CIDA — undertook projects to help women entrepreneurs in the Philippines. Likewise, Singapore-based Technonet Asia initiated a project to assist technology transfers to the Philippines. Meanwhile, the World Bank approved several billion dollars of loans, through the International Bank for Reconstruction and Development. Some of these funds were channelled to half a million family-farms in the Philippines. Also, the Asian Development Bank and Fund approved significant loans to provide credit to micro-enterprises and cottage industries.

Another important player, in the small business sector of the Philippines, is the International Fund for Agriculture Development, which channels aid to small-scale farmers. One of its technical assistance grants, to the International Rice Research Institute in Los Banos, led to research about a training programme to encourage the cultivation of azolla, which is a low-cost, natural fertiliser. Because azolla is labour-intensive, as opposed to capital-intensive, it is ideal for small-scale farmers.

Calamansi is a major fruit crop in the Philippines. Among other produce is guava. Rambutan is classified as a priority crop.

Figure 13.5 Calamansi; photograph by Léo-Paul Dana.

Figure 13.6 Guava; photograph by Léo-Paul Dana.

Figure 13.7 Rambutan; photograph by Léo-Paul Dana.

Foreign aid has also contributed to the significant improvement of the telecommunication infrastructure, especially since the 1980s, when most communities in the Philippines had inadequate access to telecommunications. The situation improved during the 1990s, when the Department of Transportation and Communication received technical assistance and training from the Philippines Telecommunications Technical Assistance Project, funded by CIDA. The same Canadian agency also sponsored a project to provide a public toll call facility in each of several communities. Today, most communications services belong to the private sector.

The Philippines traditionally practised an import substitution policy supported by high customs duties. As a result of high duties, only 20% of components in the local garment industry were sourced in the domestic market; this was true until the early 1990s. Foreign exchange controls were lifted in 1992, and the tariff structure was subsequently reformed. The Philippine Small and Medium Business Development Foundation was established in 1992, and has since been improving managerial and technical skills in small firms.

The government also planned several incentives to enhance entrepreneurial spirit. Among these are industrial estates, export processing zones and special development programmes. As well, the state created tax holidays and credits to lure entrepreneurs from overseas, especially those creating labour-intensive activity in the Philippines.

The Small Enterprises Research and Development Foundation of the Philippines (SERDEF) was established by the private sector to initiate, sponsor, promote, assist and conduct research, training and development of micro-enterprises, cottage industries, and small and medium-sized firms in the Philippines. The foundation works with a variety of organisations, forging linkages with government agencies, industry associations and educational institutions, such as the University of the Philippines Institute for Small Scale Industries. SERDEF has funded several publications.

The Institute for Small Scale Industries offers dozens of training courses to assist entrepreneurs. The institute also offers a small business-consulting course and a trainer's course. An advanced course, offered by the Institute, is the Project Appraisal, Evaluation and Monitoring Course for Small and Medium Enterprise Projects. A specialised course offering is entitled Designing and Implementing Entrepreneurship Programmes for Women.

Finally, yet another player in the promotion of entrepreneurship in the Philippines is the Philippine Foundation for Resources Management. Among its projects is the Programme on Women's Involvement in Entrepreneurship.

With a more limited scope is the Business Action Centre of the Naga City Chamber of Commerce, on the island of Luzon. It provides a variety of accounting and legal assistance as well as physical facilities, secretarial support, desktop publishing and courier services.

Constraints on Entrepreneurship

As is evident from the above, many efforts have focused on financing entrepreneurs and on developing an efficient infrastructure for them. Yet, despite efforts by governmental and non-governmental bodies to foster development in the Philippines, the national economy — except Chinese-dominated Cebu — is still characterised by inflation, underdevelopment and slow growth. According to interviews conducted by the author in the Philippines, causal variables include corruption and until recently, power shortages were a problem.

Personal relationships are very important in the Filipino business sphere, and much time is spent on *pakikisama* — the development of inter-personal ties. Among the most important ties in business are those between entrepreneurs and the government, especially a practice known as *lagacy* (a polite word for "buying personal ties"). Officials expect bribes in return for allowing entrepreneurship to flourish. Some entrepreneurs have long-established channels of bribery, and these are used to create barriers to entry. This effectively inhibits potential new entrants, and limits competition. Entrepreneurs are often approached by individuals offering "protection" for small firms, in exchange for special payments, locally known as *tong*. This is effectively a bribe.

Finally, an adequate supply of affordable energy is essential for economic development, and for a healthy entrepreneurship sector. Beginning in 1983, the Petro-Canada International Assistance Corporation began a programme of co-operation with the Bureau of Energy and Development. Loans were extended to the Philippines National Oil Company and to the National Power Corporation, to exploit an existing geothermal steam field, construct a power station and improve power transmission lines. Yet, the nation is still dependent on imported petrol.

The Entrepreneurship Sector Today

The economy of the Philippines is a blend of agriculture, fishing and light industry; small enterprises are major players. On family farms, important crops include bananas, coconuts, coffee, copra, corn, hemp, nuts, pineapples, rice, sugarcane, tapioca, tobacco, vegetables, yams, and abaca (a fibre related to the banana plant). Both subsistence farming and subsistence fishing are common to this day. Although the nation could have been self-sufficient in food, it is not. The low yields can be traced to a tradition of absentee landlords in a peasant society.

Clothing and food-processing are the most developed industries, along with the light manufacturing of home appliances. Sectors showing growth include aquaculture, furniture assembly and microcircuit production. Most exports are manufactured goods such as electrical microcircuits and semi-conductors.

Some literature (Halloran 1991; Kinyanjui, 1993) has suggested that for some countries the growth of the entrepreneurship sector is constrained by the lack of easy access to financing. This is *not* the case in the Philippines. During the early 20th century, missionaries introduced to these islands the concept of co-operatives. Basing these co-operatives on the rural credit unions of the United States, the missionaries launched a movement that eventually gained considerable popularity. Today, several hundred credit unions provide low-cost capital to entrepreneurs who lack collateral. Chinese entrepreneurs have their own credit circles. In addition, foreign entrepreneurs provide financing to informal enterprises sometimes without collateral.

Toward the Future

It has been shown that entrepreneurs in the Philippines have a great deal going for them. Several programmes were created to help small enterprises and cottage industries. Entrepreneurship is even fostered at the Iwahig Penal Colony, where prisoners are required to make and sell handicrafts.

Unlike the situation described in other countries, financing is not problematic here. Yet, Yap and Majuca (2013) noted that the lack of entrepreneurship in the Philippines is a major challenge.

Figure 13.8 Harvesting Coconuts; photograph by Léo-Paul Dana.

Case Study: Benno the Windsurfer

"I like punctuality and I want people to receive good value for what they pay," said Benno Schmieder, "and that explains my success." It was the week before Christmas and Benno was enjoying his annual eight-month holiday. In the past, he had travelled across Asia and South America. This time he was in Cape Town, and Benno was asked whether he would consider expanding his business. If so, then marketing communications would be a primary concern, such as to ensure continued success of his business.

Benno Schmieder, a German national from Munich, did his military service during the early 1980s, at a North Atlantic Treaty Organization (NATO) base in Sardinia, Italy. There, he learned how to windsurf, and took a liking to the sport. Hence, after completing his military duties, he decided to return to Italy and spend the summer giving windsurfing lessons. A problem arose, however, when Eppe Giua, the son of a wealthy Italian family, found Benno operating an unofficial school with no license to do so.

"I'll go to the police," said Signor Giua. "Or, if you want, you can pay me and use my license." Benno had noticed that there was much more bureaucracy and corruption in Italy than in Germany. Furthermore, he understood that he lacked the connections to obtain a license on his own. He therefore accepted to pay Signor Giua a percentage of the earnings of Benny's Windsurfing School. Yet, owning only four windsurf boats, Benno realised he could not make much money that way. Thus, he convinced Signor Giua that the school needed more capital investment. It was finally agreed to acquire another 10 windsurf boats.

All went well for some time, and the school could operate officially using Signor Giua's license, but two years later, the windsurf boats were showing signs of wear and needed to be replaced. This time, Signor Giua refused to invest into more boats.

Frustrated, Benno approached Signor Giua with another offer. This time Benno would pay for the boats; in return, he wanted 75% of the school and its profits. It might have been acceptable, but in fact neither Benno nor Signor Giua knew the profitability of the enterprise, as nobody had ever recorded revenues nor expenses. The school had operated for nine years, without any accounting or bookkeeping. Consequently, Signor Giua demanded a flat rate per summer, in exchange for (unofficial) permission to use the license.

Up to 1990, operations were smooth. In 1991, however, Italian port authorities sent officials to verify licenses. Meanwhile, Signor Giua had forgotten to apply for a renewal. So, Benno's school was closed down for two weeks, causing annual income to fall by about 12%.

For years, Benno was unofficially operating with Signor Giua's license; however, in order for the license to be valid, Signor Giua was supposed to be present, in person, on the beach. In reality, he came by a couple of times a year. Another concern was that although Benno had invested in the school, there was no written record of his participation in the school.

Seeking to protect himself, at the end of a season, Benno suggested to Signor Giua that they jointly incorporate International Windsurfing School S.N.C. of Eppe Giua. Each shareholder held 50% of the new company. It was agreed that the new corporate body would expand operations. Signor Giua said he would apply for an additional license to lease parasols and beach lounges, but he missed the March 31, deadline. Suffering from cancer, in June, Benno underwent surgery in Germany. This delayed his arrival in Italy. His income from windsurfing dropped, and Signor Giua's procrastination caused the firm to miss out on a company license to rent parasols and beach lounges. Benno would live all year from his summer income, and although Signor Giua was independently wealthy, Benno was angered at the opportunity cost of not having a license to rent parasols and beach lounges.

Case Study Assignment

In 2014, the time was possibly right to set up a windsurfing school in the Philippines. But where exactly? Act as a consultant to Benno and help him set up the school in the Philippines in the most optimal way.

Chapter 14

Singapore[1]

Introduction

At the tip of peninsular Malaysia lies Singapore, a city-republic covering one main island (23 kilometres from north to south and 42 kilometres wide), and some tiny islets, the latter mostly uninhabited. Its area totals under 700 square kilometres, and it is home to about 100,000 small and medium-size enterprises. The island republic is multicultural with each ethnic group having its set of traditional belief systems, and living in harmony with people from other groups. The Wenzhou people and the Chettiars have been among entrepreneurs who internationalised from Singapore, long before globalisation became a norm (Tan, 2013).

After independence, the Singapore Government perpetuated a positive investment climate, attracting multinational corporations to a free port with a business-friendly environment. Foreign firms responded; they brought their technologies, created employment, and contributed to economic development. As foreign firms began to shift operations to lower-cost locations, the Singapore Government began encouraging its own entrepreneurs to thrive. However, market saturation in Singapore soon threatened the survival of many local entrepreneurs; internationalisation of entrepreneurship became a necessity. To assist with communications, Singapore launched a national broadband project called Singapore One.

---

[1] This chapter is based on information obtained from a variety of sources, including: the Agency for Science, Technology and Research; the Building & Construction Authority; the Economic Development Board; Enterprise Promotion Centres Pte Ltd; International Enterprise Singapore; the the Singapore Tourism Board; and the Standards, Productivity and Innovation Board (SPRING). The author is also grateful to Professor Tommy Koh for personally sharing some thoughts. Travel to Singapore was provided by Nanyang Technological University. The chapter includes historical material that first appeared in Dana (1999b).

Wong, Wong, Lee and Ho (2005) identified the trend that the total entrepreneurial activity index for Singapore has been on the rise, and opportunity entrepreneurship accounts for the majority of entrepreneurial activity. Comparing early-stage entrepreneurship, in Singapore and Thailand, Minniti, Bygrave, and Autio (2006) pointed out that opportunity motives — as opposed to necessity motives — explain entrepreneurship in Singapore more so than is the case in Thailand.

Dana, Hamilton and Wick (2009) found that entrepreneurs who were opportunity seeking at start-up were likely to have responded to export 'pull' forces; in contrast it was rare for a reactive founder to have been 'pulled' into exporting. The authors concluded with some implications for policy targeting and suggestions for further research suggesting that it may well be that Singapore should focus on developing and supporting more opportunity entrepreneurs, individuals who do appear to have the same motivation towards exporting.

Historical Overview

A Chinese document from the 3rd century referred to Singapore as *Pu Luo Chung*, literally meaning, "island at the tip of a peninsula." Because of its location, at the tip of a peninsula between China and India, traders already knew this island.

While Marco Polo referred to Singapore as *Malayur* (Tamil for "Hill Town"), the Javanese called it *Temasek*, meaning "Sea Town." The harbour made it attractive to Arab, Chinese, and Indian merchants, who came to trade with entrepreneurs from Java, Malaya and Siam. The Sumatra-based Srivijaya Empire ruled the region, including the Malay Peninsula and the islands of Java and Sumatra.

In 1299, on the island of *Temasek*, a prince from Sumatra saw an animal that he could not identify. An elder said it might be a lion. It was probably a tiger, as lions have never been indigenous to this area. Nevertheless, the island came to be known as *Singapura*, meaning "Lion City" in Sanskrit. Later, the name was anglicised to its present form, Singapore.

Merchants from Arab lands, and others from India, frequently passed by Singapore. These entrepreneurs were the middlemen in the spice trade between Indonesia and Europe. During the early 1500s,

Europeans began coming to this part of the world, to obtain spices directly. In the sub-continent, the British established the British East India Company. An increase in demand for Chinese tea, silk and pottery, among European consumers, prompted the company to send expeditions from India to China.

In 1781, Thomas Stamford Raffles was born at sea, into a poor family from London. At the time, the British were interested in India for its tea, and their trading arm was the British East India Company. The firm had trading posts in Bombay (today's Mumbai), Calcutta (today's Kolkata), and Madras (today's Chennai). From India, the company sent ships to China, to obtain pottery and silk. Since the journey between India and China was a lengthy one, it was therefore decided to set up a node along the way, where British ships could stop for water, food and repairs. Accordingly, in 1786, the British East India Company set up a base in Penang.

In 1795, 14-year-old Thomas began working for the British East India Company, in London. A decade later, the company sent him to Penang, where he learned Malay. In 1811, he was put in charge of Java, where he abolished slavery. In 1818, he was transferred to Bencoolen, a British trading post on the island of Sumatra. This was before Sumatra became Dutch.

In 1819, Sir Thomas Stamford Raffles, Lieutenant-Governor of Bencoolen, selected Singapore as the location for a new port for the British East India Company (see Turnbull, 1977). The local population was estimated to be 150 people (Djamour, 1959). Raffles paid the local leaders for permission to set up a free port, and this attracted thousands of entrepreneurs. Raffles segregated different ethnic groups into assigned neighbourhoods.

When the British took full control of Singapore, in 1824, the settlement had 10,683 people, of whom 31% were Chinese. In 1826, Singapore became part of the British Straits Settlements, along with Malacca and Penang. That year, a famine in China prompted 4,000 men to come to Singapore. When Chinese men had children with Malay women, the offspring were known as Baba Chinese or Straits Chinese. Their descendants are known as Peranakans. By the late 19th century, more than 70% of Singapore's population was Chinese (Freedman, 1961).

In 1830, a group of Jewish entrepreneurs came to Singapore from Iraq, to work in the spice trade. Many followed, and Singapore became home to a thriving community of Jewish entrepreneurs, among them Baghdad-born Menasseh Meyer, reputed to be the richest Jew in the Far East (Dana, 2010).

Beginning in the 1850s, the Borneo Company Limited co-ordinated the transfer of capital and technology from Britain to Asia, and that it took responsibility for the management of such capital and technology in the foreign locations to which this investment was directed (Cox and Metcalfe, 1998). Among the locations was Singapore.

Figure 14.1 The Former Singapore Office of the Borneo Company Limited; photograph by Léo-Paul Dana.

In 1867, the Straits Settlements became a Crown Colony. The inauguration of the Suez Canal, in 1869, made Singapore an important node along the route from England to Australia. This helped the growth of Singapore as a centre of international trade. As well, Mizrahi Jews from Iraq made Singapore an important node in their international network of international business. Entrepreneurs set up go-downs (warehouses) and trading houses. Singapore became a centre for entrepôt trade.

Figure 14.2 A Former Godown (Warehouse); photograph by Léo-Paul Dana.

The British were interested in the development of modern capitalism in Singapore. They promoted trade and commerce, in an environment of minimal regulation. This attracted entrepreneurs from countries such as Burma, Iraq, Syria, and of course China.

Many migrants from China were sojourners who intended to eventually return to their homeland. Since these people had no long-term commitment to the British colony, they usually avoided capital-intensive industries, which required long pay-back periods. Thus, the ethnic-Chinese in Singapore were largely concentrated in commerce, an activity in which gains were more immediate.

Simpich wrote, "Nearly all of the trades and the retail commerce of Singapore are in the hands of the Chinese (1926, p. 268)." Gasse (1982) cited the pre-war Chinese community in Singapore as cultivating entrepreneurs more easily than others. It should be noted, however, that these entrepreneurs were mostly merchants, not industrialists.

Figure 14.3 Merchant Shophouses; photograph by Léo-Paul Dana.

On February 15, 1942, the Japanese took control of Singapore, renaming it *Syonan-to*, Japanese for "Light of the South." Although the British returned after the Japanese surrender, an independence movement began to grow. The year 1946 saw the break-up of the Straits Settlements, as Malacca and Penang joined the Malayan Union.

Under British colonial rule, the Jews of Singapore were denied full access into British society. A Jew by the name of David Marshall — president of the Maghain Aboth Synagogue on Waterloo Street — led the movement for Singapore's independence and became the Chief Minister of Singapore. In April 1956, he led a delegation to London and asked for internal self-government; on April 23, 1956, David Marshall showed Herbert Morrison signatures of 167,000 people requesting independence for Singapore. In 1959, when self-government was granted, Lee Kuan Yew became the nation's prime minister. David Marshall later served as Singapore's ambassador in France, Spain, Portugal and Switzerland.

Figure 14.4 British Architecture from Colonial Times; photograph by Léo-Paul Dana.

Figure 14.5 Artisans Made Quality Goods; photograph by Léo-Paul Dana.

Figure 14.6 Boat Quay; photograph by Léo-Paul Dana.

Singapore's Economic Development Board was formed in August 1961. In 1963, Singapore joined Malaya, Sabah and Sarawak to form Malaysia but was expelled. Turnbull wrote, "Singapore's expulsion from

Malaysia destroyed the basis on which responsible Singapore politicians had considered the state viable. She was unique among colonial countries in having independence thrust upon her unilaterally (1977, p. 297)."

On August 9, 1965, Singapore became an independent republic. In 1983, its government opened a high-tech port, and soon later merchant vessels were phased out of Boat Quay. Until 1985, the city-state relied on foreign multinational corporations to industrialise the nation and to develop the economy. A global recession that year led the government to realise the vulnerability of a domestic economy that relied very heavily on foreign capital and overseas markets.

Figure 14.7 Victoria Building; photograph by Léo-Paul Dana.

During the 1980s, focus shifted to entrepreneurship (Dana, 1987) and more recently to technopreneurship. To make way for the new, old buildings were demolished; among these was the Victoria Building, last renovated during the 1990s. In 2005, Singapore accepted a proposal to establish a youth enterprise academy, to "provide experiential programmes that focus on entrepreneurship and leadership (Zainol 2005, p. 1)." In 2013, Singapore signed a trade liberalisation deal with Taiwan.

A Multicultural Society

Singapore was built by people of numerous cultural backgrounds, including Malays, Tamils, and ethnic-Chinese from different provinces of China. Although the Armenian minority was never large here (Wright, 2003), Armenian entrepreneurs were also active in Singapore. The Raffles Hotel and the *Straits Times* were established by Armenian entrepreneurs.

Figure 14.8 Raffles Hotel; photograph by Léo-Paul Dana.

From Fujian Province came Foochows, speaking *Fuzhouhua*; Henghuas, speaking *Xinghuahua*; Hokchias, speaking *Fuquinhua*; and Hokkiens, speaking *Minnanhua*. Cantonese people speaking *Guangzhouhua*, and Teochews speaking *Chaozhouhua*, came from Guang Dong. Hainanese immigrants, speaking *Hainanhua*, came from

Hainan Island. Hakkas, speaking *Kehua*, came from Fujian and Guang Dong. The Hokkiens are the largest ethno-cultural group in Singapore.

For linguistic reasons, people tended to live among, and to work with others, who spoke the same dialect. This led to considerable occupational clustering. The Hokkiens — who had political contacts with the colonial government — became very involved in entrepôt trade. Many traded along Chulia Street. Other Hokkien entrepreneurs lived on China Street, where they sold sundry items as well as fresh greens. Telok Ayer Street was home to larger-scale Hokkien entrepreneurs who imported goods from neighbouring countries.

The Teochews dominated the rice trade across Southeast Asia. In Singapore, Teochews could be found along Circular Road, not far from the Singapore River. On Chin Chew Street, they traded spices. On Chulia Street, Teochew dealers sold bird's nest and shark's fin.

Under the leadership of Mr. Aw Boon Haw, producer of Tiger Balm, Hakka entrepreneurs dominated Singapore's medicine halls. The Cantonese were regarded as a lower class. They were clustered in the district around Kreta Ayer. Many sold cloth. Some sold furniture, musical instruments, tobacco and silk, which they imported from China. They had shops on Pagoda Street and on Temple Street. Others were artisans, goldsmiths, tailors and restaurant-owners.

To foster co-operation among people sharing the same dialect, and to promote commercial and industrial development, entrepreneurs established and joined clan associations. Mingling with other members helped individuals understand trends in product development as well as price fluctuations. Here, entrepreneurs could discuss partnerships and obtain financing. Clan associations provided social contacts, training, business ideas, market information, business concepts, start-up capital and technical assistance. This web of networking played an important role in the development of entrepreneurship in Singapore.

The Hokkien Hui Kuan (Hokkien Clan Association) donated land to build Nanyang University, which opened in 1958. This was the first Chinese-language university outside China. After independence, nationalism transcended clan loyalties, and clan associations lost their dominance.

Figure 14.9 Traditional Chinese Medicine; photograph by Léo-Paul Dana.

The behaviours and values of the Chinese in Singapore are deep-rooted in Confucian dynamism, which includes the virtues of perseverance and thrift. Both of these factors tend to facilitate entrepreneurship. Singaporeans have been discouraged from believing in extreme individualism. Instead, they have been conditioned to feel a loyalty to the family. Divorce rates are low. All these factors may be said to have contributed to the success of family business in Singapore. Singaporeans are also taught the importance of saving, frugality and hard work. These factors, when coupled with compulsory Central Providence Fund (CPF) contributions, have made Singapore's savings equal to 46% of GNP — the highest in the world. When entrepreneurs need capital for new ventures or to expand existing firms, informal financing is often available.

Figure 14.10 Preserving Chinese Culture; photograph by Léo-Paul Dana.

Confucian values have served as guidelines for social norms, which may help entrepreneurship. However, research has not found ethnic-Chinese cultural values to emphasise initiative. Although the Singapore Government once relied on foreign investors for economic growth, since 1985 there has been emphasis on encouraging Singaporeans to develop initiatives in the realm of entrepreneurship.

Singapore society, today, is quite heterogeneous. Buddhists comprise 28% of the population, while 19% are Christian, 16% are Muslim, 13% are Taoist and 5% are Hindu.

Figure 14.11 Muslim Entrepreneur; photograph by Léo-Paul Dana.

Figure 14.12 Savouring a Hindu Meal; photograph by Léo-Paul Dana.

The Singaporean Model

In 1985, BG Lee Hsien Loong, the Acting Minister of Trade and Industry and Chairman of the Committee on Small Enterprise Policy, stated: "We must have our own entrepreneurs... We need a focal point for small business, a single agency to co-ordinate these schemes, work out new ones, and provide one-stop service for small enterprises." He was introducing the Small Enterprise Bureau of Singapore, with programmes to help entrepreneurs. The Singapore Government allocated S$100 million to this end, and the Small Enterprise Bureau was established as a division of the Singapore Development Board, for the purpose of helping promising entrepreneurs.

Until 1995, the Economic Development Board was in charge of small and medium-size enterprise development. Its Small and Medium Enterprise (SME) Master Plan emphasised local entrepreneurship. That year, the Singapore Productivity and Standards Board was created. (It has since been renamed the Standards, Product and Innovation Board — abbreviated SPRING Singapore.) This agency took the responsibility to promote entrepreneurship in Singapore and it developed a three-pronged strategy to promote entrepreneurship: (i) broad-based assistance to small and medium-size firms; (ii) focused assistance to selected, promising entrepreneurs; and (iii) industry-wide assistance.

During 1996 — its first year of operations — the predecessor to SPRING provided broad-based assistance to more than 2,500 small and medium enterprises. This assistance was implemented through its Local Enterprise Upgrading Centre. The Board helped entrepreneurs to participate in a variety of Government Development Assistance Programmes. Under the industry-wide assistance scheme, it facilitated the creation of new franchises. The Board also helped entrepreneurs to harness information technology. For instance, Shopnet linked small-scale retailers with suppliers, and financial assistance was offered to entrepreneurs who wished to adopt the system. Funding came from the Local Enterprise Technical Assistance Scheme. Additional money to train entrepreneurs how to use Shopnet was available from the Skills Development Fund.

During a parliamentary debate, in November 1998, it was announced to have a special committee to promote technology-based entrepreneurship, in Singapore. Deputy Prime Minister Dr. Tony Tan saw the Asian Financial Crisis of 1998 as an opportunity to accelerate the transition of the island republic to a knowledge-based economy, and a high-powered panel was organised to create a climate conducive to boosting high-tech entrepreneurship.

Technological entrepreneurship was termed "echnopreneurship and ingredients were identified to promote it. These included: the availability of creative talent (foreign and local); low barriers to entry; easy access to capital; easy access to markets; tolerance of failure; and high gains. Dr. Tony Tan, chairman of the Technopreneurship 21 Ministerial Committee, explained, "Technopreneurs serve as the critical interface between ideas and markets, translating creative ideas into vehicles to serve market demand." In 1999, the Supreme Court unveiled a new scheme, offering contractual manufacturers a waiver of the Goods and Services Tax (GST).[2]

Leong discussed Government Development Assistance Schemes:

> Several government bodies have been tasked to support and promote SME growth. Efforts include well-structured departments able to provide assistance in all areas of operations such as monetary assistance...a month-long promotional event to create awareness of the programmes for SMEs, etc. The Economic Development Board (EDB) ... aims to develop and help multinationals and Singapore-based companies thrive and upgrade to higher value-creating operations. The Singapore Productivity and Standards Board (PSB) champions the raising of Singapore's Total Factor Productivity (TFP), promotes innovation, enhances market access, and upgrades the domestic sectors... SPRING Singapore will take over the responsibilities of PSB to spearhead the National Productivity Movement and play a lead role in raising the productivity of the domestic sector. Similarly, TDB is renamed International Enterprise Singapore (I.E. Singapore), which signifies the importance of developing local enterprises into world-class operations. It proposes to help local companies grow and internationalize by shortening their learning curve and helping them to make the right connections.... Some of the broad-based programmes and schemes that SMEs and new start-ups in Singapore common apply are SME 21, ProAct 21, Promising Local Enterprises Programme (PLEs), and Start-up Enterprise Development Schemes (SEEDs). In addition, there are new programmes and schemes such as Technopreneurship 21, Business Angel Fund, and Technopreneurship Investment Fund (TIF), which are targeted specifically at high tech startups....

[2] For a discussion about the nature of GST, see Dana (1993a).

> There are more than 60 assistance schemes available to SMEs.... LEFS aids SMEs in acquiring fixed productive assets and working capital loans to upgrade and automate their businesses and expand their productive capacity, LETAS aids SMEs in paying for the costs of engaging external consultants to upgrade their operations. Both schemes work hand-in-hand in assisting SMEs to develop and expand operationally (Leong, 2004, pp. 130–131).

Various agencies were given responsibility for the different government assistance programmes, including capital loan programmes that complemented business development grants. International Enterprise Singapore (formerly the Trade Development Board) was delegated to administer grant to assist entrepreneurs in developing their brand names. The objective of the Economic Development Board's Local Industry Upgrading Programme was to foster ties between multinational corporations and smaller-scale suppliers of parts and services in Singapore.

With the objective to assist innovators and investors to develop their concepts into commercially viable processes and products, business innovation grants such as the Innovator's Assistance Scheme were administered by the National Science and Technology Board (more recently renamed the Agency for Science, Technology and Research). Likewise, SPRING has a Technology Enterprise Commercialisation Scheme.

This section has illustrated that various loans, grants and tax incentives are available for entrepreneurs in Singapore. The wide range of programmes covers financing, business development, management, productivity improvement, manpower training, marketing, exporting, technology transfer, information technology and automation. Some programmes are for new venture start-ups, and others for expansion or internationalisation. The next section shall address government attempts to internationalise entrepreneurship from Singapore.

Internationalising Singaporean Entrepreneurs

In the late 1980s, the Singapore Government began promoting the "Growth Triangle," giving incentives for Singaporean entrepreneurs to relocate manufacturing activities to Indonesia and Malaysia. However, internationalisation was limited.

It was in 1993 that Senior Minister Lee Kuan Yew declared, "We can enthuse a younger generation with the thrill and the rewards of building an external dimension to Singapore. We can and we will spread our wings into the region and then into the wider world."

Notwithstanding Singapore's attractiveness to foreign multinational corporations, Singaporean entrepreneurs can also play a role in international business. Given the limited size of Singapore's domestic market, internationalisation would help Singaporean entrepreneurs to achieve economies of scale. Thus, internationalisation can improve local production.

The Trade Development Board (now International Enterprise Singapore) offered a Franchise Development Assistance Scheme, to encourage Singaporean entrepreneurs to develop a franchise package and to market the concept overseas.

The Association of Small and Medium Enterprises also promoted the internationalisation of Singaporean small and medium enterprises. In 1998, it launched SME Day, with networking events for entrepreneurs, under the theme Towards Globalisation.

In September 1998, the first conference on international entrepreneurship brought together leading academics from around the world. It was decided that Singapore's Nanyang Technological University would sponsor the second conference, at the Goodwood Park Hotel, in Singapore, August 15–18, 1999, and the Proceedings were published as Dana (1999c). As the domestic market in Singapore became increasingly saturated, it became increasingly important for Singaporean entrepreneurs to look beyond Singapore.

The Singapore Government has been promoting the internationalisation of Singaporean jointly with their Malaysian counterparts. The Malaysia-Singapore Third Country Business Development Fund (MSBF) is co-funded by Malaysia and Singapore, and jointly administered by International Enterprise Singapore and by the Malaysian Industrial Development Authority. Its purpose is to encourage Singaporean firms to undertake, jointly with their Malaysian counterparts, feasibility studies on pursuing joint investment and business projects in third countries.

Toward the Future

Prior to independence, entrepreneurs in Singapore thrived as merchants. The colony was an important hub of entrepôt trade, but it had few industrialists. During the 1950s, the Khong Guan Biscuit Factory produced biscuits in Indonesia. Similarly, Ho Rih Hua opened a manufacturing plant in Thailand. Yet, Singapore's entrepreneurship sector was lacking in industrialists, and was limited by a distinctly local orientation. Singaporean entrepreneurs had few foreign direct investments.

After independence, the government designed an enterprise-friendly environment to attract foreign direct investment from abroad. Multinational corporations were handed the task of industrialising Singapore. More recently, the state has been encouraging both entrepreneurship and the internationalisation of entrepreneurs.

Singapore has two types of entrepreneurs. One set is comprised of elder individuals who became entrepreneurs because they lacked formal education and could not compete in educated Singapore. These people were motivated by money. Failure would bring shame to their families, and so they worked very diligently to succeed. They attribute their success to hard work, patience, persistence and luck. Although successful in their home market, they tend not to venture abroad.

In contrast, the other set of entrepreneurs consists of young, educated individuals. Power and fulfilment motivate them in addition to money. Most importantly, they are expansion-oriented. Yet, they are not many in number.

In the future, according to then Senior Minister Lee Kuan Yew, "How well we do depends on how many entrepreneurs or wealth creators we have in our midst."[3] For years, the high salaries provided by multinational corporations lured many Singaporeans away from becoming entrepreneurs. Unlike the poor Chinese migrants who lacked alternatives in colonial Singapore, Singaporeans could become very successful in corporate life, without becoming entrepreneurs. However, entrepreneurship has since become increasingly attractive. The number of self-employed in Singapore increased from 227,400 in 1996 to 299,800 in 2010 and is likely to grow further.

---

[3] Source: *The Straits Times*, July 11, 1996.

Case Study: Poh Heng[4]

Du Zhuo Lei founded the Poh Heng jewellery store in 1948. His first shop was on North Bridge Road, around the corner from Arab Street. At that time, this was one of the main shopping areas in Singapore. According to a brochure printed in honour of its Golden Jubilee, the success of Poh Heng was "because of its uncompromising insistence on the best quality products and service." Poh Heng has since flourished under the leadership of the Du family as it has maintained the solid reputation of being a jeweller who treats its customers with absolute honesty and reliability.

The success of the company was not based solely on good management; it was also credited to the loyal and hardworking staff. In an interview, Mr. Ng Chee Choo, Poh Heng's 68-year-old master craftsman, said (in Mandarin), "I have been working at Poh Heng for more than 40 years, but I have never thought of leaving. I like working here and the bosses treat us well." Another employee, Mr. Wu Song Zhi, was only 15-years-old when he started working at Poh Heng. He joined as an apprentice, where he learned the "tricks of the trade" from his then *shi fu* (teacher). Eventually he became the *shi fu* and to an apprentice, 22-year-old Eng Kim Sia.

The tagline, "A tradition of trust and security," is the foundation of the Poh Heng company, which expanded to a chain of shops largely set up in Housing Development Board (HDB) estates. Branch managers were given full authority, being in charge of everything from window displays to the selection of gold accessories that are most suitable for customers in the area.

Over the years, the company adapted to the changing needs of its customers. This was supported by innovative designs that kept Poh Heng going, from the 1940s until today. One of the product innovations that differentiated Poh Heng from its competitors is Bianco22.

Launched in July 1997, this is a series of 22K white gold and the first of its kind to be offered in the world (white gold has traditionally been offered in 12K, and 18K). The significance of this type of white gold is that it has a high resale value, thus making older customers more receptive to it.

---

[4] This case was written by Teresa Elizabeth Dana, while Director of Marketing Communications, at Nanyang Technological University in Singapore.

The pricing of gold is very much dependent on the weight of the gold and the quality of the workmanship. Prices of gold fluctuate and Poh Heng follows the market very closely. During the late 20th century there was "underhanded" marketing by several goldsmiths in Singapore. According to the Singapore Jewellers Association, many misled customers into believing that the price of gold was cheaper in their shop. What was being done was that the price of the workmanship was hiked to compensate for the difference in gold prices. In line with their company slogan, Poh Heng stood firm with its company policy not to cheat customers, even though business was initially affected. In response to the situation, a stamp of approval by the Singapore Jewellers Association was been placed on all of Poh Heng's promotional pieces.

Target Market

Since its establishment, Poh Heng's customer base has largely been Chinese. In the 1960s and 1970s, most Chinese lived in the North and South Bridge Road areas (near Chinatown) and this was the area where Poh Heng had its shop. However, with the urban redevelopment programme by the Housing Development Board (HDB), there was a shift of influence from the central business district to different housing estates. Poh Heng adapted to these changes by opening new shops in HDB estates, like Bedok, Tampines, and Hougang. In 1980, the original shop was torn down due to a re-development plan.

In addition to the changes in where people live, Poh Heng had to adapt to the increasing level of education among the younger population. In contrast to older customers who are traditionally concerned with the resale value of jewellery, the younger generation places more emphasis on the aesthetic value of products. Thus, they prefer ornamental jewellery with trendy designs rather than genuine gold. When asked about her feelings toward jewellery, a 20-year-old undergraduate, Miss Rachel Tay responded, "I don't want to wear anything that will make me look old-fashioned. Only mothers and housewives buy gold chains. For me, I prefer 'Bits & Pieces' and 'Perlini's Silver' anytime."

According to Mr. Mah Boon Yi, the Advertising and Promotions Manager of Poh Heng, "the majority of Poh Heng's customers are

Chinese females between the ages of 25 and 40 years old." He went on to say that because Poh Heng is a traditional Chinese family business, most Chinese can identify with the company and its auspicious sounding name (*poh* is the Chinese word for jewel, and *heng* stands for luck.)

The customer base can be further subdivided into different categories. Previously, the bulk of Poh Heng's customers were "Dependent Matriarchs," "Jing Di Wa," and "Traditional Chinese." Product knowledge was not the element that brought these patrons to the stores, but rather fierce brand loyalty and the auspicious Chinese name. The people who would fall under the category of "Hard-Pressed Providers" and "Bo-Chaps" would also frequent the stores. These, however, bought gold out of a sense of duty, as it is customary to buy gold as a dowry in the Chinese culture.

During the late 20th century, Poh Heng began targeting the younger crowd, who tend to be more "westernised" in their thinking largely due to higher education and the influence of the mass media. The company introduced newer Italian designs, platinum and white gold to appeal to this segment of the population.

Change

Over the years, attitudes of people towards gold have changed. People used to be more sceptical about paper currency and thus had more faith in the value of gold. Instead of depositing their money in the bank, they would rather spend the cash on gold. During recessions, such people would hoard gold in case the currency should be devalued. In fact Poh Heng's sales rose considerably during the 1984/5 recession in Singapore.

Poh Heng always emphasised yellow gold as the main attraction. However, upon recognising the trend of wearing white gold among the younger female customers, Poh Heng came up with its Bianco22 series. The company emphasised the trendy and innovative designs of this series in order to cater to the needs of this younger target market. Consumers became increasingly demanding where presentation of the product was concerned. As a result, Poh Heng did away with the obsolete plastic container packages, which used to be suitable, in favour of a new classy-looking velvet box.

Marketing

Most of Poh Heng's advertisements were designed to create awareness for sales promotions. The company worked closely with an external public relations and advertising agency in order to publicise its products. They were also mostly placed in the newspapers and in magazines. Poh Heng also advertised on radio stations. Poh Heng generally had four sales promotions every year:

- **Chinese New Year** (January / February)
  The Chinese, in general, see gold as a symbol of wealth. During the Lunar New Year period, many Chinese will purchase gold accessories for themselves and for their families.

- **Mother's Day** (May)
  Mother's Day is one of the more significant occasions in Singapore, where children celebrate and shower their mother with gifts and/or take her (and dad) out for dinner. As filial piety is very much emphasised, Poh Heng sees this occasion as a good opportunity to promote its products. Here are some of the slogans that the company has used in its print advertisements in recent years.
  - "For a sentimental Mother's Day gift, nothing beats heavy metal."
  - "Because Mum deserves more than lunch, the Poh Heng Mother's Day pendant."
  - "This Mother's Day, Poh Heng salutes all loving daughters."

- **Collection for Next Year** (September)
  In September, the company advertises the new series of product designs that it has for the upcoming year. It is a promotion to instil excitement for the new product lines.

- **Year End Sale** (End of November)
  Many goldsmith shops in Singapore see the year end sale as a good way to promote their products. This is a time when Singaporean employees receive their year-end bonuses. For Poh Heng, this promotion is carried out in order to remain competitive in the marketplace and to create an occasion for customers to purchase gold. Purchasing gold is often not an impulse act; thus the company

seeks to provide enough reasons to buy gold. Examples of slogans that have been used in the past are:

- "Year-End Glitter. For A New Year Glamour."
- "Jewellery That's Ahead of its Time."
- "Give in to Exquisite Temptation."

50th Anniversary Promotion

In honour of its 50th anniversary, Poh Heng decided to "reward" its loyal customers by giving 50 times the original value of any piece of jewellery that was purchased 50 years earlier. All that was required was the item and the bill. The promotion was called "50 times in 50 years" and it actually brought in 82-year-old Mrs. Lim, who had purchased a ring in 1948. At that time, the ring had been priced at $50.80. She traded it in for a whopping $2,450.

Poh Heng held an exhibition in honour of its 50th anniversary in Singapore. The event featured many rare items such as 24-karat golden toothpick and ear sets. These items were used in the days where the genteel Chinese and traditional Peranakan (Straits Chinese) women of leisure used to flash their wealth by whipping out such hair-clip look-alike contraptions. The exhibition displayed gold, diamond and jade jewellery from the 1940s as well as traditional Peranakan costumes, original certificates of lifetime warranty, and old advertisements. These collectible items were not for sale.

Case Study Assignment

Poh Heng would soon be 70. The firm had become an authorised licensee for Disney characters and was producing jewellery featuring Mickey and Minnie. The idea came up to have a promotion whereby customers could be eligible for a draw, the winner of which could fly on Singapore Airlines to Tokyo and attend a celebration for Poh Heng's 70th anniversary at Tokyo Disneyland.

Create the promotional campaign.

Chapter 15

Taiwan[1]

Introduction

Taiwan is an island with an area of 35,751 square kilometres, off the coast of China. While Taiwan is home to several high-mountain Indigenous peoples, such as the Tsou,[2] the majority of the people here are Han Chinese. Many are descendants of people whose migration was encouraged by Qing emperors. Han immigrants often originated along China's southern coast, and consequently Taiwanese dialects resemble those along China's southern coast. In 2012, real GDP growth in Taiwan was 1.3%.

Each country has its mix of large businesses and smaller firms. Environmental forces, such as a government's credit policy, may greatly influence the ratio and relative importance of small enterprises to large ones. Credit policy in Taiwan has traditionally been tight; loans have been expensive and difficult to secure. Most firms in Taiwan are small, and tightly held. Entrepreneurs typically exert an over-riding influence on their enterprises. Even large companies tend to be owned by families, with a senior family member being the central decision-maker. Lin (1998) reported that of 935,000 entrepreneurs in Taiwan, 96.5% are small or medium enterprises, collectively employing 78.6% of the workforce. Taiwan has more entrepreneurs per capita than does any other nation in Southeast Asia. Taiwanese entrepreneurs are "major players in international business (Ali, Lee, and Camp, 2002, p. 29)." Aw (2002) explained that productivity gains have been high in Taiwan, as a result of low barriers to entry and exit.

---

[1] This chapter is based on information obtained from a variety of sources, including: the Board of Foreign Trade; the Directorate-General, of Budget, Accounting and Statistics; and the Ministry of Economic Affairs. Travel to Taiwan was provided by a grant from the University of Oxford; in Taipei, the author was hosted by Academia Sinica. The chapter includes historical material that first appeared in Dana (1999b).

[2] For accounts, see Hipwell (2005), Kirjassoff (1920), and Simon (2005).

Figure 15.1 From Taiwanese Waters; photograph by Léo-Paul Dana.

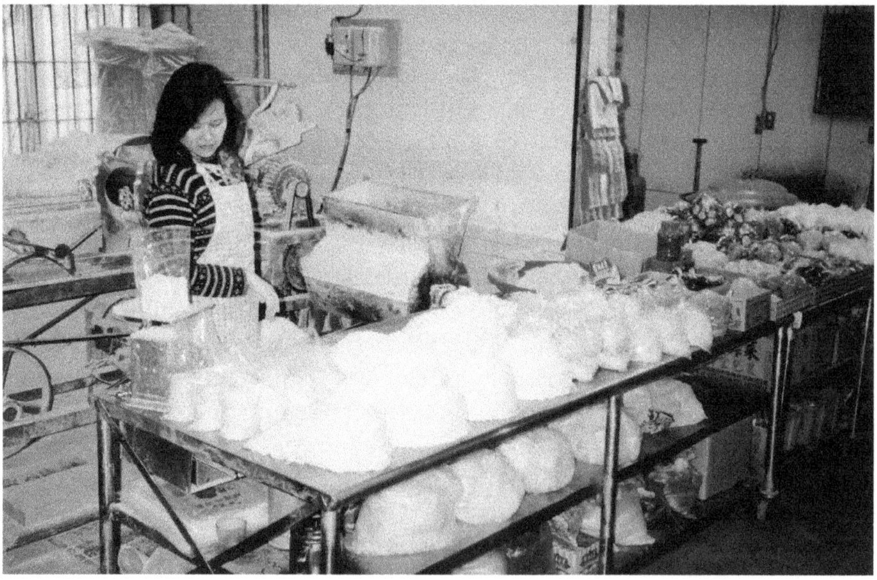

Figure 15.2 Cottage Industry; photograph by Léo-Paul Dana.

As noted by Schive and Hu, "Whilst taking advantage of …the infrastructure inherited from the era of the Japanese rule, and the aid provided by the US during the early phase of Taiwan's modern industrial development, the government undertook an active role…through the adoption of market oriented policies. This gave rise to the emergence of SMEs in the private sector (2001, p. 248)." Taiwan's cottage industries then played a significant part in the development of the national economy.

Figure 15.3 Self-employed at the Market; photograph by Léo-Paul Dana.

Traditionally, economic activites in Taiwan were organised in networks among Taiwanese firms, and cross-border networks between Taiwanese firms and multinationals (Poon, 2002). Poon explained that subcontracting networks emphasise a vertical control relationship between different units of production (contractors and sub-contractors), while cooperative networks also highlight a horizontal cooperative relationship between firms in the network. In her view, the subcontracting relationship in Taiwan is not the kind of stable exchange relationship as in a Japanese Keiretsu. Entrepreneurs often join a network because of personal contacts and inter-firm networks of Taiwanese firms are largely a function of a closely-knit relationship based on friendship, family relationships, and kinship ties. Members of a Taiwanese network are tied together in a web of social relationship and bound by degree of social obligation. She suggests that cross-border networks — the channels through which Taiwanese firms learn and assimilate technology from foreign firms — are supported by networks within Taiwan. Production flexibility of networks enable Taiwanese manufacturers to pursue a flexible-niche strategy; strategy concentrates on short product cycles, quick product delivery schedules, short production runs, and mixes of products aimed at particular market niches.

Yan (2013) showed how some entrepreneurs transform their Taiwanese firms into global enterprises.

Historical Overview[3]

The island today known as Taiwan was settled during the 14th century, by Han Chinese from southern China. The Portuguese arrived in 1517, and named it *Ilha Formosa*, literally "the island of beauty." In 1624, the island was claimed by the Dutch East India Company. Under Dutch rule, the island became a trans-shipping hub for international commerce. Its economic importance increased Chinese interest in the island, and by 1662 the Dutch were defeated and Formosa was Chinese. In 1858, the Chinese allowed the British and the French to establish trading facilities on the island. Eventually, the French occupied a piece of Formosa. In 1895, the Qing dynasty ceded this island to Japan, but on May 12, 1895, Taiwan declared its independence as the Republic of Formosa. A Japanese expedition landed on the new republic on May 28, 1895 and made Taiwan a Japanese colony. For 50 years, Japan ruled Formosa as a colony. Fiscal incentives encouraged the establishment of firms which were owned by Japanese entrepreneurs and which in turn, produced for the Japanese market.

At the end of World War II (WWII), Formosa was returned to China. When the communists took-over China, Chiang Kai-shek and almost two million followers fled to Taiwan. In 1950, Chiang Kai-shek became president of Taiwan.

[3] See also Roy (2003).

Figure 15.4 Fresh Produce; photograph by Léo-Paul Dana.

When Taiwan declared itself as its own country, it was largely agricultural, and manufacturing was limited to light industries, such as sugar refining and the production of fibres. The state nationalised assets that had been controlled by the Japanese, and the government set out to develop a comprehensive economic policy suitable for the nation's situation.

Taiwan's first national policy was known as the Four Year Economic Construction Plan. At the time, it seemed reasonable to produce for the national market. Thus, in 1953, Taiwan adopted a policy of import substitution. This boosted local, small-scale enterprise. However, the size of the Taiwanese market limited local growth. Therefore, in 1958, the government adopted a new model of export promotion.

Taiwanese entrepreneurs began to produce electric machinery for export. To facilitate export-development, a free access zone was established in Kaohsiung. The government developed export-processing zones in Nantze (an area in Kaohsiung) and in Taichung. The purpose of these zones was to encourage industrial development, to facilitate technology transfer, and to promote exports. This new policy proved very successful, and the zones still offer several incentives, such as exemptions from duties and taxes.

Figure 15.5 Skinning Snakes; photograph by Léo-Paul Dana.

Figure 15.6 Service Orientation; photograph by Léo-Paul Dana.

During the 1980s, the Taiwanese economy shifted to a service orientation. This was facilitated by the government's relaxation of laws. Beginning in 1987, entrepreneurs in Taiwan realised that their small businesses could not survive by simply undertaking local labour-intensive production. Along with economic and political factors, this contributed to the internationalisation of Taiwanese entrepreneurs to its ASEAN neighbours.

Schive and Hu wrote, “Since the mid-1990s, when Taiwan’s economy entered a period of medium growth (at a rate of approximately 6% a year), the relative proportion of SMEs has continued to ascend (2001, p. 255).” Schive and Hu also noted, “the extent to which Taiwan’s SMEs are achieving success in overseas markets might be said to be quite unique (2001, p. 270).”

By 1996, Taiwanese firms had 241 projects in Vietnam, representing $3.6 billion. This was a larger investment in Vietnam than any other single country made. Taiwanese entrepreneurs also made significant investments in other countries across East Asia.

During the early 21st century, the Taiwanese government promoted venture capital, innovation incubators, an open laboratory system, and e-commerce. This was discussed by Lee and Wang (2003).

Taiwanese entrepreneurs have also been active in China. The average Taiwanese investment in China is $800,000. Indeed, Taiwanese entrepreneurs have been contributing significantly to economic development in Asia.

Credit Policy and Entrepreneurship

Two models can be used to describe the credit policy framework of nations:

Model I

In consideration of the fact that high interest rates may cause a heavy debt burden on entrepreneurs, while decreasing the rate of new venture formation and increasing the rate of bankruptcies, the government intervenes with subsidised interest rates, helping a few favoured borrowers. Subsidised interest rates, below the market-clearing rate, help few privileged entrepreneurs, while creating jobs for the masses. This is the model which was adopted by South Korea, and which led to the growth of the *chaebols*, very diversified and powerful mega-conglomerates.

Model II

Subsidised rates are considered unjust, as low-cost money encourages capital intensive methods of production, consequently limiting employment growth. Therefore, interest rates rise with market demand. High real interest rates encourage savings and keep inflation under control by reducing demand. The formal financial systems have rigid financing regulations. This is the model adopted by Taiwan.

The Taiwanese Model

Since 1950, the economy of Taiwan has followed the path of Model II, letting its interest rates rise to high market levels. This policy resulted in the world's highest rates of savings, and efficient investment in atomised industrial structures. Savings per capita, in Taiwan, have been traditionally high. Taiwan bloomed largely because of the efforts of small-scale entrepreneurs, with thousands of entrepreneurial small businesses. Each firm had minimal debt, and entrepreneurs strive to be efficient. *The Economist* of July 14, 1990 estimated that 80% of the firms in Taiwan had fewer than 20 employees (p. 20).

Taiwan's experience with a Model II approach gave rise to a multitude of successful small businesses thriving in a healthy economy. The typical firm in Taiwan is small and equity-based. The selection of such an approach has allowed policy to remain stable with no major corrections necessary along the path to prosperity. Entrepreneurs often boast that their firms have no debt.

A shortcoming which may be attributed to a Model II approach is that small firms may lack economies of scale. However, Taiwan's low overheads, good infrastructure, and excellent network of local suppliers all help compensate for any disadvantage due to size. Local suppliers being small, a firm may be required to deal with several of them. This reduces risks, as compared to dealing with only one supplier overseas. Taiwanese SMES often link up with firms abroad, thus gaining access to marketing expertise specific to foreign markets.

Whereas South Korea's implementation of Model I has necessitated many corrections, Taiwan's success with Model II has necessitated fewer corrections. Other countries might learn from the experience of these two tigers and their contrasting styles. In both cases, a healthy small business sector comes into existence, sooner (as in Taiwan) or later (as in South Korea after corrections). However, the Asian Financial Crisis has shown that Model II is more sustainable. In contrast to the situation arising in states where subsidised credit is available, entrepreneurs in Taiwan borrow principally from the informal market, and at higher rates. This encourages them to focus on labour-intensive activities while optimising the use of capital.

Today, small industries are the backbone of Taiwan, and these small industries have become internationally competitive; 300 have become large, without government assistance.

Flexible Entrepreneurs

Entrepreneurs in Taiwan tend to combine management and ownership into one function. They like to have power over their firms, and they often prefer a sole proprietorship to other forms of enterprise. They also have a higher self-funded proportion of capital than do large-scale enterprises.

As a consequence of a Model II type policy in Taiwan, Taiwanese entrepreneurs have relied relatively little on loans. Consequently, they have coped with the Asian Financial Crisis better than have their neighbouring counterparts. By limiting external sources of income, Taiwanese entrepreneurs have reduced their risks. On the other hand, limited capital has also limited their opportunities for economies of scale.

To compensate for the lack of scale, economies of scope have been emerging. Entrepreneurs in Taiwan are willing to produce a large variety of similar products, albeit in relatively small quantities. For example, the process of production is similar for steel car-plates and machinery-shells. Therefore, one firm can easily make both items. Nevertheless, entrepreneurs usually do so only after receiving specific orders.

In contrast to large corporations, which have heavy capital investments, entrepreneurs in Taiwan have relatively less fixed production equipment. This makes it easy to adapt facilities in order to modify products or to produce different items, as necessary. This allows Taiwanese entrepreneurs to adapt rapidly to changing needs.

Entrepreneurs in Taiwan also respond quickly to changes in purchasing power. Owner-managers are often involved in sales as well as in production. They know their costs, and can rapidly adjust prices according to market demand. This ability is very helpful during crises.

Large-scale enterprises, which tend to be more formal in their organisational structure, have depth and breadth. In contrast, entrepreneurs in Taiwan tend to have few employees outside family members and friends. Furthermore, in a traditional Taiwanese firm, the founder is generally the role model for employees. These factors allow entrepreneurs to lean toward emotion for the smooth operation of their firms. Emphasis is on team-work.

The situation in Taiwan is such that manufacturing processes are flexibly organised among entrepreneurs, each optimising on efficiency brought about by the division of labour among firms. Although the division of work among firms is clear, the division of labour within a small firm is vague. Employees are often asked to do more than required by their respective job descriptions, and they usually comply. This includes personal sacrifice, when the entrepreneurs need extra input. In turn, this reduces costs and contributes to the profitability of entrepreneurship in Taiwan. During the crisis, employees have been asked to make due with less.

As discussed by Lin (1998), successful entrepreneurs in Taiwan have focused on people-related issues rather than structure or technology, and there has been more concern with attitudes and skills than with equipment. Entrepreneurs, here, do not perceive a need to be the vanguard of technological innovation. As long as there is a demand for existing goods, made with existing technology, entrepreneurs are not hasty to change production methods.

Toward the Future

Taiwanese entrepreneurs often prefer to have a small family business than to lose control and obtain growth via delegation to professional outsiders. The tendency is to seek a niche, and entrepreneurs in Taiwan seldom produce a complete product from start to finish; most have prospered as suppliers of parts. Many have concentrated on the manufacturing of consigned components; in these cases, mass marketing has not been an important concern, because an entrepreneur needed few clients.

Growth-oriented entrepreneurs in Taiwan often expect to encounter challenges. Banks are reluctant to lend capital to SMEs in Taiwan, especially those lacking a sound accounting system. As discussed by Luo (1997), entrepreneurs, in Taiwan, rely very much on personal networks, for market information, for suppliers, for clients and for employees. This approach combines the economic and social activities of entrepreneurs.

Among economic and social activities is gift-giving. Gifts are very symbolic in Taiwan, and neglecting an opportunity for gift-giving may be perceived as poor conduct.

Figure 15.7 After a Long Day at Work; photograph by Léo-Paul Dana.

Although small — by world standards — Taiwanese firms serve their purpose. Neither government nor financing is central to entrepreneurship in here. The focus is on people. The establishment of a new venture creates jobs for the entrepreneur's family, and sometimes for strangers who become adopted as family members of the firm. The small size of most firms facilitates communications. A friendly, teacher-apprentice relationship is superimposed on the entrepreneur-employee relation.

The future scenario is likely to see much relocation of manufacturing from Taiwan to locations overseas. An agreement signed in June 2013 by China and Taiwan is also likely to have an impact on the future.

Case Study: Beauty Tourism

Vacation time can be allocated to many different types of activities and places. The classic vacation is heading to the beach for a little rest and relaxation. The sun is a natural healer, but as more reports about ozone depletion come out, precautions should be taken. Touring different cities and countries as well as discovering new cultures and foods, are great vacation plans which sometimes leave the tourist more tired when the trip is over. Adventure holidays, such as sailing, diving, hiking, rock climbing and visiting tribal villages, are increasing in numbers. People are constantly seeking new ideas, and the list of vacation options goes on and on.

Israel is surrounded by the Mediterranean Sea to the west, Lebanon and Syria to the north, Jordan to the east and Egypt and the Red Sea to the south. The country is 450 kilometres (280 miles) in length and 135 kilometres (85 miles) at its widest point. Including its administered territories, this country is approximately 28,000 square kilometres (11,000 square miles).

Despite its small land mass, Israel encompasses almost all types of geographical terrain. The Jezreel valley, an agricultural area, separates the mountains of Galilee (in the north), from Samaria and the Judean hills in the centre. The Coastal Plain, a narrow, sandy shoreline, runs parallel to the Mediterranean. The south of Israel is an arid desert, known as the Negev; it consists of flatlands and limestone mountains. It stretches southward from the Judean Desert, where irrigation has made agriculture possible and productive. In the east is the Jordan Valley; it connects the Sea of Galilee with the Dead Sea. The area which reaches from the Dead Sea to the Red Sea is a long, arid valley — Arava — developed for intensive agriculture.

In general, Israel has two main seasons: a hot, dry summer, and a rainy winter, the latter between November and March. Climatic conditions also vary depending on the region. For example, Mount Hermon in the north receives an average yearly rainfall of about 100 cm, while Elat, in the south, may average less than one inch. Winters are milder along the Mediterranean coast and colder in the more mountainous regions. Summers have, on the whole, subtropical conditions which are hot, humid and void of rain.

Located 425 metres (1,300 feet) below sea level, at the base of the Judean Desert, south of the Jordan River, and north of the Red Sea, the Dead Sea is the lowest point on earth. Therefore, the concentration of oxygen is very high and the weather is warmer here than at other points along the same latitude. It is a major source of minerals, including bromide, magnesium and potash. The air is dry and the water of the Dead Sea is hot; the sea is constantly evaporating, enabling the concentration of minerals to remain very high — so high that no form of life can be sustained in these waters. Of what use is a sea in which there is no life? Fish could never be introduced here, and Israel breeds fish on its fish farms, further west.

Swimming and other water sports have been integral to Israel's other beaches, along the Mediterranean (from the border of Lebanon at Rosh Hanikra, to the Gaza Strip); at the northern tip of the Red Sea (Elat); and all along the Sea of Galilee (Lake Kinneret). At the Dead Sea, however, the concentration of minerals is so high that one cannot swim; one can simply lie on the water and float. Immersing one's face in the water can cause irritation to the eyes, and ingestion of the water, in large dosages, can be fatal. Nonetheless, since Cleopatra's time, the Dead Sea has been cherished for its therapeutic, mineral-rich mud and the healing power of its minerals. It was the site of Sodom, the Biblical city.

The aromatherapy of salty air and the rejuvenating qualities of sea mud, clay and salts, fills the senses while soothing the mind and body. The thick, black mud of the Dead Sea has properties that claim to work wonders on the skin. When smeared and left to dry on the skin for a minimum of 15 minutes, many people assert that their face becomes firmer, their wrinkles less visible, and their skin smoother.

The same way that iron (Fe), when exposed to the elements, oxidises and becomes rust, so too is the skin transformed with age. Lipids, or fats, congregate on the skin's surface, where they can oxidise, changing the appearance of exposed body surfaces. Once oxidised, the otherwise harmless secretions become free radicals due to such pollutants as second-hand smoke. Then, the free radicals cause damage to the surface upon which they cling — human skin.

Just as copper (Cu) loses its lustre and changes colour after oxidation, the face loses its youthful appearance, due to lipid oxidation on the skin's surface. Mud is especially effective for those with oily skin, as mud is a safer alternative to cleaning than is soap. Mud is gentle, non-irritating and its crystalline structure allows it to retain both oil and water. Therefore, mud is especially effective for facial treatments, absorbing excess oil while moisturising. This slows down the chemical reactions of free radicals which otherwise hasten facial aging.

As mud slows down the aging of healthy cells, sea clay (rich in minerals) has the natural ability to destroy and absorb dead skin cells. Simultaneously, clay draws out toxins, thus firming and tightening the skin tissue. Some clays also fight skin irritations.

Around the world, there is a variety of clays. Red, green, white and other colours of clays, each have a different set of mineral contents. Some contain more calcium (Ca), while others have richer concentrations of magnesium (Mg), or potassium (K). Also, sea salt (NaCl) is a disinfectant which can be used to clean cuts and/or to lubricate the skin. When added to almond or olive oil, coarse salt cleanses small particles out of pores. Salt, on its own, can dehydrate skin, but combined with oil, contributes to a healthy epidermis. The Dead Sea contains salts, and oils, making it very therapeutic.

Each year, thousands of tourists flock to the shores of the Dead Sea, to smear mud on their faces and all over their bodies. Many drape themselves on rocks, virtually mummified in layers of dark clay. Others lie flat on the water, reading the latest novels and sometimes not so recent newspapers; cuts sting, but will heal most rapidly thanks to the minerals of the Dead Sea. Not far from the shore are outdoor showers, and people stand under the faucets to rinse off the excess minerals, clays and muds. It can be a lengthy process, depending on the thickness of the layers. Egged buses from Jerusalem and from Elat pick up and drop off these healthy-skin enthusiasts throughout the day. Tour groups also find themselves congregated at this unique health location.

Figure 15.8 Dead Sea Facial Treatment; photograph by Léo-Paul Dana.

Case Study Assignment

1. Prepare a business plan for a new travel agency in Taiwan, with a focus on specialties including beauty tourism.

2. Prepare a business plan for a new shop to sell luxury beauty products in Taiwan.

Chapter 16

Thailand[1]

Introduction

Neighbouring Cambodia, Laos, Myanmar and Malaysia, the Kingdom of Thailand covers 514,000 square kilometres. An independent, sovereign state for over seven centuries, Thailand is the only country in Southeast Asia that has never been colonised. During the latter half of the 20th century, the nation's industrial structure was transformed from that of a primary product producer to a major manufacturer. Under the Ministry of Commerce, the Department of Export Promotion was established to promote Thai exports overseas. In 1984, devaluation helped boost Thai exports. Textiles surpassed rice exports and were for some time the leading product exported from Thailand. In 1997 the fall of the baht initiated the Asian Financial Crisis.

Compared to their counterparts elsewhere, entrepreneurs in Thailand have been given greater leeway, and this has resulted in a vibrant entrepreneurial verve, reinforced by the Thai interpretation of Buddhist values. Thailand has long had a free-market culture, and entrepreneurs, along with their efficient work force, have contributed greatly to the Thai economy. Yet, while multinationals have been in the limelight, the potential of entrepreneurs has been underestimated. The Global Entrepreneurship Monitor study revealed that in 2005, Thailand

[1] This chapter is based on information obtained from a variety of sources, including: the Bangkok Bank; the Board of Investment; the Board of Trade of Thailand; the Department of Industrial Promotion; the Department of Technical and Economic Cooperation; the Federation of Thai Industries; the Industrial Finance Corporation of Thailand; Khon Kaen University; the Ministry of Commerce; the Ministry of Information and Communication Technology; the National Economic and Social Development Board; the Siam Commercial Bank; the Thai Bankers Association; and the Thailand Development Research Institute. Travel to Thailand was provided by the Asian Institute of Technology (AIT). The chapter includes historical material that first appeared in Dana (1999b).

had an exceptionally high score in the Established Business Index, when compared to Singapore and the United States. "With respect to early-stage entrepreneurial activity, countries such as… Thailand (20.7%)…exhibit very high rates of individual involvement compared to other countries such as …Japan (2.2%)…(Minniti, Bygrave, and Autio, 2006, p. 10)."

Historical Overview

The original Thai kingdom came into existence in 1220, as a result of a Thai rebellion against the Khmers. King Ramkhamhaeng, who reigned from 1278 to 1318, adapted the Khmer alphabet to the Thai language. Monks from Ceylon were brought in to form a different form of Buddhism than that practised by the Khmers. The Thais subsequently adopted the Hinayana School of Orthodox Buddhism. When Ayutthaya was the national capital of the Thais (from the mid-14th century until 1767), it was known as the Baghdad of the East — a thriving area for trade. Merchants reported that it was larger than was London at the time.

During the 19th century, the Thai kingdom — known as Siam, at the time — ceded some land to Britain (currently the north of peninsular Malaysia) and to France (currently part of Cambodia and Laos). Nevertheless, Siam succeeded in being the only country in the region to escape European colonial rule.

The country became a constitutional monarchy in 1932. In 1939, Siam changed its name to Thailand. During the next several decades, Thailand received considerable assistance from the United States. In 1991, Thailand embarked on a programme of economic deregulation and liberalisation.

The Asian Financial Crisis caused growth to slow down during the latter years of the decade. By 2006, the economy had picked up and $1 traded at 40 baht. In 2012, real GDP growth in Thailand was 6.4%. In 2013, $1 traded in the range of 32 baht.

Influence of the Hinayana School of Orthodox Buddhism

Buddhism is more than a religion in the Western sense; it is also a philosophical system. With 94% of Thais being Buddhist, this way of life dominates culture and society in Thailand. Yet, since tolerance is central to Buddhist beliefs, Buddhism has never led to fanaticism or religious war.

Buddhism's tolerance has also allowed the survival of ancient Thai beliefs. Thus, Buddhism, as it is practised in Thailand, coexists with beliefs in omens. Stars and spirits are principal forces in daily life. Entrepreneurs consult astrologers — many of them self-employed Chinese — to determine the most auspicious time to expand their firms. Similar to the eye in Arab countries, or to garlic in Greece or Turkey, amulets are said to protect the Thais from misfortune.

Many firms in Thailand have a spirit house. This is an ornate, miniature temple, where spirits can be comfortable. This applies to all business enterprises — even brothels. In contrast to Christianity, which links sensual pleasure to sin, Buddhism involves a partnership of piety and pleasure. While good spirits do no harm, entrepreneurs often fear that bad spirits may hurt their business. To counter this, tattoos are used to keep away bad spirits.

The same philosophical system contributes greatly to entrepreneurship in Thailand, as it instils values that appear to encourage entrepreneurial spirit. The importance of tolerance extends beyond religion, to a respect for business competition.

Likewise, the prevalent philosophy in Thailand discourages abuse and envy. Buddhism in Thailand encourages: (i) asceticism; (ii) self-reliance; (iii) taking initiative; (iv) love of work; (v) diligence; (vi) patience; (vii) frugality; and (viii) efficiency. These qualities are very compatible with entrepreneurship. Since a young age, Thais are taught that Buddha left the comforts of his home to live a life of asceticism. The importance of asceticism is not unique to Buddhism; Weber (1904-5) linked entrepreneurship to asceticism. Self-reliance is emphasised through Buddha's teaching, "Make of yourself a light. Rely upon yourself. Do not depend upon anyone else." Indeed, many Thais become self-employed, not to depend on others for employment. Bandura (1982) and Bandura and Adams (1977) reported a correlation between self-efficacy and subsequent task performance.

Figure 16.1 Learning to be Ascetic; photograph by Léo-Paul Dana.

Buddha noted that people believing that everything happens by chance consequently lose hope and neglect to act wisely. Likewise, teachings discourage the belief in destiny, as the existence of destiny would imply that human plans and efforts for improvement and innovation would be in vain. Thais are taught not to rely on chance or fate. Instead, it is important to take initiative. There is an emphasis on an internal locus-of-control. Hull, Bosley and Udell (1980) found a correlation between an internal locus-of-control and entrepreneurial activity. Brockhaus (1982) and Begley and Boyd (1987) contended that entrepreneurs have a more internally oriented locus-of-control, than do non-entrepreneurs.

The teachings of Buddha specify that foolish people are avaricious for good results, but are too timid to go after them, and therefore fail. This is interpreted as emphasising the importance of a strong work ethic. Like asceticism, Weber (1904–1905) linked work ethic to entrepreneurship.

Figure 16.2 Determined to Sell Her Wares; photograph by Léo-Paul Dana.

Figure 16.3 Self-reliant; photograph by Léo-Paul Dana.

It is said that a man, who is satisfied with the progress he has made by little effort, relaxes his effort and becomes proud and conceited, falling into idleness and failure. This teaches people the importance of continuous efforts and determination. Hornaday (1982) noted that perseverance and determination are among the entrepreneurial characteristics most reported in academic surveys.

It is explained that a farmer cannot expect to see buds today, plants tomorrow and harvest the day after. The Thais learn that patience is a virtue. King Udayana once asked Ananda what he was going to do with 500 garments he had just received. Ananda replied:

> I am going to distribute them among my brothers in rags.
> What will you do with the old garments?
> We will make bed covers out of them.
> What will you do with the old bed covers?
> We will make pillowcases.

What will you do with the old pillowcases?
We will make floor covers out of them.
What will you do with the old floor covers?
Use them for foot towels.
And the old foot towels?
Use them for floor mats.
And the old ones?
Tear them into pieces, and
Mix them with mud and plaster the house-walls.

The moral of the parable is that frugality is desirable. Again, frugality is a quality that Weber (1904–1905) linked to entrepreneurship.

Buddhism, as it is taught in Thailand, also teaches the importance of efficiency. A parable recounts the story of a traveller who came across an obstacle to his journey: a river. He therefore built a raft and safely crossed the river. Upon reaching the other bank, the man decided that despite its weight, he would keep the raft, "I will not abandon it to rot, but will carry it with me." Buddha explained that this was not efficient. Even a valuable asset should be discarded, when the cost of keeping it is greater than the benefit it provides.

Visible Hands

The first National Economic Development Plan of Thailand (1961–1966) was greatly biased in favour of large enterprises. Its goal was to stimulate economic growth by providing large-scale investments via the Board of Investment and the Industrial Finance Corporation of Thailand. Small-scale enterprises were given limited encouragement. The governor of Udorn helped small-scale farmers by introducing sorghum to them. While rice sold for 100 baht ($5 at the time) per acre and required 210 days to mature, sorghum needed only 90 days to yield 200 baht per acre. Eventually, policy-makers identified the need to upgrade existing small-scale enterprises, and in 1966, the Small Industry Service Institute was formed. Supported by the United Nations Development Programme (UNDP), its purpose was to provide technical assistance in order to modernise small-scale industries.

Figure 16.4 Working Elephant; photograph by Léo-Paul Dana.

Thailand's second economic development plan (1967–1971) largely replicated the first. Industrial estates were provided for small-scale industries, outside Bangkok. However, no assistance was provided to entrepreneurs. The third economic development plan (1972–1976) perpetuated the concern with the importance of relocating industries outside the capital city. Incentives were promised. However, the oil crisis and the recession, which it caused, both contributed to delays.

The year 1977 witnessed the Investment Promotion Act, which developed the legal foundation for Thailand's Board of Investment. This government agency was empowered to grant preferential status to enterprises engaged in a variety of designated activities which were singled out including agriculture; mining and related industries; heavy industry; manufacturing; and services.

Figure 16.5 Elephant at Work; photograph by Léo-Paul Dana.

Figure 16.6 Efficient Travelling; photograph by Léo-Paul Dana.

Projects attracting the most generous incentive packages include: those expected to generate substantial employment; those located outside Bangkok; those which conserved energy; those which involved substitutes for imported fuel; those with the potential for foreign exchange earnings; and those deemed complementary to the development of basic industries. Qualifying entrepreneurs may be granted exemptions from import duties, from withholding taxes and from income tax. In addition, the Investment Promotion Act empowered the Board of Investment to provide guarantees against competition from new state enterprises. Finally, tariff protection may be introduced, and in some cases, the products of foreign competitors may be banned.

The Board of Investment evolved over time. In its early years, it served as an incentive-granting agency, dedicating much of its resources to monitoring the tax incentives granted to enterprises. Eventually, it established a "One Stop Centre" and took on the role of business advisor, providing technical expertise to entrepreneurs.

Like its predecessor, Thailand's fourth economic development plan (1977–1981) was also concerned with the importance of relocating industries outside Bangkok. However, the facilities in the estates continued to be minimal, and operating costs were high.

The fifth economic development plan (1982–1986) ushered in a new era for Thailand, marking a shift in policy direction. This time, the government emphasised the need to promote small-scale industry as the pillar of industrial development in Thailand. Policy-makers expected that providing specific incentives to small-scale enterprises would result in these firms growing faster than the rate of growth among large corporations. Also, if small firms were concentrated outside the nation's capital, then growth would be decentralised outside Bangkok. This new approach was consistent with the state's long-term objective of narrowing the gap between Bangkok and the less developed regions of the country.

The state-owned Transport Company, Ltd. controlled 10% of the total traffic on buses linking Bangkok and the provinces. In a bold move, this company gave franchises to local entrepreneurs. This turned out to be highly profitable for the franchiser, as well as for the franchisees.

During the mid-1980s, large enterprises achieved unexpected success in expanding their export performance. This prompted policy-makers to change their strategy again. Rather than providing policies to promote small industries, it was decided to focus on promoting exports. Consequently, Thailand's sixth economic development plan (1987–1991) was not concerned with small firms. In September 1990, the Royal Thai Government reduced tariffs on machinery, from 20% to 5%. This stimulated latent demand among price-elastic entrepreneurs, thereby facilitating the transfer of technology.

Of particular concern to entrepreneurs was the structure of the tax system at the time. Personal income tax rates were very high, especially compared to those in neighbouring Malaysia. Furthermore, the cascading nature of the business tax discouraged backward linkages. Consequently, a Value Added Tax (VAT) was introduced in January 1992, replacing the old system of business taxes. In April 1992, Thailand announced that it wanted to slow down tariff cuts to which it had agreed the previous year.

Propelled by manufactured exports, Thailand became the world's fastest growing economy. A problem, however, was that the manufacturing sector became top heavy, *i.e.*, strong in final assembly but less so in supply industries. This led to a bottleneck, as firms developed a dependence on imported raw materials and machinery. Supply and support industries have a major impact on a nation's industrial sector, because their role is to feed manufacturing operations.

Thailand's seventh economic development plan (1992–1996) explicitly emphasised a commitment to the rapid development of key support industries, and this was of special interest to entrepreneurs. Countless small firms are the core of the domestic support industries in Thailand. Yet, they often suffered from a lack of economy of scale or the lack of technology to be globally competitive. Although components could be produced in Thailand, local firms lacked the resources to produce the quantities for which demand existed. Therefore, the Board of Investment implemented a special programme to promote the growth of small and medium scale Thai companies in the area of support industries. The Board of Investment Unit for Industrial Linkage Development (BUILD) devised a scheme to market the concept of backward linkages to smaller firms, whereby small firms acquire technology from multinationals, in order to supply them with components.

The Bank of Thailand and also the Industrial Finance Corporation of Thailand gave preferential financial assistance to entrepreneurs. Priority was focused on rural entrepreneurs using local raw materials to produce exports. In early 1996, the baht was showing signs of weakness.

Thailand's eighth economic development plan (1997–2001) coincided with difficult times. In July 1997, the baht collapsed, prompting a domino effect across the Far East. Almost two million people lost their jobs and unemployment surged from almost nil, to 6%. In November 1997, a new coalition government was elected, headed by Prime Minister Chuan Leekpai. He proved himself an honest man, eager to implement economic reforms proposed by the International Monetary Fund, along with a $17.2 billion package. Within a few months, the Royal Thai Government closed over 50 finance companies, nationalised four failing banks, and opened the financial industry to foreigners. These government actions were followed by an announcement that Bangchak Petroleum, Thai Airways International and the Electricity Generating Authority of Thailand were scheduled to be at least partially privatised. Not surprisingly, this led to opposition from labour. Meanwhile, the Asian Development Bank led a consortium of banks, which lent $1 billion to Thai exporters.

In 1998, the Royal Thai Cabinet approved the Industrial Restructuring Master Plan, prepared by the Ministry of Industry. The National Economic and Social Development Bureau, which is the economic planning body of Thailand, prepared a privatisation plan, to shift economic functions from the state to private enterprises.

With financial assistance from the International Labour Organisation and from the United Nations Special Fund, the Small Industries Service Institute evolved into the Industrial Services Division of the Ministry of Industry's Department of Industrial Promotion. Initially, its scope was to modernise small-scale industries across the board; by the 1990s its mandate was to focus on enterprises in specific sectors, regardless of firm size. The Industrial Services Division was organised into three sub-divisions: (i) the Furniture Industry Sub-Division; (ii) the Miscellaneous Industries Sub-Division; and (iii) the Design Promotion Sub-Division. This allowed the Division to allocate its resources across six industrial sectors: (i) furniture; (ii) agro-industry; (iii) jewellery; (iv) packaging; (v) toys; and (vi) industrial design. These sectors were selected because they were "particularly beneficial" to the industrial and economic development of the nation. Entrepreneurs and potential entrepreneurs interested in the above sectors were entitled to a wide range of services from the Industrial Services Division. These included training courses, seminars, exhibitions, technology, acquisition, product testing, analysis, design promotion, consultancy and industrial studies.

Individual nations also made contributions. The Canadian International Development Assistance (CIDA) programme established the Small and Medium Enterprise (SME) Project — administered through the Royal Thai Department of Industrial Promotion — to support the growth of SMEs in north-eastern Thailand, including the provision of credit as well as advisory services. CIDA also designed the Northeast Fisheries Project, to assist small-scale fishing operations. In addition, CIDA funded a community-based Integrated Rural Development project, helping small-scale farmers and cottage industries. Finally, CIDA launched the Enterprise Collaboration Project, aimed to support joint ventures between Canadian and Thai entrepreneurs.

Thailand's ninth economic development plan (2002–2006) formally adopted the principle of sufficiency economy as guiding philosophy.This was reiterated in the tenth economic development plan (2007–2011). Thailand's eleventh economic development plan (2012–2016) promoted balanced development.

Pluralism & Minorities

Chinese traders have long been active in Thailand. This is especially so in Bangkok, the nation's main port. Two groups of ethnic-Chinese became prominent — the Hokkiens and the Teochews. The former spoke *Minnanhua* — a dialect from Fujian Province — while the latter spoke *Chaozhouhua* — a dialect from Guang Dong Province. Hokkiens found employment as tax collectors for the royal family, during the 18th century. Teochews became entrepreneurs. Throughout the 20th century, more ethnic-Chinese entrepreneurs migrated to Thailand, and became prominent in business.

Whereas religious and cultural differences prevented the Chinese from assimilating smoothly into Muslim countries, this was not the case in Thailand. A common religion (Buddhism) and the lack of discrimination helped them blend into Thai society. Unlike Burma, Indonesia, Malaysia and Vietnam, Thailand never favoured its Indigenous people at the expense of the ethnic-Chinese community. As explained by respondents interviewed by the author, "We don't feel any different whether they are Thai or Chinese." Thailand's tolerance of entrepreneurship, in its Chinese community, contributed to a healthy national economy. In 1999, 14% of Thailand's population was Chinese, and ethnic-Chinese entrepreneurs controlled 90% of manufacturing in Thailand (Yeung, 1999).

Through marriage to Thai women, Chinese men integrated well into their host society, and it became fashionable to adopt Thai names. Barth (1981) argued that when two groups interact, they begin sharing values. In the case of Thailand, although the government limited the number of Chinese schools, the community preserved its cultural values, a desire for education and its diligent work ethic. Silcock (1967) described the Chinese of Thailand as the "Jews of the East." Thailand also has a community of Jews, many of them entrepreneurs.

The most powerful Chinese family in Thailand was formerly the Tejapaibul family, owners of a banking, distilling and real estate empire. Chin Sophonpanich, owner of hospitals and plantations and father of the Bangkok Bank, was a prominent leader of the Chinese community in Bangkok, until his death in 1988. Also among the prominent ethnic-Chinese entrepreneurs, in Thailand, was Chuan Ratanarak.

Figure 16.7 Bangkok; photograph by Léo-Paul Dana.

Chuan Ratanarak was born in China in 1920, and was brought to Thailand by his parents, in 1926. In 1945, he was still a wage-worker at the port of Bangkok. He then established his own firm, loading sea vessels. In time, he progressed to banking and manufacturing, as did numerous ethnic-Chinese entrepreneurs in Thailand. By the 1990s, he controlled the Bank of Ayudhya and Siam City Cement.

Other important families of Chinese entrepreneurs in Thailand include the Chearavanonts, the Chokwatanas and the Shinawatras. The Chearavanonts established the Charoen Pokphand (CP) group. This involved animal feed, petrochemicals and a joint venture with British Telecom.

Thiam Chokwatana started out with one shop in 1942. This evolved into the Saha Pathana group, including 60 companies producing a variety of goods from clothing to detergents. Although a third of these came to be listed on the stock market, each of Chokwatana's sons has kept control of at least one listed corporation. The family business proved to be very successful, despite competition from Colgate, Procter & Gamble, and Unilever.

Thaksin Shinawatra, an ethnic-Chinese from Chiang Mai, started out as a distributor of IBM computers. He later set up a cable-television network and then decided to establish his own cellular telephone operation.

More than half of Bangkok's seven million people have Chinese blood, and they tend to be active in entrepreneurship. They are involved in a wide range of activities, from manufacturing to retailing. Some are bakers. Others are self-employed astrologists and palmists, respected occupations in this superstitious society. Entrepreneurs in Bangkok's Chinatown tend to sell cloth, gold and noodles.

In addition, hundreds of entrepreneurs from Taiwan have been contributing to foreign direct investment across Thailand. There are about eight million ethnic-Chinese in Thailand. Although they comprise only 14% of Thailand's population, they control four-fifths of the market capital in Thailand. Over half of them are Teochew.

Figure 16.8 Woman Entrepreneur; photograph by Léo-Paul Dana.

Women Entrepreneurs

Although Thai women are often portrayed as being subservient to men, Thai culture fosters a relatively egalitarian status for men and women. According to the culture, both genders are equally important. Traditionally, Thai women have had leadership roles in community health, education and earning family income. More recently, women have become very visible in Thailand's entrepreneurship sector. Many are owner-managers of small firms; others own enterprises which have grown into larger-scale businesses.

One woman entrepreneur owns a golf course. Another — this one from Chiang Mai — operates a large antique business. Women operate a bus company in Bangkok, along with a fleet of ferryboats.

Toward the Future

Several development plans have recognised the potential of entrepreneurs; yet, programmes to foster entrepreneurship have been over-shadowed by politics encouraging multinationals. In some cases, this has been at the expense of local entrepreneurship. During the latter decades of the 20th century, Thailand became an export base for multinationals, which enjoyed low labour costs in an open economy. However, little was done to supply these corporations from within Thailand. Much production activity was little more than assembly work. In the future, the use of local suppliers will increase cost-effectiveness for multinationals, while allowing local entrepreneurship to play an increasingly vital role in the Thai economy. The regional economy will also contribute to entrepreneurship in Thailand. Already, Thai entrepreneurs have been engaging in business with Laos and Myanmar.

Figure 16.9 Thailand is a Producer of Jackfruit; photograph by Léo-Paul Dana.

Case Study: Bangkok's Best Garment[2]

Best Garment was a custom tailor for men's and women's clothing, in Bangkok. Any design could be put together using fabrics chosen from the available selection of cottons and silks; garments could also be made by using materials obtained from another store, from markets or elsewhere. Some of the finest cloths may be obtained in Thailand. Best Garment's factory was located at 296/3-4 Silom Road, one of the busiest main roads in Bangkok's downtown core. Its two retail outlets were located nearby, one at 145 River City, and the other at 52/6 Suriwong Road. Many of Best Garment's clients were tourists, staying in nearby hotels. Concerns, however, were that many big Western-style department stores were opening in the area, with ready-made clothing.

[2] This case was written by Teresa Elizabeth Dana, formerly at Thammasat University, Thailand.

Changes in the Nature of Retailing

Retail institutions have gone through much change over the past century, from little shops to giant mega-complexes. North America and Europe have been trend setters in retailing patterns and as their markets become saturated, they are beginning to enter new ones with considerable force either by themselves or through joint ventures/alliances. Theories have been developed to depict the pattern of changes that have gone on in the retail industry (mainly the Western patterns) from its inception in the 19th century. Such theories not only set the stage for trends in the industrialised world but also demonstrate the spill-over effects that such trends have in the developing world.

Successful retailers require the ability to anticipate shifts in demographics and consumer attitudes and the adapt accordingly. The evolution of change in retailing at one time was local, but as infrastructures began to develop and travel was made easier, competition increased as it was drawn from a wider audience. This territory is increasing more and more to the point where almost all businesses are affected by globalisation in one form or another. Products, from colas to jeans, are gaining recognition on the international scene at a rapidly increasing pace and retailers world-wide are following such trends to meet the demand.

Consumers in the West have come to depend on retail institutions to buy almost anything they desire in the way that suits their lifestyles. However, such customers have not always demanded their products in the same ways nor have they always had the means to acquire such a diverse selection of items. Demographic, social, economic and cultural changes constantly affect the character of consumers and their purchasing patterns. These shifts, along with evolving technology and increasing competition greatly affect the operations of retail establishments. All aspects must be kept under regular scrutiny in order for any firm, large or small, to adjust its positioning and excel in the marketplace.

Thailand falls into a category of high growth potential and low competitive strength, a much desired entry market for foreign competition. Local retailers in Thailand must therefore be aware of the imposing trends and to an extent, must turn to the natural selection theory to adapt, defend and strengthen their position in their own native markets. Soon, even the most remote small business operator will be affected by globalisation. Retailing practices in the large metropolitan areas of developing countries already resemble those of retailing stores in the large cities of industrialised countries.

Report on Thailand's Retail Market

According to Bank of Thailand (BOT) figures, department stores are at the core of the retail market. Competition is tough especially in Bangkok, however there is room for large domestic retailers to compete on margins with the big international chains if operations are planned thoroughly. One strategy that is emerging for retailers is to by-pass the saturated Bangkok market in order to reach the underdeveloped provincial. This is causing a serious threat to local businesses who are not prepared for the influx of such retailers.

Thailand has experienced in years what took decades to happen in the West. The retail market has moved very swiftly through the normal evolution of department and discount stores, convenience stores and straight to big super-centres. As a result of this rapid transition, retailers in Thailand have had to become very competitive.

There is a lot of activity going on in terms of the changing character of consumers, improvements in technology and intensifying competition. Free Trade Agreements and the increased role of local and international advertising are also playing key roles in the growth of this country's retail industry. Only time will tell whether a homogeneous Western-style retail market will emerge and whether or not traditional small firms in Thailand will be able to remain differentiated, given the increasing impact of globalisation.

Values

Traditionally, cultural values in Thailand stressed the spiritual side of a person as well as the group to which he or she belongs. Personal growth would relate to social well-being. A person was taught to respect other living beings, including animals and plants. Personal achievement at the expense of others was frowned upon. Exploitation, confrontation and competition are to be avoided, while unity, communality, and harmony were encouraged. The rich and powerful were expected to treat others kindly and with respect. Conspicuous consumption was scorned. The rich exhibited their wealth only on certain festival days. In everyday life, they ate and dressed the same as everyone else.

It would seem that Thai people are moving away from such basic notions as they become wealthier and more influenced by the Western ways of the world. With the rise in incomes, more children study abroad where they usually become entrenched into the Western way of life. It is these people, through their liberalisation as well as through the influx of foreign business ventures, films and communication that are now changing the cultural values of this country.

Consumption Patterns

Consumers are using a good portion of their increase in income to buy bigger-ticket items. Interestingly enough, many Thais are drinking Scotch whisky like water and Mercedes-Benz cars are increasing their presence on Bangkok roads, exponentially. This pattern of conspicuous consumption is great for high priced retailers but may be an alarming pattern in the long-term.

In order to keep up with image, many Thais began to carry at least one credit card. These cards have a strong appeal for the Thai materialism factor. According to Dr. Thanawan Sangsuwan at Chulalongkorn University, credit cards and member cards respond to five basic consumer needs: convenience, prestige, safety, savings, and performance. Already the Mall Department store has reported that the majority of transactions are made via credit cards. There are also increasing numbers of member cards for shops and debit cards such as the ones that can be used when taking a micro bus in Bangkok.

Retail Environment

Changes in retail buying habits as well as the rapid growth of the residential communities in and around the market area have led to the development of different types of retailers. At present, Thailand's formal retail environment consists of five major segments: department stores and malls, convenience stores and minimarts, cash-and-carry wholesalers, super-centres and stand-alone supermarkets.

The department store trade is dominated by few major retailers. The cash-and-carry wholesale segment came to be controlled by the Charoen

Pokphand group (CP) through its Makro stores. Supermarkets have generally been located within department stores and are used as lost leaders to attract people to buy there. In terms of stand-alone supermarkets, Foodland is the only existing major chain at the moment however the Central group is moving in to this segment with their Central Supermarket.

One of the trends of this decade is for many retailers to adopt the "All-in-One" concept, whereby customers can find everything they need in one central location. This is not only in response to the time-restrictions that seem to be imposed on Thai society these days but also in response to the increasing need for convenience and accessibility. Traffic congestion has made the average Bangkok consumer spend from four to six hours traveling to and from work. Pressures on time and increasing disposable income are propelling Thais to alter their shopping habits.

The total supply of retail space available in Bangkok tripled in a five year time span. Thailand's retail market is becoming more and more competitive and is expanding dramatically as the big retailers are investing heavily in development. To survive in this business, retailers have diversified themselves into several types of outlets.

It is important to note that the local naming of retail stores must be kept in mind when looking for similarities and differences between markets as names can be misleading. Although department stores and supermarkets can now be found in many developing countries, the types of customers attracted are different to those of the same name in industrialised countries and vice versa. For example, most department stores in North America attract the middle class customer, whereby a good portion of Thai department stores target the upper-income class. In addition a word like "drugstore" can be misleading as those under this nomenclature in the US stock more than just pharmaceuticals. Nevertheless, the concepts are similar as they have simply been taken to be adapted to this new climate. Supermarkets in Thailand are located inside a department store whereas in North America, they tend to be situated as anchors for shopping centres.

Department Stores and Malls

Department stores are large retail stores that carry a wide variety of good quality, fashionable and relatively expensive merchandise, from clothing to electronics to furniture. Many of the goods are quality brand name items that are properly displayed. Clothes are placed neatly on shelves, hangers as well as on mannequins for optimal selling. Samples of furniture and household goods are removed from boxes and generally placed in room settings. A lot of merchandising time and effort is put into the way each product is presented to the clientele. Customer service is a priority and typically a large number of staff is required to service the customers adequately as well as creating and maintaining displays.

Department stores can be stand-alone or as seen more recently, can serve as anchor tenants to big mall complexes, which are big shopping attractions where smaller specialty stores are set up to surround this bigger retailer. Customers frequenting a mall know that if they cannot find what they are looking for in the department store, they have many smaller shops to choose from. As this set-up is clearly taken from the West, many Western-style specialty shops are located in such malls. Popular specialty franchises include Body Glove, Body Shop, Marks & Spencer, and TAB.

Food courts are usually set up in department stores or in mall complexes in Thailand. In newer establishments that are appealing largely to the needs of the middle and upper class, the food courts consist of franchises with high brand name recognition like McDonald's, KFC, Daidomon and Black Canyon. In traditional and older department stores, which generally cater to the lower-middle class or to the "C-class," the food courts consist of Thai cuisine served at little kiosks. The variety offered differs between stall, however one can not always find the same dishes at the same stalls from day to day. For these operations, coupons are purchased from a central vendor and are redeemed when food and beverages are bought. Thus, the department store controls sales of each unit.

Central Department Store, targeting the upscale consumer, holds approximately 25% of the market, followed by Robinson, targeting the middle income segment with 15% market share, followed by the Mall and Imperial. Some of the more popular mall complexes would include Siam Square, Siam Center and the World Trade Center. According to industry sources, the Japanese upscale department stores, Isetan, Sogo, Tokyu and Daimaru have approximately 20% of the market. Now that Central and Robinson have merged, they have an estimated combined shared of over 40%.

Department stores have flourished in Bangkok for the same reasons that they became popular in the West — the growth of cities, improvement in transportation systems, a rise in the standard of living, increased capital, the coming of the electrical age, development of plate glass and of retail advertising. Department store sales in Bangkok slowed down a few years ago however seem well positioned to take off again.

Unofficial Economic Activity

Much care must be taken when using and interpreting data on retailing patterns, especially in developing countries as unlicensed shops and street vendors, representing major segments, go unreported in statistics. In addition, some retail sales are often not disclosed or are underreported so as to reduce taxes or avoid payoffs to local government officials. Therefore, the large informal sector in Thailand must be addressed; its role is significant as it provides a steady source of income for much of the lower class and it is an integral part of Thailand's make-up. Formal retail trends as well as the increasing Western influence affect this economy to a large degree.

Unofficial economic activity plays an important role in most developing countries' economies and its influence often goes unreported in statistics because of its very nature. This sector comprises three types of activities that can be classified as legal, quasi-legal and illegal.

The internal category includes such activities that yield goods and services generated in subsistence production but where no market transaction is involved. The value of housework as well as agriculture for personal consumption are examples of this and represent an extremely important part of the survival strategy for the poor, especially in rural areas.

Street vendors sell everything from imitation designer clothes to hand-made hill tribe costumes. Unfortunately, buying such hand-made items usually means supporting child-labour and other abusive work practices. Buying directly from the hill tribes may cost a little more, but the proceeds go straight to their communities. Because it is very normal to buy almost anything from street vendors and at markets, buyers are never really sure of the means by which the merchandise has been acquired, or in some cases if they are indeed getting what they paid for. In Bangkok and a few other bigger cities, jewels, tour offerings and other scams are integrating nicely into the new ways of business activity. There are no laws regarding prices that can be charged and therefore buyers must beware of the products being offered.

Food stalls are set up along almost every street. Drinks are poured into bags and tied by an elastic band with a straw and all kinds of delicious foods are served on plastic, reusable dishes. Passers-by can eat standing by the vendor or can sit down at tables and plastic chairs. Even in the worst of floods, these food vendors can be found grilling prawns, octopus, chicken or pork and serving them to their local clientele standing knee-deep in water. These moveable stalls are an integral part of the cities' tapestry and yet it was reported that local authorities did remove many of them temporarily when foreign investors were arriving in Bangkok for a government investment program. Anyone taking a train or bus in Thailand can be sure that food vendors will be available selling everything from their home-made specialties to cans of Singa beer or Coca-Cola. Of special interest, even though data is not available on sales of food-stall vendors and tuk-tuk/taxi drivers, there is an imposed restriction. The only people allowed to perform these tasks must be of Thai origin. This is a sharp contrast to patterns in the West, where it is usually immigrants who are involved in such sectors.

The Illicit Category differs from the aforementioned one in that the type of goods and services offered are illegal, such as drugs trafficking and prostitution. Thailand is internationally renowned for its activities in this unofficial sector mainly because they really thrive in tourist areas. It is big business for many who are willing to take advantage of value systems. The more that foreigners frequent the "red light" districts of Pat-Pong, Pattaya, Chiang Mai, etc., and partake in such activities, the more the innocent children of Thailand will be exploited. Young girls are taken from their homes, mainly in the northern regions, raped and then disowned by their parents due to the loss of their virginity. They are sold to local restaurant owners and in many cases are forced to "perform." As long as demand increases, supply will be met.

Changes in Retailing

Every retail outlet is, at one time or another, influenced by changes in the environment. An area can be extremely lucrative at a certain point and then due to "acts of God," zoning laws, demographic shifts, etc., buyer traffic can slow down considerably or even completely. This is true for retail outlets worldwide. However, when looking at the situation in

Thailand, one can observe that it is not only local regulations and environmental effects that have caused changes to its retail structure. Huge forces by global firms, mainly from North America, Europe and Japan, entering or threatening to enter the market, are also key variables compelling small and large firms to change strategies and adapt to new market conditions. These global forces have brought with them new dimensions of competition as well as changes in market demand through the increased availability of products and services via new channels of distribution. For many Western retailers, bringing their well-developed concepts to a developing country such as Thailand, is a market expansion opportunity, and part of the next phase of their retail evolutionary cycle. It is pushed not only by expanding territory, but because an overall business phenomenon is happening.

More and more Western businesses are entering developing markets with the good intention of helping improve the standard of living of the people through technology transfers and education. With this however, the people who are sent to set up plants and businesses tend to want some of the comforts of home and introduce different ways of doing things to their native counterparts, who in turn demand some of these products and facilities. Retail outlets slowly began to cater to such needs. At present, such demand has increased so much that there are plans to implement many new Western-like retail structures. And thus, the other theories will begin to play integral roles in the changes that happen in Thailand now and in the future. The process is accelerating quickly and so big retailers like Central, Robinson and the CP Group have been working diligently on competitive strategies both amongst themselves and in preparation for potential new market players. Many are entering joint ventures with Western firms or holding companies and thus are creating strategic alliances for the future.

There are many reasons to explain the high cluster of outlets in the growth stage of the lifecycle for Thailand. They range from the increasing strength of the economic environment, higher incomes and spending as well as changes in demand for products and how they are offered. Many outlets, however, which are not at the same stage of the lifecycle as those in the West would have differed in their explanatory theory in the introductory stage of their evolution as they had been given somewhat of a jump start by outside forces. As these outlets catch up with their Western counterparts, the trends will tend to be more strongly correlated to the prevailing Western theory.

Many Thais now have more money in their pockets and as a result are becoming socially geared towards spending for a "better" lifestyle. Any Thai will say that they are a very discerning people, taking only the good they find in Western practices and learning from them while maintaining their traditions. Time will tell just how integrated Western ways will permeate Thai traditions.

The Thai People's Respect Authority and the Class Structure

In the past, a Thai's position was inherited, not achieved. This is changing within the social realm. With education, especially a Western one, as well as a job in the business sector or with the government, one can raise one's status. Increasingly, material possessions are indicative of class, and items of material value, especially authentic ones, help support the whole notion of face. Another determinant of status is the colour of one's skin. The whiter it is (*i.e.*, closer to the Chinese tone), the higher the perceived role in society. On the other hand, when one's skin colour is darker (*i.e.,* of Siamese background), the lower one is placed on the social ladder. Darker skin is associated with the field labourer, who works outside under the burning sun. It is therefore uncommon to find Thais sunbathing. Other physical traits that are highly valued are a bridge on the nose and eyelids, two very distinctive Western traits. Plastic surgery is increasing as a result of these desired traits.

Women are moving away from factory work to jobs that require higher education. They have more discretionary income and less time to spend it. Their needs are changing in that they want more convenience and cleanliness.

There are many new international names entering the Thai market, generally through established Thai retailers, joint ventures, or franchising. Companies such as Marks & Spencer are represented through the Central Group. Fast-food chains such as Kentucky Fried Chicken and Pizza Hut are now household names in Thailand and most families in urban areas now eat fast-food on a regular basis. Thailand has always been very quick at seizing new initiatives and experimenting with Western business, and now the market seems primed for international giants like WalMart and KMart to enter. This is a big fear for many existing retailers. The Central/Robinson merger was one tactic adopted by Thai firms to be more competitive when such international industry giants inevitably try to enter the market.

The market environment is changing drastically as a result of the influx of Western style retailers. It is changing the nature of competition as well. Traditional selling practices resemble that of a bazaar economy where a sliding price system exists. Competition takes place between the buyer and the seller mainly through haggling.

It is quite fascinating to witness first hand the incredible changes and chaos that exist in everyday living, especially in a city like Bangkok. Most Westerners find themselves stressed beyond imagination at the way systems work or (for them) more appropriately, do not. But the Thais smile, wait and simply say "Mai Pen Rai" when things do not go smoothly. Mai Pen Rai means "never mind" or "no worries" and is perhaps the basis for the reason why although the chaos is seemingly intolerable, things do not blow up. They are a solution oriented people as are the Japanese who remain very calm under what a Westerner, especially those that fall under the expressive category, would view as a stressful situation and where everything is problematic. Thais find such reactionary attitudes amusing and it is rare that one would ever see a Thai display such openly expressive emotions.

Case Study Assignment

1. As a consultant for Best Garment, create a report including suggestions for dealing with the changing retail environment in Thailand.

2. As the owner of Best Garment, write a letter to the government, listing your concerns as to what is happening in the retail industry.

3. Acting as a policy maker for the Thai government, with regard to the regulation of the entry of foreign multinationals into the country, create a report to insure the survival and promotion of local small businesses in the country.

4. Design a promotion campaign for Best Garment, keeping the desired target market in mind.

5. As a consultant for Best Garment, create a report including suggestions for dealing with the changing retail environment in Thailand.

Chapter 17

Vietnam[1]

Introduction

The Socialist Republic of Vietnam covers 329,560 square kilometres. With shores on the Eastern Sea — also known as the South China Sea — the country borders Cambodia, Laos and China.

Until the 1980s, Vietnam had an economic policy that conformed to the command system. Leaders at the national level made centralised decisions about local production, often without knowledge of local conditions. Produce raised or goods manufactured in one locality were shipped to the central level and then distributed back to the localities, creating huge inefficiencies and losses, due to mould, rats and slippage. Manufacturing was very limited because the French colonialists had concentrated on extracting raw materials and emphasised neither industry nor infrastructure. Manufacturing equipment was old and rusty. In addition, the US-led embargo that started in 1964, prevented people and firms in Vietnam from legally replacing industrial parts patented in the United States. In late 1986, Vietnam launched its *Doi-Moi* Model — literally "renovation" — laying the path to a free-market economy. Under the command economy, farming had been done through farm co-operatives. These were privatised in 1988, with the land divided among families of the community. The result was a stunning surge in productivity.

[1]This chapter is based on information obtained from a variety of sources, including: the General Statistics Office of Vietnam; the Ministry of Industry and Trade; the Planning and Trading Department of Artex Saigon; and the Vietnam Trade Promotion Agency. Travel to Vietnam was provided by McGill University. The chapter includes historical material that first appeared in Dana (1994a; 1994b; 1994c; 1999b; 2002), and benefitted greatly from the personal assistance of Lady Borton, Field Director, American Friends Service Committee, in Hanoi.

Farmers who had once lolled about on their production teams worked their own fields from "dew to dew." Within a year, Vietnam began to export rice; by 1989, villagers and city people were no longer gaunt. Up to 1990, most trade was with socialist block countries. Until the late 1980s, the state-supported currency differed widely with the real market value, and this led to a parallel rate.

Figure 17.1 Working in the Fields; photograph by Léo-Paul Dana.

The state concentrated its efforts on agriculture, the rural economy and the domestic market. Thus, changes of *Doi-Moi* took place first in the agricultural sector. In the attempt to ensure domestic growth, Vietnam implemented a drastic programme of economic reform. Regulations that formerly limited the private sector, were substantially reduced and Vietnam moved away from being a very highly centralised command economy. By 1995,Vietnam had joined the Association of Southeast Asian Nations (ASEAN), signed a treaty with the European Union, and established diplomatic relations with the United States.

Smith-Hunter (2006) noted that only 20% of women entrepreneurs in Vietnam receive training, compared to nearly a half of their male counterparts. In a study of bribery focusing on 606 entrepreneurs in Vietnam, De Jong, Tu, and Van Ees (2012) found that bribery allows entrepreneurs to develop and foster a network of informal relationships with public officials, and reap the accompanying benefits.

Historical Overview

Tonkin, the northern part of today's Vietnam, was originally inhabited by different ethnic groups with the Viet predominating. It was conquered by the Chinese in 111 BC and became a province of the Chinese Empire. Further south was the Kingdom of Champa, founded in the 3rd century. It eventually came to be under the control of the Viet peoples, as they expanded from the north. After a lengthy civil war, the Vietnamese kingdom was split into two in 1660. The extreme south of Vietnam, known as Cochin-China, remained under Khmer rule until a century later. Finally, the whole of Vietnam was unified in 1802, by the Nguyen dynasty. Its capital was Hué.

The people of the north are of a Sino-Tibetan race that has strong Han influences, from many years of Chinese domination; the people of the south tend to have been exposed to slightly more Dionysian and fewer Promethean values. While the people of the north adopted a northern sect of Buddhism, those of Cochin-China included followers of a southern sect, with some Hindu influence.

In 1859, in order to protect persecuted Catholic missionaries and their economic interests in the region, France invaded the south. In 1867, Cochin-China became a colony. In 1885, France established a protectorate over Tonkin and to the south. Hence, France controlled all of today's Vietnam, which it grouped with Cambodia and Laos to create a new entity called *Indochine française* — French Indochina. In 1887, Hanoi became the seat of the French colonial government. Many resented French rule, and Confucian scholars led some of the earliest revolutionary movements. Particularly famous is Phan Boi Chau, whose "Go East Movement" sent young revolutionaries to study in Japan. One candidate decided to go west instead; Nguyen Tat Thanh, later known as Ho Chi Minh — Ho the Enlightened — left Sai Gon (later Saigon) in 1911 on a French steamer, on which he worked as a cook's assistant. In 1930, using the name Nguyen Ai Quoc, *i.e.,* Nguyen the Patriot, he got together with other revolutionaries in Hong Kong, where they established the Indochinese Communist Party, with the hope of overthrowing the French colonial administration. In the fall of 1940, Japan invaded, but the Japanese kept the French administration in place. Ho Chi Minh returned to the region in early 1941, and lived in a cave in Pac Bo, in Cao Pang Province, on the Vietnamese side of the Chinese border. In 1941, he formed Viet Minh. When, during the war, the Japanese army confiscated rice from Vietnamese peasants, two million Vietnamese people starved to death (Dinh, 1989).

Figure 17.2 France Provided Infrastructure; photograph by Léo-Paul Dana.

Figure 17.3 French Colonial Architecture; photograph by Léo-Paul Dana.

On August 16, 1945, within days of the Nagasaki bombing, Viet Minh gathered at Tan Trao, in the northern highlands, where they planned the August Revolution; on August 19, they seized key buildings. On August 25, Emperor Bao Dai yielded to the Viet Minh in Hué. After the revolution, Ho Chi Minh entered Hanoi and wrote the *Declaration of Independence* while hidden in the second floor of an import-export company. The declaration was read before 500,000 people in Hanoi, on September 2, 1945. Ho Chi Minh declared himself president of a newly independent country, but his government faced huge challenges. Only 5% of the population was literate. In accordance with the Potsdam Conference Agreements, Nationalist Chinese occupied Hanoi along with French troops.

Less than three weeks after the declaration of independence, the French landed again in the south, taking over Saigon and regaining control of its former colony of Cochin-China. The Associated States of Viet Nam — formerly Tonkin, Annam, and Cochin-China — became a member of the French Union. The spirit of entrepreneurship thrived, and the nation welcomed refugees from communist China.

Long described the sidewalks of Saigon, "Barbers hang mirrors on trees, unfold stools, and are ready for business. Dentists pull teeth and fit gold replacements before admiring audiences. Physicians cup and massage their patients...Squatting vendors sell anything from American cigarettes to lottery tickets and incense sticks (1952, p. 289)."

Following their defeat at Dien Bien Phu, in 1954, the French were expelled from the region. The cease-fire of July 22, 1954 led to an armistice agreement, in Geneva, creating the Democratic Republic of Vietnam — North Vietnam — north of the Ben Hai River, and the Republic of Vietnam — South Vietnam — to its south. Small-scale landowners and Catholics fled from the north to the south. Samuels (1955) reported that about forty civilians moved from the south to the north; interviewees suggest that there were many more who went north for regrouping, expecting to return home after elections that were scheduled to take place in 1956.

In accordance with the Geneva Agreement, the Viet Minh took control of Hanoi on October 10, 1954, and of Hai Duong on October 30. Hanoi, formerly the administrative capital of Indochina, became the capital of North Vietnam. Saigon became the capital of South Vietnam. At the suggestion of Cardinal Spellman, Ngo Dinh Diem — who had been living in the United States for over three years — was brought back to Saigon to lead the government of the South. In North Vietnam, the government — led by Ho Chi Minh — instituted a programme of land reform. The First Five-Year Plan, 1961–1965, put emphasis on basic heavy industries.

The Viet Cong — South Vietnamese who sympathised with the North — fought a civil war, with weapons and leadership from communist North Vietnam and "the Viet Cong ruled nearly half of Viet Nam (White, 1961b, p. 447)." During the war, Sochurek reported, "Despite 30 guards to a train, Viet Cong guerrillas take a fearful toll: Mines and ambushes have killed or injured hundreds of passengers, railroad employees, and soldiers, and have wrecked scores of cars and engines (1964, p. 414)." By 1967, more Americans had died in Vietnam than in the American Revolution of 1776 (White, 1967). In 1975, South Vietnam, formerly a rice exporter, was living off daily airlifts of rice from Louisiana. This major source of food ceased in April 1975, when the communists took over. All bank accounts in former South Vietnam were frozen, and its people were told they had twelve hours to take their cash to the banks, as their currency would become valueless. Each family was limited to a maximum saving, the equivalent of approximately $200.

All firms were nationalised. Government newspapers replaced the existing dailies. Private homes were raided and "decadent" literature was burned. Schools of bourgeois learning were closed, as Hanoi spread its Marxist ideology. With the new regime came a shortage of foreign exchange, resulting in a shortage of imported inputs, new materials and spare parts. Domestic supply could not satisfy consumer demand. Further constraints in capacity utilisation were brought about by shortages in energy production and a weak transportation network. Furthermore, state firms in Vietnam lacked access to modern technology. Their costs of production were high, relative to the quality of products. Chinh explained, "The State of the Socialist Republic of Vietnam is a proletarian dictatorship state…it represses counter-revolutionaries, eliminates the comprador capitalist class and the remnants of the feudal landlord class, carries out socialist transformation of the ... private capitalist economic element…(1977, p. 1)."

Figure 17.4 Promoting Nationalism; photograph by Léo-Paul Dana.

Toward the *Doi-Moi* Model

The Second Five-Year Plan (1976–1980) set a 16–18% targeted annual growth rate for industrial production; actual outcome was 0.6%. In 1978, the Sino-Vietnamese War prompted an exodus of ethnic Chinese from Vietnam. In 1979 and 1980 there were shortages of basic consumer goods including food, as well as shortages of inputs to the industrial sector.

Liberalisation, in 1981, helped industrial output to grow beyond 9% annually during the early 1980s. Growth was primarily generated by small and medium-sized enterprises, some in the private sector. A Three-Plan System made this possible. Enterprises operating under Plan A were required to produce using state-supplied inputs and to sell their outputs to the state at low command prices. Plan B permitted firms to acquire inputs on their own, and to sell their outputs independently, provided that the profits were used to purchase additional inputs. Plan C permitted entrepreneurs to diversify and to sell "minor" products with no centrally planned external control.

In 1982, the Fifth Party Congress officially adopted its new economic orientation, recognising the need to: shift emphasis from heavy to light industry; transfer resources to the agricultural sector; and promote exports. As production activities were partially deregulated, individual enterprises were granted some autonomy. In 1984, the government further relaxed restrictions. When a new currency was introduced, in 1985, old dong were exchanged at a rate of 10:1, but only up to a set quantity. Also in 1985, consumer price subsidies were replaced by wage adjustments. Most prices remained under central control, determined by an average cost-plus formula; however, some costs were not accurately assessed.

The nation's economic development followed an import substitution model. Industrial policy in Vietnam was influenced by that of the former Soviet Union. Centrally planned industrialisation was aimed at the domestic production of heavy industry such as capital goods. The state supplied the input and capital requirements of enterprise and set quantitative output targets. Policy typically leaned towards achieving self-sufficiency, but neglected opportunities for international trade.

Coupled with fighting and the embargo, the command economy led to desperate poverty. The attempt to be self-sufficient had led to insufficient specialisation. Investment had been scattered over too many projects, in a haphazard fashion. Despite vertical integration, there was a lack of horizontal integration.

Innovation and creativity were stifled. Research, science and technology for industry were weak. Energy supplies were lacking.

Export-oriented activities were not being given enough attention and there were insufficient links between foreign markets and Vietnamese producers, the latter lacking awareness about international quality, prices and demands. There was more incentive for a farmer to chop down a mango tree and use it for firewood than to harvest the fruit. Aggravating the situation for producers in Vietnam, there were constant limitations on capital resources and raw material supplies, especially imported ones. Construction periods were typically overrun and numerous projects remained unfinished. Reform or more specifically "renovation" became a necessity.

Major change was introduced towards the end of December 1986, when the Sixth Congress of the National Representatives of the Communist Party of Vietnam approved economic reforms that eliminated much of the basic apparatus of control. This programme was called *Doi-Moi*. Individual entrepreneurs obtained the right to get involved in light industry. Profits were defined as the difference between the value of sales and *allowable* costs; enterprises remained liable for taxes on profits. Restrictions on wages were abolished and firms were given the right to recruit as per their needs.

In contrast to the experiences in Eastern Europe and in the former Soviet Union — where a market economy was decreed to have replaced communism without a long transition period — *Doi-Moi* evolved slowly and gradually, ushering in entrepreneurship initially as a *complement* to state enterprise, rather than as a *replacement*. The *Doi-Moi* Model marked the path to: transition to a market economy; openness to the West; openness to overseas Vietnamese (Viet Kieu); and greater personal freedom. In 1988, the state divided huge co-operative farms into private holdings, releasing private initiative. In July 1988, the Resolution of New Regulation for the Non-State Economic Sector called for making entrepreneurs important components of the national economy. On September 5, 1988, the Council of Ministries adopted Decree 139, regulating the implementation of the Law on Foreign Investment in Vietnam; this set forth procedures relating to foreign investment and the corresponding tax structure. In the case of a joint venture, the foreign party usually contributes capital and technology. A breakthrough in the reintroduction of market-oriented policies followed in 1989, when the predominantly rural population was granted the right to sell output at market prices; furthermore, this right could be inherited.

Whereas Vietnam had been near starvation prior to this reform, the nation soon became the world's third largest rice exporter. Without abandoning Marxist ideals, young intellectuals came to the conclusion that a market economy with a private small business sector and entrepreneurship is the quickest means to attain the benefits sought out by socialism. The result has been a unique blend of socialist and free enterprise policies whereby the entrepreneur is the agent for social change as described by Barth (1963; 1967), but in a socialist state, *i.e.*, the government affirmed its commitment to socialism. New billboards began to promote *Doi-Moi*, while others continued urging workers to follow socialism.

Most prices in Vietnam were released from centralised control, in 1989. Exceptions were electricity, petrol and transport. This policy enabled entrepreneurs and the small business sector to begin setting prices as a function of market forces, while keeping energy and transportation costs artificially low, thus indirectly subsidising entrepreneurship. That same year, the State Committee for Co-operation and Investment was established, as the body responsible for foreign direct investment and for providing guidance to foreign entrepreneurs. Taiwanese entrepreneurs were among the first to arrive in Vietnam *en masse*, and Singaporeans soon followed.

In 1990, the Ministry for External Economic Relations was absorbed into the Ministry of Commerce. The former had already issued about 100 permits to provincial and local enterprises — and a similar amount to central government firms — permitting them to export directly and allowing them to keep a substantial proportion of the foreign exchange earned. Also in 1990, the Council of Non-State Enterprises was established, specifically to promote the interests of the private sector. Very significant was Decree 28, adopted by the National Assembly on June 30, 1990. The new legislation was named the "Law on Amendments and Additions to a Number of Articles of the Law on Foreign Investment in Vietnam." Towns and cities sprouted into a plethora of street stalls, restaurants and hotels; by late 1990, Hanoi had a reliable telephone system. Motorcycles, taxis and private cars competed for space. Formerly quiet towns became bustling cities.

Relaxation of regulations made it possible for foreign entrepreneurs to hold 100% of the equity of a business in Vietnam. The Law of Foreign Investment was enacted to protect assets of foreign enterprises from nationalisation. Legislation also made new foreign-owned ventures income-tax exempt for the first four years of operations.

Figure 17.5 Private Initiative; photograph by Léo-Paul Dana.

Vietnam established that all enterprises belonging to the socialist state would develop plans directed by the market. Between June 24 and June 27, 1991, the Seventh Congress of the National Representatives of the Communist Party of Vietnam — also known as the Seventh Party Congress — reaffirmed its commitment to *Doi-Moi*, showing support for economic reform, while maintaining political stability was held. On the agenda were concerns such as "serious inflation; unstable production; increasing unemployment; wages and salaries below subsistence level ... widespread corruption and other evils ... an erosion of cultural, spiritual and moral values; and declining confidence in the Party and the State (Communist Party of Vietnam, 1991, p. 150)." Confirming the leading role of the Communist Party of Vietnam, and its adherence to Marxist-Leninism, the Seventh Party Congress renewed the strategy of *Doi-Moi*: "The overall objectives of this strategy up to the year 2000 are to emerge from crisis, stabilise the socio-economic situation, strive to overcome the condition of poverty and underemployment, improve living conditions for the country to develop more rapidly in the early 21st century (Communist Party of Vietnam, 1991, p. 157).

In 1991, the Viet Kieu community, numbering 700,000 in the United States alone, contributed approximately $500 million to the Vietnamese economy. In 1992, the Labour Ministry announced a new reform aimed at encouraging new jobs. The minimum wage for employees of foreign firms was *reduced* to $30 monthly. Also in 1992, the government began the process of privatising state enterprises. The first to be offered to the private sector was the Legamex garment factory, run by Ms. Nguyen Thi Son in Ho Chi Minh City. This firm exported 1,700,000 jackets to Germany in 1992. The embargo still in effect at the time, entrepreneurs ordered clothing in Hanoi, shipped them to South Korea where South Korean labels were put on them, and re-exported to the United States under their quota.

A tight economic policy succeeded in reducing inflation from over 700% in 1986, to about 10% in 1993. In 1994, the United States dropped its trade embargo, and American companies rushed into Vietnam (Dana, 1997a). Per capita income jumped from $190 in 1994, to $275 the following year. In July 1995, Vietnam became the seventh member of ASEAN. Also in 1995, the National Assembly adopted a new Civil Code, which laid the foundation for a market economy. That same year, import duties of 60% were reduced. A government resolution, on October 21, 1995, established the Ministry of Planning and Investment.

The Eighth Congress of the Representatives of the Communist Party of Vietnam took place in June 1996. The 1996-2000 Plan called for $21 billion, in foreign investment, to complement an equal amount in local investments.

In 1997, Vietnam's exports grew by 24%, while inflation was 4%. Although the Vietnamese dong depreciated by about 20% compared to the dollar, exports grew by only 3.5% between January and October 1998. Inflation approached 10%. The Asian Financial Crisis had hit Vietnam, and this was of concern because 70% of Vietnam's exports depended on neighbours in the region (Rondinelli and Litvack, 1999).

The state's Central Committee convened in October 1998, to outline a new strategy. In contrast to policy that had, in recent years, designated entrepreneurs as economic engines of growth, the Central Committee decided that state-owned enterprises would lead the Vietnamese economy, giving priority to the local market. The state was neither rushed to privatise state firms, nor to reform the almost obsolete banking sector. Instead, the government decided to focus its efforts, during 1999, on agricultural development, the rural economy and the domestic market. In April 2001, the Ninth Congress initiated further reforms.

Infrastructure

In 1989, Hanoi's electrical system still fluctuated between 80 and 360 volts, and there was not yet a reliable domestic telephone system. Most Vietnamese had yet to see a computer or a photocopier. Because of the embargo, the banking system could handle few transfers; funds were routed via Laos. The state-owned banks favoured state-owned firms.

In July 1992, Banque Indosuez of France and Bangkok Bank of Thailand became the first two foreign banks to open branches in Ho Chi Minh City. By 1993, the ANZ Bank had a branch in Hanoi as well as a representative office in Ho Chi Minh City. Other banks, which were quick to enter Vietnam, included Banque Nationale de Paris, Credit Lyonais, Nordbanke, and the Export-Import Bank of Japan. Thus, the banking infrastructure began taking shape and commercial credit slowly began to evolve. Yet, personal cheques for domestic accounts were still unheard of, and most entrepreneurs paid their employees in cash. With the dollar worth over 10,000 dong, and 200-dong notes being common, cash transactions were sometimes bulky. Meanwhile, foreign banks expressed their concerns: they could only repatriate 30% of their capital, and they were not given the three-year tax holiday granted to foreign entrepreneurs. Furthermore, there was a high tax structure for banks: 50% income tax as well as a turnover tax.

By 2002, a plentiful and reliable source of electricity made possible many developments. Computer literacy had long surged with personal computers in urban households and neighbourhood Internet cafés offering affordable rates. International organisations, businesses and foreigners used standard bank transfers. Most international organisations transferred salary payments directly into the private bank accounts of staff.

The Impact of the *Doi-Moi* Model

Vietnam's model of economic transition has been stunning; it is quite a unique model, as it has achieved a harmony between government firms still operating under a system of centralisation, and the small business sector operating independently, yet having access to state alternatives as specified by Resolution No. 16. Whereas transition from centralised planning to market economy in the Soviet bloc was very abrupt and economic reform in Yugoslavia very violent (Dana, 1994d; 2005), the *Doi-Moi* Model of evolutionary change introduced a gradual and smooth transition in Vietnam. Private enterprise is thriving side by side a state-controlled sector.

While many co-operatives have been privatised, most of those still in existence are small to medium-sized businesses. As well, there are countless micro-enterprises in the handicraft and agriculture sectors. The small business sector, including handicrafts as well as small industry, accounts for a significant part of industrial production and exports. Current exports include: bamboo products, bicycle tires and tubes, cotton yarn, glass products, handicrafts, processed forestry products, rubber gloves, and silk yarn.

As a result of *Doi-Moi*, the small business sector in the Socialist Republic of Vietnam now includes co-operatives; family businesses; other private enterprises; and joint ventures between state and private interests. The first three operate free from state control; in the fourth, government influence is limited to contractual agreement. Although the Socialist Republic of Vietnam has chosen to *retain* socialist ideals, to the ethnographer, Vietnam appears to be thriving more on free enterprise than on Marxist ideology. There is a constant buzz of mercantile energy.

Entrepreneurs optimise the use of their minimal resources, and make due despite a poor infrastructure. The spirit of entrepreneurship is in the air, even at the subsistence level. One villa advertises — with a spelling mistake — "Telex Coffee Dansing Massage." Not far, a man sits by the roadside with a pump and fills tires, while another rents out the use of a scale.

In Ho Chi Minh City, one is overwhelmed by entrepreneurial activity; even children sell a variety of merchandise, including pocket video games, T-shirts, cigarettes, fans, money from French Indochina, and stamp collections. The young peddlers follow their prospective clients, for blocks on end, in an attempt to sell their goods. Nearby, one shed is a pancake restaurant when it is not being used as a bus depot. "Mr. Fix-It" earns his living by selling a wide variety of inventory, ranging from motorcycles and caviar to tiger skins. Not far, a woman sits on the sidewalk, feathering ducks. A man unloads fresh pork from a wooden container onto the street. Nearby, fish are being laid out in tidy rows; some of the fish are still flopping on the merciless, hot pavement. At the market, items for sale include bananas, coconuts, dragon fruits, grapes, guavas, mint leaves, oranges, papayas, pineapples, and jeruk — green pomelos sweeter and larger than grapefruit. Chicken, duck, fish and pork are sold alive or dead, or in between. Also for sale is a mixture of green peas, coconut and cane sugar wrapped in palm leaves fashioned into tiny boxes held together by bamboo toothpicks. Self-employed vendors sell food to passengers on state-run trains. While some children run along the aisles fanning passengers. Others sell sodas; they open the bottles with their teeth.

Where the train stops in the morning, locals have washcloths for rent as well as buckets of water for passengers to refresh themselves. Through the windows of the train, merchants sell bread, coconut water, fruit, juice, pastries and sodas. Blind musicians come on board the train to sing or play a melody, while an assistant usually holds out a cap for donations. Simultaneously, one may buy a chicken breast with rice cooked in chicken fat, served on a palm leaf, and eaten with one's fingers. Other passengers prefer to crunch a raw, fertilised duck egg, just prior to hatching, feathers, bones and all, lightly salted. Still other passengers enjoy having a local cook board the train and flame a fish at their seat.

Figure 17.6 Entrepreneur Selling Breakfast to Passengers; photograph by Léo-Paul Dana.

Figure 17.7 Young Locksmith; photograph by Léo-Paul Dana.

A glance out of the open window supplies passengers with constant stimulus. Catholic churches line the railway tracks side by side with Buddhist temples still in use. Farmers in rice fields, with water buffaloes as tractors, work their land in utter peacefulness while but a few kilometres away remnants of a bloody war fill the landscape. Graves with crosses, and graves with dragons adorning them dot the landscape, with the sorrow of war still hanging about them.

Figure 17.8 Ambulant Vendor Making Sidewalk Sale; photograph by Léo-Paul Dana.

Some people live a few feet from the railroad tracks in shacks with no kitchen, toilet or running water. Subtle hands reach into the passenger compartment of the train. Others sling a hammock under the railway cars and alight where they choose, while still others enjoy a warm breeze sitting on top of the wagons as clandestine passengers.

In Hoi-an, an untouched heritage site, the market is the life of the town. For sale at the market are *chuoi tieu*, a variety of bananas with an attractive colour and taste. A few minutes away, peaceful serenity reigns. Lining the waterfront are storefronts untouched for 200 years or more and buildings inscribed with Chinese characters dating back to the era prior to French rule. Along the road to Hanoi — in addition to modern petrol stations — stalls display one-litre Coca-Cola bottles filled with kerosene or petrol for sale. Others sell fuel for cigarette lighters.

Figure 17.9 Work Ethic; photograph by Léo-Paul Dana.

Every day, 50,000 peddlers transport goods between Vietnam and China. Women carry wicker baskets, each balanced at the end of a pole leaning across the shoulders. In the baskets are cats and dogs destined for Chinese dinner tables.

Pluralism

Ever since the French era, the Hoa — a significant ethnic Chinese minority — were very active in the small business sector of Vietnam; the French — not wanting to deal directly with those they had colonised — encouraged the Hoa to serve as "middleman" entrepreneurs in the region. These continued to dominate sectors of the economy after 1954. Auster and Aldrich (1984), Bonacich (1973), Cherry (1990), Dana (1997b), and Loewen (1971) discuss middleman entrepreneurship.

The Chinese in Vietnam — of whom 57% are Cantonese — comprise about 3% of this country's population, but they control a disproportionate percentage of the local economy. Cho Lon — the Chinatown of Ho Chi MinhCity — was founded by Chinese immigrants in the 18th century, and the settlement was fused into Saigon in 1932 (Long, 1952). With the exception of scooters, there are relatively few motor vehicles, so *cyclos* can weave their way through traffic. En route, one encounters motorcycles bound for market, carrying bunches of ducks and chickens. Feathers seem to appear everywhere. On many street corners, food is served, including rice soup, fish, duck, chicken, pork, vegetables and coconut paste. Most dishes are served in re-used plastic bowls, not necessarily washed between users.

Most people in Vietnam are Buddhists, Confucians or Taoists. During colonial rule, the French converted 1,600,000 Vietnamese to Catholicism and many of these fled from the north to the south, in 1954 and 1955 (Samuels, 1955).

Toward the Future

In 1952, George W. Long, writing for *National Geographic*, noted a young lieutenant in Vietnam raising his glass and saying: "To our American visitors. I hope they will return someday. And when they do, I hope they will find this country happy, prosperous, and at peace (Long, 1952, p. 328)."

Three score later, Vietnam is at peace, its people appear happy, and prosperity is spreading — although not at an equal rate. The Vietnam-US Bilateral Trade Agreement established guarantees against expropriation, and mechanisms for dispute resolution. Yet, there is still some concern about property rights.

As discussed by Dollar (1999), it would be misleading to think of Vietnam as having state-sector households distinct from private-enterprise households. Instead, it is common for employees of the state to supplement their incomes with self-employment. Although large state enterprises may be inefficient, people in Vietnam demonstrate a strong work ethic. In contrast to China, where individuals dare speak up against their boss, the Vietnamese tend to be very disciplined, and with a mild temperament. As the state enterprises gradually lose their monopolies, a new middle class of *nouveau-riche* entrepreneurs is emerging.

The small business sector will continue to be important to development of the Vietnamese economy in the future. Firms may be established rapidly, and they can produce quick returns on investment. Given the low level of wages, new ventures are likely to utilise labour-intensive technology, creating considerable employment. Small enterprises are flexible as to location, and may be situated in rural areas, thereby reducing development imbalances.

There are nevertheless constraints. Tan and Lim (1993) reported that 80% of business people surveyed in Vietnam found bureaucracy and corruption to be major obstacles to enterprise. More recently, Venard explained:

> Vietnamese corruption arises from four factors: strict relations between the government and some private interests, decentralisation to regional governments which makes them more powerful and less controllable, under-payment of state employees, and vague laws governing commercial transaction (1998, p. 87).

The government is faced with the challenging task of dismantling bureaucratic structures no longer relevant to the economic model of *Doi-Moi.* In addition, Vietnamese entrepreneurs are faced with a complex tariff scale; local taxes; business turnover tax; and a high personal income tax. Entrepreneurs often prefer to bribe an under-paid tax collector than to pay the taxes that they owe. Whereas Vietnamese entrepreneurs are heavily taxed, foreign direct investment is encouraged. Vietnamese entrepreneurs are therefore getting "foreign devil companies" set up in Hong Kong on their behalf. Profits are made in Hong Kong, resulting in less tax and less bureaucratic interference. A reduction in government intervention would allow entrepreneurs to concentrate more on business than on avoiding government regulation. Furthermore, given that Vietnam still has considerable import duties and that large-scale smuggling is known to occur, the entrepreneur who imports legally finds himself at a disadvantage. Appropriate government action should correct this.

Figure 17.10 Cycling a Toshiba Delivery; photograph by Léo-Paul Dana.

Exports of the Socialist Republic of Vietnam were traditionally destined to former East Germany and other socialist countries where demand exceeded supply. Quality, marketing and advertising were not concerns. Vietnamese entrepreneurs have since learned about a service orientation and about marketing, but they do not necessarily understand long-term environmental and sustainability issues. Nor have they come to terms with the fickle nature of capitalism, as their coffee rides the market one year but not the next. Government promotion of entrepreneurship should include the training of entrepreneurs, provision of industrial estates and common facility services, including consultant services and labour relations services. Also beneficial would be access to financing for development, industrial research, and assistance in procuring inputs.

Vietnam has introduced reforms, but has maintained a hands-on approach. Until recently, considerable resources were being expended, in order to spread the socialist model throughout Vietnam. The *Doi-Moi* Model allowed entrepreneurship to gradually play an increasingly important role — without overthrowing the socialist establishment. Institutions and regulatory frameworks are slowly, but continuously, being adapted to the needs of the future.

Figure 17.11 Manufacturing Panasonic Products; photograph by Léo-Paul Dana.

Taiwanese entrepreneurs are important investors in Vietnam. They bring technology, they create jobs, and they allow Vietnam to benefit from their marketing skills and networks abroad, contributing to exports. However, these people are concerned about what they perceive to be excessive government intervention in the economy.

Meanwhile Vietnamese entrepreneurs have been venturing abroad. Thai and Chong (2013) examined internationalisation of SMEs from Vietnam.

Case Study: Vo Quy Beverages[2]

Figure 17.12 Delivery of Coca-Cola; photograph by Léo-Paul Dana.

Report on the Beverage Sector

Under French colonial rule, Les Brasseries et Glacières d'Indochine was established and it became the leading beverage manufacturer; with the independence of Vietnam, its name was changed to Chuong Duong Beverage Factory, and it maintained itself as Vietnam's largest producer of carbonated beverages (Dana and Dana, 1999).

In 1954, Vietnam was divided into the Democratic Republic of Vietnam (North Vietnam) with Hanoi as its capital; and the Republic of Vietnam (South Vietnam), with Saigon as its capital. Only in South Vietnam did free enterprise survive. Until the surrender of Saigon, Chuong Duong Beverage Factory bottled Coca-Cola, and the Vietnamese consumed 500 million bottles of Coke annually. In 1975, South Vietnam

---

[2] This case was co-authored with Teresa Elizabeth Dana, formerly at Thammasat University, Thailand.

was overrun by North Vietnam. With the advent of communism, the name of Saigon was changed to Ho Chi Minh City. American investments were nationalised and Coca-Cola was officially banned from Vietnam. The United States responded with an embargo. Nevertheless, cans of Coca-Cola were smuggled into Vietnam, as shown in the Table below.

Table 17A Coca-Cola available in Vietnam during US Embargo

Country of Origin	Producer	Format	Ingredients
Indonesia	PT. Pan Java Bottling Company, Semarang, Indonesia	330ml can	Carbonated water, sugar, Coca-Cola concentrate
Singapore	Fraser & Neave (S) Pte Ltd., 457 Jalan Ahmad Ibrahim, Singapore 2263	325ml can	Carbonated water, sugar, caramel colour, phosphoric acid, caffeine and other flavourings

Speculation about the ban being removed led to serious negotiations. In July 1993, the Vietnam Ministry of Light Industry's Chuong Dong Beverage Factory, in Ho Chi Minh City, agreed to enter a joint venture after the eventual removal of the US embargo; the partner of the Chuong Dong's Beverage Factory was Coca-Cola Indochina Pte. Ltd., a Singapore-based joint venture between F&N Coca-Cola Pte. Ltd. of Singapore and Thai Pure Drinks Ltd. (partially owned by the Coca-Cola Company). Negotiations resulted in agreement about a joint venture, 60% held by Coca-Cola Indochina Pte. Ltd. This was the plan to produce, bottle, and distribute 90 million litres of Coca-Cola annually, in the south of Vietnam. This agreement was subject to: (i) removal of the embargo; and (ii) approval by the State Committee for Cooperation and Investment.

In the north of the country, Indochina Pte. Ltd. applied to establish Coca-Cola Ngoc Hoi Soft Drink Co. Ltd., a joint venture with Vietnam National Foodstuff Import-Export Co., also known as Vinalimex. This project, 16 kilometers south of Hanoi, would have an annual capacity of 8.5 million cases. The accord stipulated that after the embargo would be lifted, then Vinalimex would contribute a plot of land 15 kilometres south of Hanoi in exchange for 30% of this new venture, producing, bottling, and distributing Coca-Cola, Sprite and eventually Fanta Orange, for the north of Vietnam. Annual production capacity was projected to reach one million litres.

Also in 1993, PepsiCo signed an exclusive bottling agreement with International Beverage Company, a joint venture between Hong Kong-based Macondray Co. Inc. and Saigon General Service & Manufacturing Co. This would come into effect once the US embargo would be lifted. Not to be confused with the IBC of the United States (Independent Beverages Company), the Vietnamese International Beverage Company (IBC) was a relatively small business in Tan Thoi Hiep, a village near Ho Chi Minh City, in Vietnam. IBC was a relatively insignificant soft drink firm, with 200 employees. IIBC general director, Pham Phu Ngoc Trai, explained, "In 1993, our market share was very insignificant as we were able to produce and sell only about 5 million litres."

On February 3, 1994, the United States lifted the 19-year embargo against Vietnam was lifted[3]. On February 4, Pepsi-Cola bottles began rolling off the assembly line at International Beverage Company, near Ho Chi Minh City.

Both Coca-Cola and PepsiCo launched impressive marketing campaigns, including billboards, television advertisements, dancing cola cans, giant, inflatable cola bottles, and promotional pageants. While Ogilvy & Mather produced a television ad for Pepsi-Cola, McCann-Erickson prepared a commercial for Coca-Cola. However, the government's State Committee for Cooperation and Investment denied the application for Coca-Cola Indochina Pte. Ltd. to produce their soft-drinks in Ho Chi Minh City. In response, Coca-Cola approached the Pacific Beverage Company to produce Coca-Cola products for consumers in southern Vietnam, subject to government approval, of course.

The rejection of Coca-Cola's Chuong Duong plans gave Pepsi a head start in Ho Chi Minh City. Although Coca-Cola's joint venture near Hanoi was approved, it would take months to build a factory. As long as Coca-Cola could not be produced in Vietnam, IBC grew and prospered, making, bottling and distributing Pepsi and 7-Up. Within weeks, IBC's market share jumped from an insignificant proportion to 55%. IBC

[3] The US placed an embargo against North Vietnam from 1964–1975. After the Vietnam War in 1975, the superpower placed an embargo on the entire country until the year 1994.

increased its staff from 220 employees in 1993 to 700 in 1994. In 1994, IBC production exceeded 32 million litres and sales soared from 27 billion dong in 1993 to 171 billion dong in 1994. During the mid-1990s, IBC had two production lines in Tan Thoi Hiep village, near Ho Chi Minh City. One produced 600 glass bottles per minute and the other 300 cans each minute. Coca-Cola was lagging far behind. This put Coca-Cola at a serious disadvantage, as PepsiCo claimed 55% of the country's soft-drink market. Mr. Victor Akiro, the general director of Coca-Cola Indochina Pte. Ltd., realised that it would be awhile before his Hanoi production could begin. A $20 million bottling plant had yet to be built. With respect to his Ho Chi Minh City project, he had expected to receive a government license before the arrival of summer 1994. (All foreign investments required a permit from the State Committee for Cooperation and Investment.)

Although the permit was received to build a Coca-Cola bottling plant 15 kilometres from Hanoi, Coca-Cola's proposal to produce near Ho Chi Minh City was rejected. Coca-Cola responded by importing canned Coke from Singapore. A problem arose, however, as a bottle of Pepsi-Cola retailed in Ho Chi Minh City at half the price of a can of Coca-Cola. Furthermore, Coca-Cola's Fanta Orange would only be launched in 1995, while 7-Up entered Vietnam in early 1994. Due to Coca-Cola's late re-entry into the Vietnamese market, PepsiCo was able to gain much market share. The Vietnamese are brand loyal and PepsiCo was able to win many hearts.

Thus, International Beverage Company (IBC), bottlers of Pepsi and 7-Up, became the largest soft-drink firm in Vietnam, with two production lines at its factory in the village of Tan Thoi Hiep, near Ho Chi Minh City; one plant produced 600 glass bottles per minute, and the other, 300 cans per minute. Coca-Cola lagged significantly behind, with only 39% market share.

In 1995 and in 1996, IBC received the Pepsi-Cola International bronze medal for product quality. By 1997, IBC was producing Orange Crush, Pepsi-Cola, Schweppes and 7-Up. Its investors included Macondray and Company Inc., of Singapore.

The Youth Market

Drinkers of cola in Vietnam tend to be young. People under 20 years of age make up 50% of the population here. The secondary market would include those in their twenties. These youths are part of a generation for whom hope for a better tomorrow is the primary reason for living. They grew up in a "controlled" environment for a good part of their formative years, and are now anxious for freedom and for all which they associate with it.

Success, independence, and living in harmony are very important to Vietnamese youth, who believe very much in the future of their country, and who have strong nationalistic pride. Traditional family values are looked highly upon and ultimate respect is given to one's parents. Vietnamese parents differ from their children, largely due to the fact that they have lived through the war. The youth have different goals and aspirations but do not rebel against their parents due to the strong family bond, as well as the financial security of living at home. The family is the strongest influence in anyone's life, even stronger than the police, the government or peers. The father is the nominal head; however, it is the mother who controls the purse strings.

The northerners desire independence much more than do their southern counterparts; the latter look for stability in their lives. These feelings seem to be direct consequences of the change from communism in the north and the effect of losing the war in the south.

Many young Vietnamese admire cultures which they perceive as more civilised, cultured, free and vast — for example, those of Japan, France, Australia and America. Such countries are seen as helping out to rebuild Vietnam.

Cultural Norms

Assumptions which can be made in the West are often irrelevant in Vietnam, and vice-versa. For instance, age in the West is determined according to one's birthday; in Vietnam, it is a function of a lunar new year's day, Tet Nguyen Dan. In the West, an index finger may be used to call someone; this is rude in Vietnam. To summon someone (within visible range), the polite procedure, in Vietnam, is to wave four fingers with the palm down.

When people from the country visit city folk, in Vietnam, it is common to bring a gift such as a chicken (alive) or rice (especially the sticky variety). When urban residents go to the villages, bread and tea are typical gifts. During the visit, people normally drink tea, and sometimes a meal is served. When passing food (or anything else), it is polite to use both hands. During a meal, rice bowls are held in the hand because it is considered rude to eat from a rice bowl which is on a table — only lazy persons would do such a thing. It is very disrespectful to leave food in one's bowl. After a meal, it is expected of female guests to offer to assist female hosts with washing the dishes.

Although it is socially unacceptable for members of the opposite sex to show affection in public, it is common for individuals of the same gender to hold hands while walking. It is important not to touch anybody's head, in Vietnam, as this is the body's most spiritual point.

Trust is very important in Vietnam, and can be obtained by earning people's respect and affection. The family — the strongest bond for any Vietnamese — is an extremely complex unit and quite difficult to influence. Loyalty, togetherness, harmony and nationalism are important values to understand, as they relate to the Vietnamese. Traditions include the importance of Tet and other festivals, as well as the traditional dress — the *ao dai* (a long silk or velour dress, worn over flowing pants), and the *non la* (conical hat).

Vietnam is a country of festivals, and Tet Nguyen Dan (the new year celebration) is the most respected of all. It is a time for family bonding, observing traditions and gift-buying. Festivals vary across regions, districts and provinces, and they are numerous. The Vietnamese word for festival is le hoi, and the literal translation means prayer-gathering; thus, festivals have a spiritual tone. Ritual offerings take place and many games are played. Village festivals have processions and each celebration is based on a myth. There are countless festivals which take place. Some follow a lunar calendar, while others follow the solar one.

Marriage is the most important event in a Vietnamese girl's life, even though she knows that once married, a life of intense hardship begins. Courting in this country can be described as that of the dating process of the 1950s in America. Shyness and inexperience with relationships lead to very innocent dating which typically begins only at the age of twenty. The family has complete authority over the entire process, and premarital sex (for women) is virtually non-existent. Dates generally take place at schools, at parks, at the movies, in the home and at pagodas. Girls look for a successful, intelligent and faithful partner, while men seek a caring, comforting and understanding woman. Being attractive and not asking too many questions also help women find a mate. The longer the hair of the woman, the more virtuous she is. While women place very high emphasis on honouring their marriage, it is common for men to openly have a mistress. Vietnamese women are generally very jealous of this.

Internationally branded items are viewed by Vietnamese youth, as a sign of the future, of economic prosperity and of internationalism. No matter how "local" an advertisement can be for an international brand, such products will have generic values attached to them.

Image is crucial for any product and the Vietnamese are quite literal when viewing advertisements. The unique selling point of a brand must be stated when launching a new product.

Confucian influence is strong and thus group values such as camaraderie, family, leadership and courage are highly regarded. Signs of prosperity and a positive future of togetherness are important. Anything that illustrates loneliness, individualism or rebellious images, would not be well received in Vietnamese culture.

Bottled or canned drinks are generally not consumed directly from the bottle or can. Instead, they are served with straws, in a plastic bag or in a glass filled with ice. High levels of dust in the cities make it attractive not to consume a beverage directly from its container. Ice is used because many vendors do not have refrigerators. If vendors sell a soft drink in the bottle or can, they will expect the customer to return the container immediately after drinking the contents. They will even follow the consumer until the drink is finished.

Promotion in Vietnam

Until October 1996, give-away promotions were illegal in Vietnam; Toshiba, for example, was shut down for having a lucky draw. New legislation made promotions legal, provided that permissions would be obtained. In 1997, Coca-Cola offered 300 ml. bottles for the same price as 200 ml. bottles, but this prompted accusations of price dumping.

Later, Coca-Cola proposed a mountain bike give-away. Bottle caps would be printed with a picture of one of six parts of a real mountain bike. In Hanoi, the Ha Tay People's Committee approved this promotion. In Ho Chi Minh City, however, the media claimed that promotional campaigns were not undertaken in good faith. Examples included a manufacturer which did not print all necessary parts which had to be collected in order to win; this made winning impossible.

Although the Ho Chi Minh City People's Committee approved of a Tiger Beer promotion, the committee rejected Coca-Cola's application.

(The rejection was not a surprise to those who realised that the committee had equity interest in IBC.)

Table 17B Ingredients of Colas Bottled in Vietnam

Coca-Cola[1]	Water, carbon dioxide, sugar, phosphoric acid, artificial colour 150d, caffeine, natural resources.
Pepsi[2]	Water, carbon dioxide, sugar, caramel, phosphoric acid, caffeine, natural flavour.

[1] Source: Fraser & Neaves (S) Pte. Ltd., 457 Jalan Ahmad Ibrahim, Singapore 2263.
[2] Source: International Beverage Company, Tan Thoi Hiep, Vietnam.

Table 17C Ingredients of Coca-Cola

Note: A typical Coca-Cola contains 180 kj/100 cm.[3]

Australia	Carbonated water, sugar, colour (caramel), phosphoric acid, flavour, caffeine.
Austria	Water, sugar, carbonation, caramel colouring, stabiliser E338, flavour, caffeine.
Belgium	Carbonated water, sugar, colour E150, food acid E338, natural flavours, caffeine.
Bolivia	Carbonated water, sugar, authorised colour, authorised acidulent, vegetable extracts.
Botswana	Carbonated water, sugar, caramel, phosphoric, flavourants, and caffeine.
Bulgaria	Water, sugar 100 g/l, carbon dioxide, caramel, mineral acid, flavour, caffeine max. 0.15 g/l.
Canada	Carbonated water, sugar/glucose-fructose, caramel colour, phosphoric acid, natural flavours and caffeine.
Chile	Carbonated water, sugar, caramel colour, phosphonic acid, natural flavours, caffeine.
Denmark	Water, sugar, carbonation, colour E150, stabiliser E338, flavour, caffeine.
France	Carbonated water, sugar, colour E150, food acid E338, vegetable extracts, caffeine.
Germany	Water, sugar, carbonation, colour E150, mineral acid E338, natural flavour and caffeine.
Greece	Water, sugar, carbon dioxide, colouring E150, acidifier E338, flavour, Coca-Cola extract, caffeine up to 0.013%.
Hong Kong	Carbonated water, sugar, caramel colour, phosphoric acid, caffeine and other flavourings.
Indonesia	Carbonated water, sugar, Coca-Cola concentrate.
Israel	Water, sugar, CO_2, caramel, acidifier, flavours and caffeine.
Italy	Water, sugar, CO_2, caramel colour, phosphoric acid, natural flavours, caffeine.
Jordan	Carbonated water, sugar, caramel colour, phosphoric acid, natural flavourings, caffeine.
Kenya	Carbonated water, sugar, caramel colouring, phosphoric acid, flavouring and caffeine.
Mexico	Carbonated water, sugar and concentrate.
Moldova	Water, sugar, carbon dioxide, caramel, mineral acid, natural flavour, caffeine.
Mozambique	Carbonated water, sugar, caramel, phosphoric acid, caffeinc, flavourings.
Namibia	Carbonated water, sugar, caramel, phosphoric acid, flavourings and caffeine.
Netherlands	Carbonated water, sugar, colour (caramel), phosphoric acid (E338), flavourings, caffeine.
Portugal	Water, sugar, CO_2, caramel colourant, acidulant E338, natural flavour, caffeine.
Romania	Water, sugar, carbon dioxide, caramel, mineral acid, flavour, caffeine.
Singapore	Carbonated water, sugar, caramel colour, phosphoric acid, caffeine and other flavourings.
South Africa	Carbonated water, sucrose, caramel, phosphoric acid, flavourants and caffeine.
Sweden	Carbonated water, sugar, colour E150, phosphoric acid, natural flavour, caffeine.
Switzerland	Water, sugar, carbonation, caramel colouring, mineral acid, caffeine, natural flavours.
United Arab Emirates	Carbonated water, sugar, caramel colour, ortho-phosphoric acid, natural flavours, caffeine.
United Kingdom	Carbonated water, sugar, colour (caramel), phosphoric acid, flavourings, caffeine.
United States	Carbonated water, high fructose corn syrup and/or sucrose, caramel color, phosphoric acid, natural flavors, caffeine.

Table 17D Sweetener of Low-Calorie Coca-Cola Products			
Market	**Product Name**	**Generic Description**	**Sweetener**
Bolivia	Diet Coca-Cola	Low calorie beverage	Aspartame and saccharine
Botswana	Diet Coke	Low joule beverage	Sodium saccharide and calcium cyclanate
Canada	Diet Coke	Diet soda	Aspartame
Chile	Diet Coca-Cola	Pleasant beverage	Aspartame
Denmark	Coca-Cola Light	Refreshing drink	Aspartame
Fiji	Diet Coke	Compound beverage	Cyclamate and saccharine
France	Coca-Cola Light	Refreshing vegetable extract beverage	Aspartame and acésulfame K
Israel	Diet Coca-Cola	Sugar-free dietetic beverage	Aspartame
South Africa	Diet Coke	Artificially sweetened soft drink	Acésulfame K and aspartame
Sweden	Coca-Cola Light	Soft drink	Aspartame
Switzerland	Coca-Cola Light	Low-calorie soft drink containing caffeine with sweeteners	Aspartame
United Kingdom	Diet Coca-Cola	Low calorie soft drink with vegetable extract	Aspartame
United States	Diet Coke	Diet cola	Aspartame

Table 17E Ingredients of Pepsi-Cola as Listed in Sample Markets

Abu Dhabi	Carbonated water, sugar, caramel colour E150, phosphoric acid, caffeine, natural flavourings.
Bolivia	Carbonated water, sugar, caramel colour, phosphoric acid, caffeine, Arabic Aum, natural flavours.
Bulgaria	Sugar 111 grams/litre, caffeine 0.1 grams/litre, phosphoric acid, natural essential oils, caramel colour and water.
Canada	Carbonated water, sugar, colour, phosphoric and citric acids, caffeine, flavour.
Chile	Carbonated water, sugar, caramel color, phosphoric acid, caffeine, natural flavours.
Dubai	Carbonated water, sugar, caramel colour (E150), phosphoric acid, caffeine, natural flavourings.
France	Carbonated water, sugar, caramel (E150), acidifier E338, caffeine, vegetable flavouring.
Greece	Water, sugar, carbon dioxide, colour E150, phosphoric acid, caffeine, vanilla flavouring.
India	Carbonated water, sugar, permitted flavours.
Jordan	Carbonated water, sugar, caramel, natural flavourings, caffeine, phosphoric acid.
Mexico	Carbonated water, sugar, Pepsi concentrate and artificial acidifier.
Moldova	Water, sugar, carbon dioxide, natural colorant, food acid, natural flavour.
Namibia	Carbonated water, sugar, caramel colour, phosphoric acid, flavourants, caffeine.
Netherlands	Carbonated water, colour E150, acid E338, natural flavourings, caffeine.
Poland	Carbonated water, sugar, caramel color, acidifier (E338), vegetable flavouring extracts, caffeine.
Romania	Treated water, sugar, carbon dioxide, natural colorant, caffeine, natural essential oils, food grade phosphoric acid.
United Kingdom	Carbonated water, sugar, colour (caramel), phosphoric acid, flavourings (including caffeine and extract of cola nuts).
United States	Carbonated water, high fructose corn syrup and/or sugar, caramel color, phosphoric acid, caffeine, citric acid and natural flavorings.
Vietnam	Water, carbon dioxide, sugar, caramel, phosphoric acid, caffeine, natural flavour.

Table 17F Ingredients of other Pepsico Products

Market	Product	Generic Description	Ingredients
Canada	Diet Pepsi	Sugar-free low calorie cola	Carbonated water, caramel colour, phosphoric acid, aspartame, sodium benzoate, caffeine, natural flavour, acesulfame.
Germany	Pepsi-Cola Light	Low calorie caffeine soft drink	Water, carbonation, colour E150, artificial sweetener aspartame, acidifier E338, acidity regulator E331, caffeine, stabiliser, natural flavour, acidifier E330.
Jordan	Diet Pepsi	Carbonated beverage	Carbonated water, caramel, aspartame, caffeine, phosphoric acid, natural flavourings.
Netherlands	Pepsi Light	Soft drink with cola extract	Carbonated water, colouring (caramel), artificial sweetener (aspartame), acidifier (E338), acidity regulator (E331), flavour (natural), caffeine.
United Kingdom	Diet Pepsi-Cola	Low calorie cola flavour drink	Carbonated water, colour (caramel), artificial sweetener (aspartame), phosphoric acid, preservative (sodium benzoate), flavourings (including caffeine, citric acid).

Case Study Assignment

An entrepreneur is seeking to launch a new venture, Vo Quy Beverages, to produce cola for the Vietnamese market. A friend of his was able to compile the information in appendices above. As his consultant, prepare a report on alternatives available and your recommendations. As well, prepare a business plan and a marketing plan for Mr. Vo Quy's new venture.

Chapter 18

Conclusion

Success depends on good timing, a proper environment and people in harmony.

— Chinese proverb

This book has surveyed the evolution of public policy on entrepreneurship in different contexts. Although governments across Asia recognise the importance of entrepreneurship, their respective promotion efforts differ greatly, reflecting national priorities, demographic factors and cultural values. Likewise, the entrepreneurship sector reflects historical and cultural factors, as well as public policy; in addition, social norms and education have an influence on entrepreneurship.

In Cambodia, the Khmer Rouge extinguished entrepreneurship, a sector that is re-establishing itself, in an environment of uncertainty. In China, entrepreneurship is being promoted as a supplement to the socialist economy. In India, entrepreneurs and their SMEs are helping the country become a superpower. In Indonesia, where the Chinese minority has been at the forefront of entrepreneurship, the state has been trying to promote entrepreneurship among the Indigenous *pribumis*. In Japan, small-scale entrepreneurship complements large corporations, and cultural values propagate inter-firm linkages. Credit policy in South Korea resulted in *chaebols* squeezing many entrepreneurs out of business; government measures have since intervened to assist small-scale entrepreneurship. In Laos, cultural values discouraged entrepreneurship among Lao men, resulting in opportunities for women and foreigners. In response to the domination of entrepreneurship in Malaysia, by ethnic-Chinese entrepreneurs, Malaysia adopted a policy of giving preferential treatment to Indigenous *bumiputras*. The Chinese minority also dominates the entrepreneurship sector of the Philippines.

Myanmar is rich in natural resources, but its people are not prosperous. Despite its lack of natural resources, British Singapore's strong legal system, the educational system and security brought prosperity to its immigrants; later, multinationals saturated the domestic markets forcing the internationalisation of formerly local entrepreneurship.

Like in Singapore, Taiwan provided law and order and this in turn facilitated entrepreneurship. Taiwan has more entrepreneurs per capita than has any of its neighbours. The Thai government's vision is to make Thailand a knowledge-based society through entrepreneurship and innovation by 2010. In Vietnam, entrepreneurship was introduced as a complement to socialism.

It appears that the ability to produce wealth is more important than simply being endowed with natural resources. The production of wealth, however, requires institutions and the efforts of individuals.

Implications for Public Policy

Different governments have designed a variety of programmes to promote the development of entrepreneurship. Much spending, however, is in vain, as entrepreneurship development programmes alone are insufficient. Programmes may be useful to those who know about them; often, those who could use them the most are unaware of their existence. Furthermore, policies that are not implemented fairly consequently fail to have the desired effect on society. In some economies, bribery, excessive taxation and regulation can inhibit entrepreneurship. Factors that could facilitate entrepreneurship include: education; reductions in barriers to entry; the reduction of excessive regulation, bureaucracy and corruption; flat taxes (as discussed by Forbes, 2006); and the freedom to compete. Also beneficial is a stable legal framework, as discussed by Smith (1892).

A priority for governments should be to determine the appropriate degree of regulation to enact and to enforce, such that the benefits to society exceed the costs of compliance. John Stuart Mill (1869) argued that the only purpose for which power can be rightfully exercised over a member of society, against his will, is to prevent harm onto others. While some regulation is required to ensure order, excessive intervention is counter-productive. Where import duties are considerable, smuggling becomes popular — as is the case in Myanmar and in Vietnam. Any society benefits from the optimal level of regulation and government intervention.

It appears that the optimal level of regulation and government intervention is culture-specific. Policy-makers should therefore keep in mind that the success of a policy or programme in the West does not guarantee equal success elsewhere. For this reason, it is crucial to avoid trans-locating these from one environment to a different one. To be effective, policies and programmes should be appropriate to the culture of a society. As summarised by Lewis, "If a religion lays stress upon material values, upon thrift and productive investment, upon honesty in commercial relations, upon experimentation and risk-bearing…it will be helpful to growth, whereas in so far as it is hostile to these things, it tends to inhibit growth. Where Theravada Buddhism is the backbone of social and cultural values…it may have a restraining effect on the accumulation of wealth and the rise of an entrepreneurial class (1955, p. 105)." Policy-makers should be aware of the cultural attributes of different ethnic groups, and policy should take these differences into account.

Economic development programmes have been introduced in different contexts. Experts have become sceptical of targeted economic development programmes, because these often subsidise the wrong people, with no lasting benefits. It appears that micro-finance programmes will have greater success. In any case, no funding should be distributed in transitional economies without post-loan or post-grant training. Recipients should be familiarised with finance, tax and payroll issues. Otherwise, of what use is capital unless there is knowledge to invest it?

A problem facing many economies is that social inequities may limit economic development in the future. The challenge facing these countries is to identify ways to broaden participation in economic development. Priorities should include:

- Reduction of poverty, by accelerating agricultural development, and in some cases by controlling population growth;
- Improvement of training and vocational education;
- Improvement of property rights;
- Improvement of the legal basis for commerce;
- Improvement of infrastructure;
- Further liberalisation of trade;
- Revision of policies to attract foreign investment;

- Improvement of the management of government expenditures; and
- Reform of tax policies such as to broaden the state's revenue base, in a fair manner.

Implications for Management

If there is one generalisation that can be made about doing business in Asia, it is that across these vast countries, transactions and profits are a function of networks and relationships. Preferential treatment — when reciprocal — reduces overall transaction costs, thus increasing efficiency, competitiveness and profitability. This is generally true, regardless of the specifics of an environment. Nevertheless, one must again be cautious in attempting to generalise across cultures.

In the West, where the firm-type sector prevails, societies tend to take a form specific to them (Geertz, 1963). They resemble each other in their value system, class structure, family organisation, governance, and economic models. Parsons (1951) identified this over half a century ago. It is just as true today, and we have come to refer to this as globalisation. Modern economies in the Occident are democratic and their mainstream society is secular.

Across the nations of Asia, there is more diversity than is the case in other parts of the world. Capitalism in Asia does not necessarily come with democratisation. Political reform is not necessarily part of economic transition. Some governments choose to have greater control than do others.

Likewise, some societies are more religious than others, and there are important differences between religions. Attitudes toward business also vary greatly (Guiso, Sapienza, and Zingales, 2003). Zingales argued that, according to him, "Buddhism and Christianity seem most conducive to capitalism, and Islam least (2006, p. 228)." He wrote, "Jews, Buddhists, Catholics and Protestants (in that order) support competition, while Muslims and Hindus are strongly against it (Zingales, 2006, p. 229)." Nevertheless, capitalism has been very successful in Indonesia and in Malaysia, as demonstrated in the respective chapters in this book. Badawi explained, "Islam is well suited to economic, social and personal development...as long as we interpret it correctly (2006, p. 208)."

Perhaps the most valuable advice one can give to potential investors is that the importance of cultural differences must never be underestimated. There is *neither* one Asian culture, nor one Asian model. Just because people live in the same region, it does not mean that they share the same views about entrepreneurship. Likewise, there is not one standard approach to transition in Asia. This is further complicated in pluralistic societies, where unlike cultures each have their own implicit and explicit assumptions. Risk also varies with different types of pluralism. Melting pot pluralism — the situation prevailing when minorities adapt to a secular mainstream society — is stable. In contrast, when ethnic groups do not share a mainstream society, polarisation can result in violence, as has been the case in Indonesia, Myanmar, and elsewhere. There is no consistency across nations.

Nor is there consistency across time, and managers should keep in mind that in some transitional economies — such as Myanmar — the newly emerging private sector lacks professional, financial and economic structure. Rules change frequently. What is legal today may be banned tomorrow, and vice versa. Also, the ownership of property is not clearly documented, and the liquidity of immoveable assets is often delayed. Where acquisition is not practical, foreign investors may enter markets via networks. Given that communist planners traditionally emphasised vertical integration, managers might find it necessary to explain how, in a market economy, synergy often comes from horizontal integration.

Western management has mastered the art and science of doing business in the firm-type sector. In Asia, many opportunities are to be found in the bazaar and in the state-controlled planned sectors. In the bazaar, the movement of raw materials, processing, distribution and sales are intertwined activities. The focus on relationships supersedes the products and services that are being exchanged. A sliding price system results in prices that are negotiated, reflecting not only the cost or perceived value of a good or service, but also negotiating skills, the relationship between the buyer and the seller, and possibly the time, as well. Also important is an understanding of the parallel sector.

Implications for Educators

Much education has been aimed at teaching managerial content. This is inadequate. As noted by Dana (2001b), programmes should reflect the needs of each host environment. Emphasis should also be placed on values, as well as technical content. In the absence of the values related to sustainable long-term entrepreneurship — such as asceticism, frugality, thrift and work ethic (Weber, 1904-5), managerial skills are not being put to optimal use.

Where privatisation and downsizing of state-owned enterprises cause mass unemployment, there is often a mismatch between market demand and skills available in the workforce. The workforce needs retraining in skills that are in demand. Consequently, the technical content of courses needs to be adapted to changes in the economy.

Due to the lack of employment opportunities, and in the absence of appropriate retraining, many people have become self-employed, often in informal or covert activities; legitimate entrepreneurship is confused with illegal transactions. It would be beneficial, therefore, for educators to promote acceptance of entrepreneurship.

Where a vibrant entrepreneurial class is absent, this may be due to the public policy environment, or to the lack of inherent entrepreneurial characteristics. Where entrepreneurial spirit exists, new venture programmes may further enhance the environment for entrepreneurship, as is the case in the United States. However, in a transitional society with little experience of legitimate entrepreneurship, education should first focus on encouraging an entrepreneurship-friendly ideology.

As the economy of a nation becomes increasingly complex, marketing functions will mature and become more specialised. Training will be required to help managers solve new problems of planning, distribution and transportation. Cheng, Chan, and Mahmood (2009) suggested that entrepreneurship education in Malaysia is not matching students' skill expectations with skill acquisition; in future, it should. Shinato, Kamei, and Dana (2013) observed an improvement in entrepreneurship education in Japan. Continued improvements would be welcome.

Toward Future Research

Entrepreneurship does not guarantee prosperity for a nation. It is important to examine the broader picture. While economic growth has been prescribed as the remedy for poverty, experience shows that growth creates problems of its own. Of what good is rapid transition if its adverse effects are uncontrolled? It is useful to look not only at the creation of wealth, but also at its distribution. Myanmar is an example of rich country with a population that is mostly poor. Class mobility, in such an environment, is often a function of access to bribes rather productive creativity or economic innovation.

It would be a fallacy to attempt to understand entrepreneurship or innovation in isolation. What must change and what need not? The answer depends upon historical context and current situation, as well as the result desired. A variety of models are means to achieve different results. This is where more research is needed.

Classic theories cannot simply be taken and injected into transitional economies, in neglect of the environment in which they are to be placed. Even among members of ASEAN, there are important differences. Historical, socio-cultural and economic contexts appear to be important factors affecting the environment for business; societies cannot all adopt legitimate entrepreneurial systems at an equal pace, nor should they be expected to.

In each economy, the nature of entrepreneurship will evolve in time, but one should *not* expect entrepreneurship to converge across societies. There is no one formula for a "best" policy to promote entrepreneurship. Entrepreneurship is embedded in society, and the latter is affected by historical experience and cultural values. To understand the global nature of entrepreneurship, we must move beyond a universal model or a Western model; entrepreneurship must be understood in the context of national development, and importantly, policy-makers should take note that to be relevant, policies must be culturally sensitive.

The findings of this book suggest that factors that facilitate entrepreneurship include cultural attitude, as well as laws that protect property and facilitate business. Culture is central in explaining the social acceptability and perceived utility of entrepreneurship.

Case Study: Industrial Parks in Israel

"The idea of the Tefen-model industrial parks," explained Mr. Arieh Dahan, Director, "is to provide a holistic environment for the entrepreneur and the worker, eliminating the artificial divisions that have traditionally separated industry from aesthetics, labour from life. Work should be uplifting and satisfying." On the premise that a free environment promotes free enterprise, the goal was for the parks to provide an atmosphere, which would improve the quality of work and life. Perhaps this was easier said than done.

It all started with a vision of Mr. Stef Wertheimer, founder and president of Iscar Ltd. "The key word, today, needs to be creativity," he asserted. "The economy is a servant of the capacity to create." The prototype of his vision, Tefen Industrial Park, was founded in Israel with the aim of providing an environment that would enable scientists, engineers and innovators to launch enterprises with minimum paperwork and interference. During its first year of operations, Tefen Industrial Park housed two exporting start-up companies. The concept soon gained popularity and other parks were set up, along the same lines as Tefen Industrial Park: Tel Hai Industrial Park, and later Omer Industrial Park. By the end of the 20th century, the firms operating in Tefen-style industrial parks, in Israel, were employing 600 people and producing $150 million in annual revenues. The contribution of these industrial parks to the national economy prompted the establishment of similar parks in Izmir, Turkey, and elsewhere.

Context

Israel covers 20,325 square kilometres. Its neighbours are Egypt, Jordan, Lebanon, Syria and the Palestinian Authority territories. While Hebrew and Arabic are official languages in Israel, English, Russian, French and Spanish are widely spoken.

During most of its history since independence, Israel was governed by its Labour Party The economy was dominated by agriculture and by labour-intensive industries. More recently, the state focused on educating its youth and in integrating highly-skilled immigrants. As a result, Israel was ranked third in the industrialised world (behind the United States and the Netherlands), in terms of university degrees per capita. Israel has 135 scientists and technicians per 10,000 workers — more than has any other industrialised country. Israel also has an impressive number of engineers per capita. While the United States has 8 engineers per 1,000 workers, and Japan has 7.5, Israel has 14 qualified engineers per 1,000 workers. High expenditures on research and development (R&D) helped Israel become a highly advanced society, with a technology-driven economy.

Israel developed diplomatic relations with 160 nations. The nation became the first, country in the world to have free trade agreements with the European Union, and with the 3 NAFTA members. Prudent fiscal and monetary policies, the liberalisation of trade, deregulation, privatisation, and the removal of exchange controls, greatly boosted the economy. Israel became characterised by an excellent infrastructure, per capita GDP at par with western European economies, and growth rates as high as Asia's tigers.

Israel was the first nation to launch m-Commerce. This technology made it possible to use mobile phones to activate fuel dispensers and to pay for petrol at service stations.

During its 50th year of existence, Israel exported software amounting to $1.5 billion. In 1999, the number of mobile phone service subscriptions surpassed the number of land-based subscriptions in Israel.

On May 26, 2000, Israel was invited to join the Western Europe and Others Group (WEOG) of the United Nations. This made the country eligible for nomination to several committees, including the Security Council. Consensus was secured by all 26 member-nations for Israel to join Canada, the United States, Australia, New Zealand, and western European countries in this grouping.

According to *Israel, A Scientific Profile,* compiled by Leora Frucht-Eren and published by the British Council, Israeli researchers have been responsible for several major contributions, including the following: discovery of a bacterium that is toxic only to mosquito larvae, and adopted by the World Health Organisation to control malaria; the first demonstration of the effectiveness of deprenyl in treating Parkinson's Disease; the first demonstration of the clinical diagnosis of aminocentesis, used to identify abnormalities in a fetus; invention of affinity chromatography; design of an instrument to scan and sort cells, to detect cancer at an early stage; design of a strategy to fight parasitic weeds, which has already saved crops in Africa and the Middle East; design of an encoding technology for protecting computer-generated data, used in smart-cards; crystallisation of the ribosome; and revelation of the three-dimensional structure of acetlylcholinesterase, the enzyme responsible for nerve impulses.

As well, Israeli researchers developed the following: a drug for Alzheimer patients, currently being tested in North America; a new method of transplanting bone marrow from non-compatible donors; a paediatric heart surgery technique; lithium substitutes for psychiatric use; a protein to treat chronic hepatitis and herpes; a medical procedure to treat earthquake victims crushed under rubble; a method to heal shattered bones; and a drug to control multiple sclerosis.

While the nation is host to the Digital Equipment Corporation, IBM, Intel, Microsoft, Motorola and National Semiconductors, local new ventures dominate its export-oriented high-tech industry. The economy of Israel is being led by scientific and industrial R&D. High-tech products and services account for three-quarters of exports.

Tefen Industrial Park

Tefen Industrial Park was founded in 1985, in the northern Israel region known as the Galilee, not far from Lebanon. The park has become home to Tefen Entrepreneur College, as well as headquarters for thirty companies. Another thirty firms expanded into the adjacent industrial zone.

Tel Hai Industrial Park

Tel Hai Industrial Park was established in 1992, in the Upper Galilee, near Syria. This park is restricted to non-polluting industries, geared to export markets. Among its firms is Kedumim Personnel Ltd., founded by an American immigrant to Israel, Elaine Levitt. “We never ceased to be inspired to excellence by our surrounding,” she exclaimed. Her enterprise has eight offices across the country.

Omer Industrial Park

Following the success of its sister parks, Omer Industrial Park was launched in 1995, along the lines of the same Tefen model. In contrast to its northern counterparts, Omer Industrial Park is situated in the south, near Beersheva, where the park has a close relationship with Ben Gurion University of the Negev.

Omer Industrial Park is home to Luzzatto & Luzzatto Ltd., patent attorneys. Originally from Milan, the Luzzatto family has been providing legal services since the 19th century.

Laron Industrial Park

Fourth in the Tefen family, Laron Industrial Park was designed to integrate a residential community and an educational institution in addition to incubator facilities.

Case Study Assignment

What could entrepreneurs and governments across Asia adopt from the Tefen experience? Be specific with a plan for each country studied.

Bibliography

Abercrombie, Thomas J. (1964), "Cambodia, Indochina's 'Neutral' Corner," *National Geographic* 126 (4), 514–551.

Acs, Zoltan J., and Léo-Paul Dana (2001), "Contrasting Two Models of Wealth Redistribution," *Small Business Economics* 16 (2), 63–74.

Adas, Michael P. (1974), *The Burma Delta: Economic Development and Local Change on an Asian Rice Frontier 1852–1941,* Madison: University of Wisconsin.

Ahlstrom, David, and Gary D. Bruton (2002), "An Institutional Perspective on the Role of Culture in Shaping Strategic Actions by Technology-focused Entrepreneurial Firms in China," *Entrepreneurship Theory and Practice* 26 (4), pp. 53–69.

Ahmad, Syed Zamberi, and Siri Roland Xavier (2012), "Entrepreneurial Environments and Growth: Evidence from Malaysia GEM Data," *Journal of Chinese Entrepreneurship* 4 (1), 50–69.

Aldrich, Howard E., Trevor P. Jones, and David McEvoy (1984), "Ethnic Advantage and Minority Business Development," in Robin Ward and Richard Jenkins, eds., *Ethnic Communities in Business: Strategies for Economic Survival*, Cambridge: Cambridge University Press, pp. 189–210.

Aldrich, Howard E., Ben Rosen, and William Woodward (1987), "The Impact of Social Networks on Business Foundings and Profit in a Longitudinal Study," *Frontiers of Entrepreneurship Research*, Wellesley, Massachusetts: Babson College, pp. 154–168.

Aldrich, Howard E., and Roger David Waldinger (1990), "Ethnicity and Entrepreneurship," in W. Richard Scott and Judith Blake, eds., *Annual Review of Sociology* 16, 111–135.

Aldrich, Howard E., and Catherine Zimmer (1986), "Entrepreneurship Through Social Networks," in Donald L. Sexton and Raymond W. Smilor, eds., *The Art and Science of Entrepreneurship*, Cambridge, Massachusetts: Ballinger, pp. 3–24.

Ali, Abbas J., Mona Lee, and Robert C. Camp (2002), "Export Attitudes of Taiwanese Executives," *Journal of Global Marketing* 16 (1–2), 27–46.

Almilia, Luciana Spica, Pepie Diptyana, Sasongo Budisuset, Sasongko Budisusetyo, and Riski Aprillia Nita (2013), "Comparative Managerial Practice and Export Potential of Small Medium Enterprises in Indonesia," *International Journal of Entrepreneurship and Small Business* 20 (1), 35–62.

Almor, Tamar, and Orly Yeheskel (2013), "Footloose and Fancy-free: Sojourning Entrepreneurs in China," *Journal of Enterprising Communities: People and Places in the Global Economy* 7 (4), 354–372.

Anderson, Alistair R., Jin-Hai Li, Richard T. Harrison, and Paul J. A. Robson (2003), "The Increasing Role of Small Business in the Chinese Economy," *Journal of Small Business Management* 41 (3), 310–316.

Anderson, Paul H. (1995), *Collaborative Internationalisation of Small and Medium-Sized Enterprises*, Copenhagen: DJOF.

Arnold, General H. H. (1944), "The Aerial Invasion of Burma," *National Geographic* 86 (2), 129–148.

Auster, Ellen, and Howard E. Aldrich (1984), "Small Business Vulnerability, Ethnic Enclaves and Ethnic Enterprise," in Robin Ward and Richard Jenkins, eds., *Ethnic Communities in Business: Strategies for Economic Survival*, Cambridge: Cambridge University Press, pp. 39–54.

Aw, Bee Yan (2002), "Productivity Dynamics of Small and Medium Enterprises in Taiwan," *Small Business Economics* 18 (1–3), 69–84.

Badawi, Abdullah Ahmad (2006), "Islam and Development," *Global Agenda: The Magazine of World Economic Forum Annual Meeting* 4, 208–209.

Bah, El-hadj M., and Geoff Cooper (2012), "Constraints to the Growth of Small Firms in Myanmar," available online at http://homes.eco.auckland.ac.nz/ebah002/pdf/Bah_Myanmarfirms.pdf.

Bainbridge, Oliver (1907), "The Chinese Jews," *National Geographic* 18 (10), 621–632.

Balakrishna, Ramachandra (1961), *Review of Economic Growth in India*, Bangalore: Bangalore Press.

Bandura, Albert (1982), "Self-Efficacy Mechanism in Human Agency," *American Psychologist* 36, 122–147.

Bandura, Albert, and Nancy E. Adams (1977), "Analysis of Self-Efficacy Theory of Behavioral Change," *Cognitive Theory and Review* 1, 287–310.

Barth, Frederik, ed., (1963), *The Role of the Entrepreneur in Social Change in Northern Norway,* Bergen: Norwegian Universities' Press.

Barth, Frederik (1966), *Models of Social Organization*, London: Royal Anthropological Institute.

Barth, Frederik (1967a), "Economic Spheres in Darfur," in Raymond Firth, ed., *Themes in Economic Anthropology*, London: Tavistock, pp. 149–174.

Barth, Frederik (1967b), "On the Study of Social Change," *American Anthropologist* 69 (6), 661–669.

Barth, Frederik (1981), *Process and Form in Social Life,* London: Routledge and Kegan Paul.

Beach, William W., and Gerald P. O'Driscoll (2001), "Factors of the Index of Economic Freedom," in Gerald P. O'Driscoll, Kim R. Holmes, and Melanie Kirkpatrick, *2001 Index of Economic Freedom,* New York: The Wall Street Journal.

Becker, Jasper (2004), "China's Growing Pains: More Money, More Stuff, More Problems," *National Geographic* 205 (3), 68–95.

Begley, Thomas M., and David P. Boyd (1987), "Psychological Characteristics Associated With Performance in Entrepreneurial Firms and Smaller Businesses," *Journal of Business Venturing* 2 (1), 79–93.

Bhagwati, Jagdish (2006), "The Big Debate: Setting the Business Agenda," Statement at the World Economic Forum, Davos, January 25.

Bishop, Isabella L. (1899), *The Yangtze Valley and Beyond,* London: John Murray.

Boissevain, Jeremy, and Hanneke Grotenbreg (1987), "Ethnic Enterprise in the Netherlands: The Surinamese of Amsterdam," in Robert Goffee and Richard Scase, eds., *Entrepreneurship in Europe: The Social Processes,* London: Croom Helm, 105–130.

Bonacich, Edna (1973), "A Theory of Middleman Minorities," *American Sociological Review* 38 (5), 583–594.

Booth, Anne (1994), "Repelita VI and the Second Long-Term Development Plan," *Bulletin of Indonesian Economic Studies* 30 (3), 3–39.

Boulnois, Luce (1963), *La Route de la Soie*, Paris: Arthaud.

Brenner, Gabrielle A., and Jean-Marie Toulouse (1990), "Business Creation among the Chinese Immigrants in Montreal," *Journal of Small Business and Entrepreneurship* 7 (4), 38–44.

Brockhaus, Robert H., Sr. (1982), "The Psychology of the Entrepreneur," in Calvin A. Kent, Donald L. Sexton, and Karl H. Vesper, eds., *Encyclopedia of Entrepreneurship*, Englewood Cliffs, New Jersey: Prentice Hall, 39–57.

Brown, Josephine A. (1944), "6,000 Miles over the Roads of Free China," *National Geographic* 85 (3), 355–384.

Brown, MacAlister, and Joseph Jermiah Zasloff (1999), *Cambodia Confounds the Peacemakers, 1979–1998*, Ithaca: Cornell University Press.

Brown, MacAlister, Joseph Jermiah Zasloff, and Richard F. Staar (1986), *Apprentice Revolutionaries: The Communist Movement in Laos, 1930–1985*, Hoover Institution Press.

Cantillon, Richard (1755), *Essai sur la Nature du Commerce en Général,* London and Paris: R. Gyles; translated into English in 1931, by Henry Higgs, London: MacMillan and Co.

Carsrud, Alan L., Connie Marie Gaglio, and Kenneth W. Olm (1986), "Entrepreneurs — Mentors, Networks and Successful New Venture

Development: An Exploratory Study," *Frontiers of Entrepreneurship Research*, Wellesley, Massachusetts: Babson College, 229–243.

Castle, William R., Jr. (1932), "Tokyo To-day," *National Geographic* 61 (2), 131–162.

Chadwick, Douglas H. (1987), "At the Crossroads of Kathmandu," *National Geographic* 172 (1), 32–65.

Chadwick, Douglas H. (2005), "Thailand's Urban Giants," *National Geographic* 208 (4), 98–117.

Chamard, John, and Michael Christie (1996), "Entrepreneurship Education Programs: A Change in Paradigm is Needed," *Entrepreneurship, Innovation, and Change* 5 (3), 217–226.

Chandler, David P. (1999), *A History of Cambodia*, Boulder, Colorado: Westview Press.

Chandler, David P., Ben Kiernan, and Chanthou Boua (1988), *Pol Pot Plans the Future*, New Haven: Yale.

Chandra, Nayan, and Rodney Tasker (1992), "The Gem Stampede," *Far Eastern Economic Review*, July 30, p. 20.

Chantrabot, Ros (1993), *La Republique Khmère (1970—1975)*, Paris: Les Editions L'Harmattan.

Chapman, H. Owen (1928), *The Chinese Revolution 1926—27: A Record of the Period Under Communist Control as Seen from the Nationalist Capital, Hankow,* London: Constable & Co.

Chen, Kuang-Jung (1997), "The Sari-Sari Store," *Journal of Small Business Management* 35 (4), 88–91.

Cheng, Ming Yu, Wai Sei Chan, and Amir Mahmood (2009), "The Effectiveness of Entrepreneurship Education in Malaysia," *Education + Training* 51 (7), 555–566.

Cherry, Robert (1990), "Middleman Minority Theories: Their Implications for Black-Jewish Relations," *The Journal of Ethnic Studies* 17 (4), 117–138.

Chetwode, Penelope (1935), "Nepal, the Sequestered Kingdom," *National Geographic* 67 (3), 319–352.

Chinh, Truong (1977), "Firmly Grasp the Proletarian Dictatorship," *Vietnam* 225, September, p. 1.

Chitty, J. R. (1922), *Things Seen in China,* London: Seeley, Service & Co.

Chow, K.W. Clement, and W. K. Eric Tsang (1995), "Entrepreneurs in China: Development, Functions and Problems," *International Small Business Journal* 1, 63–77.

Christian, John LeRoy (1942), *Modern Burma: A Survey of Political and Economic Development*, Berkeley, California: University of California Press.

Christian, John LeRoy (1943), "Burma: Where India and China Meet," *National Geographic* 84 (4), 489–512.

Clark, Milton J. (1954), "How the Kazakhs Fled to Freedom," *National Geographic* 106 (5), 621–644.

Communist Party of Vietnam (1991), *Seventh National Congress Documents,* Hanoi: Vietnam Foreign Languages Publishing House.

Coville, Lilian Grosvenor (1933), "Here in Manchuria: Many Thousand Lives Were Lost and More Than Half the Crops Destroyed by the Floods of 1932," *National Geographic* 63 (2), 233–256.

Cox, Howard, and Stuart Metcalfe (1998), "The Borneo Company Limited: Origins of a Nineteenth Century Networked Multinational," *Asia Pacific Business Review* 4 (4), 53–69.

Cummings, Scott, ed., (1980), *Self-Help in Urban America: Patterns of Minority Business Enterprise*, Port Washington, New York: Kennikat, pp. 33–57.

Curzon-of-Kedleston, Marquess (1924), "In the Diamond Mountains," *National Geographic* 66 (4), 353–374.

Dahles, Heidi, and John Ter Horst (2012), "Institutionalising Chineseness: Legacies of Chinese Commercial Hegemony in the Cambodian Silk Industry," *Journal of Contemporary Asia* 42 (2), 210–229.

Dalgic, Tevfik (1998), "Dissemination of Market Orientation in Europe," *International Marketing Review* 15 (1), 45–60.

Dana, Léo-Paul (1987), "Industrial Development Efforts in Malaysia and Singapore," *Journal of Small Business Management* 25 (3), 74–76.

Dana, Léo-Paul (1992), "Entrepreneurship, Innovation and Change in Developing Countries," *Entrepreneurship, Innovation, and Change* 1 (2), 231–242.

Dana, Léo-Paul (1993a), "A Goods and Services Tax (GST) and the Small Business Sector: Some Canadian Reflections," *Australian Journal of Public Administration* 52 (4), 457–464.

Dana, Léo-Paul (1993b), "An International Survey of Entrepreneurship Education," *Journal of Enterprising Culture* 1 (1), 67–92.

Dana, Léo-Paul (1994a), "A Marxist Mini-Dragon? Entrepreneurship in Today's Vietnam," *Journal of Small Business Management* 32 (2), 95–102.

Dana, Léo-Paul (1994b), "Economic Reform in the New Vietnam," *Current Affairs* 70 (11), 19–25.

Dana, Léo-Paul (1994c), "The *Doi-Moi* Model: An Ethnographic Account of Entrepreneurship, Innovation and Change in Former French Indo-China," *Entrepreneurship, Innovation, and Change* 3 (1), 61–84.

Dana, Léo-Paul (1994d), "The Impact of Culture on Entrepreneurship, Innovation, and Change in the Balkans: The Yugopluralist Model," *Entrepreneurship, Innovation, and Change* 3 (2), 177–190.

Dana, Léo-Paul (1995a), "Entrepreneurship in a Remote Sub-Arctic Community: Nome, Alaska," *Entrepreneurship: Theory and Practice* 20 (1), 57–72.

Dana, Léo-Paul (1995b), "Small Business in a Non-Entrepreneurial Society: The Case of the Lao People's Democratic Republic (Laos)," *Journal of Small Business Management* 33 (3), 95–102.

Dana, Léo-Paul (1997a), "Pepsi, Vietnam," *Management Case Quarterly* 2 (3), 11–13.

Dana, Léo-Paul (1997b), "The Origins of Self-Employment," *Canadian Journal of Administrative Sciences/Revue Canadienne des Sciences de l'Administration* 14 (1), 99–104.

Dana, Léo-Paul (1997c), "Vongpackdy, Laos," *Management Case Quarterly* 2 (3), Autumn, pp. 29–32.

Dana, Léo-Paul (1998a) "Small Business in Xinjiang," *Asian Journal of Business and Information Systems* 3 (1), 123–136.

Dana, Léo-Paul (1998b), "Small But Not Independent: SMEs in Japan," *Journal of Small Business Management* 36 (4), 73–76.

Dana, Léo-Paul (1999a), "Entrepreneurship as a Supplement in the People's Republic of China," *Journal of Small Business Management* 37 (3), 76–80.

Dana, Léo-Paul (1999b), *Entrepreneurship in Pacific Asia: Past, Present & Future,* Singapore, London and Hong Kong: World Scientific.

Dana, Léo-Paul, ed. (1999c), *International Entrepreneurship: An Anthology*, Singapore: ENDEC.

Dana, Léo-Paul (1999d), "Kentucky Fried Chicken in Shanghai," *British Food Journal* 101 (5–6), 293–495.

Dana, Léo-Paul (1999e), "The Development of Entrepreneurship in Macao and Hong Kong: A Comparative Study," *Public Administration and Policy*, 61–72.

Dana, Léo-Paul (2000a), "Creating Entrepreneurs in India," *Journal of Small Business Management* 38 (1), 86–91.

Dana, Léo-Paul (2000b), *Economies of the Eastern Mediterranean Region: Economic Miracles in the Making,* Singapore, London and Hong Kong: World Scientific.

Dana, Léo-Paul (2000c), "International Management: Culture is of the essence in Asia," Invited Essay in *Financial Times*, Mastering Management Special Section, 12–13.

Dana, Léo-Paul (2001a), "Networks, Internationalization and Policy," *Small Business Economics* 16 (2), 57–62.

Dana, Léo-Paul (2001b), "The Education and Training of Entrepreneurs in Asia," *Education + Training*, 43 (8), pp. 405–416.

Dana, Léo-Paul (2002), *When Economies Change Paths: Models of Transition in China, the Central Asian Republics, Myanmar, and the Nations of Former Indochine Française*, Singapore, London and Hong Kong: World Scientific.

Dana, Léo-Paul (2005), *When Economies Change Hands: A Survey of Entrepreneurship in the Emerging Markets of Europe from the Balkans to the Baltic States*, Binghamton: International Business Press.

Dana, Léo-Paul (2006), *Entrepreneurship & SMEs in the Eurozone: Toward a Theory of Symbiotic Enterprises,* London: Imperial College Press.

Dana, Léo-Paul (2009), "Religion as an Explanatory Variable for Entrepreneurship," *International Journal of Entrepreneurship and Innovation* 10 (2), 97–109.

Dana, Léo-Paul, ed. (2010), *Entrepreneurship and Religion,* Cheltenham: Edward Elgar.

Dana, Léo-Paul, and Teresa Elizabeth Dana (1999), "Coca-Cola Indochina Pte Ltd," *British Food Journal* 101 (5–6), 441–446.

Dana, Léo-Paul, Hamid Etemad and Richard W. Wright (2000), "The Global Reach of Symbiotic Networks," in Léo-Paul Dana, ed., *Global Marketing Co-operation and Networks*, Binghamton: International Business Press, pp. 1–16.

Dana, Léo-Paul, Hamid Etemad and Richard W. Wright (2004), "Chapter 1: International Entrepreneurship in the New Economy," in Marian V. Jones and Pavlos Dimitratos, eds., *Emerging Paradigms in International Entrepreneurship*, Cheltenham, United Kingdom: Edward Elgar, pp. 19–36.

Dana, Léo-Paul, Hamid Etemad, and Richard W. Wright (2008), "Toward a Paradigm of Symbiotic Entrepreneurship," *International Journal of Entrepreneurship and Small Business* 5 (2), 109–126.

Dana, Léo-Paul, Robert T. Hamilton and Kirsten Wick (2009), "Deciding to Export: An Exploratory Study of Singaporean Entrepreneurs," *Journal of International Entrepreneurship* 7, 79–87.

De Jong, Gjalt, Phan Anh Tu, and Hans Van Ees (2012), "Which Entrepreneurs Bribe and What Do They Get from It? Exploratory Evidence from Vietnam," *Entrepreneurship Theory and Practice* 36 (2), 323–345.

Deering, Mabel Craft (1933), "Chosen – Land of Morning Calm," *National Geographic* 64 (4), 421–448.

Desjardins, Thierry (1997), "Le Cambodge, royaume de la corruption," *Figaro,* January 1, p. 4B.

Dilke, Charles Wentworth (1894), *Greater Britain: A Record of Travel in English-speaking Countries,* London: Macmillan and Co.

Dinh, Tran Van (1989), "Hue," *National Geographic* 176 (5), 595–603.

Djamour, Judith (1959), *Malay Kinship and Marriage in Singapore,* London: Athlone.

Dollar, David (1999), "The Transformation of Vietnam's Economy: Sustaining Growth in the 21st Century," in Jennie I. Litvack and Dennis A. Rondinelli, eds., *Market Reform in Vietnam: Building Institutions for Development*, Westport, Connecticut: Quorum, pp. 31–46.

Drabble, John H. (1973), *Rubber in Malaya, 1876–1922: The Genesis of the Industry*, Kuala Lumpur: Oxford University Press.

Dubini, Paola, and Howard E. Aldrich (1991), "Personal and Extended Networks are Central to the Entrepreneurship Process," *Journal of Business Venturing* 6 (5), 305–313.

Dunung, Sanjyot P. (1995), *Doing Business in Asia*, New York: Lexington Books.

Dyer, Linda M., and Christopher A. Ross (2000), "Ethnic Enterprises and Their Clientele," *Journal of Small Business Management* 38 (2), 48–66.

Ear, Sophal (1995), "Cambodia's Economic Development in Historical Perspective: 1953–1970," *Berkeley NcNair Journal* 3, Summer, pp. 25–37.

Ear, Sophal (2011), "Growth in the Rice and Garment Sectors," in Caroline Hughes and Kheang Un, eds., *Cambodia's Economic Transformation,* Copenhagen: Nordic Institute of Asian Studies Press, pp. 70–93.

Edwards, Mike (2004), "Han Dynasty," *National Geographic* 205 (2), 2–29.

Eigner, Julius (1938), "The Rise and Fall of Nanking," *National Geographic* 73 (2), 189–224.

El-Namaki, M. S. S. (1988), "Encouraging Entrepreneurs in Developing Countries," *Long Range Planning* 21 (4), 98–106.

Evans, Joel R., and Richard L. Laskin (1994), "The Relationship Marketing Process: A Conceptualization and Application," *Industrial Marketing Management* 23 (5), 432–452.

Far Eastern Economic Review (1994), "Indochina," May 5, p. 60.

Feige, Edgar L., and Katarina Ott (1999), eds., *Underground Economies in Transition: Unrecorded Activity, Tax, Corruption and Organized Crime*, Aldershot: Ashgate.

Forbes, Steve (2006), "Flat Taxes, Higher Revenues," *Global Agenda: The Magazine of World Economic Forum Annual Meeting* 4, 118–119.

Freedman, Maurice (1961), "Immigrants and Associations: Chinese in Nineteenth-century Singapore," *Comparative Studies in Society and History* 3, 25–48.

Furnivall, John Sydenham (1956), *Colonial Policy and Practice: A Comparative Study of Burma and Netherlands India*, New York: New York University Press.

Furnivall, John Sydenham (1957), *A Study of the Social and Economic History of Burma*, Rangoon.

Gadar, Kamisan, and Nek Kamal Yeop Yunus (2009), "The Influence of Personality and Socio-economic Factors on Female Entrepreneurship Motivations in Malaysia." *International Review of Business Research Papers* 5 (1) , 149–162.

Gadgil, Dhananjaya Ramchandra (1959), *Origins of the Modern Indian Business Class,* New York: Institute of Pacific Relations.

Garrett, W. E. (1971), "Pagan, on the Road to Mandalay," *National Geographic* 139 (3), 343–365.

Garrett, W. E. (1974), "The Hmong of Laos," *National Geographic* 145 (1), January, 78–111.

Gasse, Yvon (1982), "Elaborations on the Psychology of the Entrepreneur," in Calvin A. Kent, Donald L. Sexton, and Karl H. Vesper, eds.,

Encyclopedia of Entrepreneurship, Englewood Cliffs, New Jersey: Prentice Hall, pp. 57–66.

Geertz, Clifford (1963), *Peddlers and Princes: Social Development and Economic Change in Two Indonesian Towns*, Chicago, Illinois: University of Chicago Press.

Ghosh, Ratna, Meenakshi Gupta, and S. Nina Dhar (1998), "Women and Entrepreneurship in India," in Rabindra N. Kanungo, ed., *Entrepreneurship & Innovation: Models for Development,* New Delhi: Sage, 156–175.

Glinkina, Svetlana (1999), "Russia's Underground Economy During the Transition," in Edgar L. Feige and Katarina Ott, eds., *Underground Economies in Transition: Unrecorded Activity, Tax, Corruption and Organised Crime*, Aldershot: Ashgate, 101–116.

Gomes-Casseres, Benjamin (1997), "Alliance Strategies of Small Firms," *Small Business Economics* 9 (1), 33–44.

Goodnow, Frank Johnson (1927), "The Geography of China: The Influence of Physical Environment on the History and Character of the Chinese People," *National Geographic* 51 (6), 651–664.

Grandadam, Sabine (2013), "Economie: Le monde en breves," *Magazine Air France* 194, 44–45.

Gray, Denis D. (2001), "Working Elephants Make Last Stand in Myanmar," *The Jerusalem Post*, March 13, p. 7.

Griffis, William Elliot (1923), "The Empire of the Risen Sun," *National Geographic* 44 (4), 415–443.

Griffis, William Elliot (1933), "Japan, Child of the World's Old Age: An Empire of Mountainous Islands, Whose Alert People Constantly Conquer Harsh Forces of Land, Sea, and Sky," *National Geographic* 63 (3), 257–301.

Gronroos, Christian (1989), "Defining Marketing: A Market-Oriented Approach," *European Journal of Marketing* 23 (1), 52–59.

Grossman, Gregory (1977), "The Second Economy of the USSR," *Problems of Communism* 26 (5), 25–40.

Guiso, Luigi, Paola Sapienza, and Luigi Zingales (2003), "People's Opium? Religion and Economic Attitudes," *Journal of Monetary Economics* 50 (1), 225–282.

Hagen, Everett E. (1962), *On the Theory of Social Change: How Economic Growth Begins*, Homewood, Illinois: Dorsey.

Hagen, Toni (1960), "Afoot in Roadless Nepal," *National Geographic* 117 (3), 361–405.

Hakansson, Hakan, ed. (1982), *International Marketing and Purchasing of Industrial Goods: An Interaction Approach,* Chicester: John Wiley and Sons.

Haley, George T., and Usha C. V. Haley (1998), "Boxing With Shadows," *Journal of Organisational Change Management* 11 (4), 301–320.

Haley, George T., Chin Tiong Tan, and Usha C. V. Haley (1998), *New Asian Entrepreneurs*, Oxford: Butterworth-Heinemann.

Halloran, James W. (1991), *Why Entrepreneurs Fail,* New York: Liberty Hall.

Hamel, Bernard (1993), *Sihanouk et le Drame Cambodgien*, Paris: L'Harmattan Broché.

Harvey, Charles, and Boon-Chye Lee (2002), "The Study of Small and Medium Sized Enterprises in East Asia," in Charles Harvey and Boon-Chye Lee, eds., *Globalisation and SMEs in East Asia,* Cheltenham, United Kingdom: Edward Elgar, pp. 1–9.

Haskell, Martin R., and Lewis Yablonsky (1974), *Crime and Delinquency*, Chicago: Rand McNally.

Hazlehurst, Leighton W. (1966), *Entrepreneurship and the Merchant Castes in a Punjabi City*, Durham, North Carolina: Duke University Commonwealth Studies Center.

Henker, Julia Kreisinger (1999), "Hot Breads," in Richard G. Linowes, ed., *Portraits of Business Practices in Emerging Markets: Cases for Management Education,* Washington, DC: Institute of International Education and US Agency for International Development, Volume 2, pp. 174–180.

Henry, Stuart (1978), *The Hidden Economy: The Context and Control of Borderline Crime*, London: Martin Robertson.

Herald Tribune (1988), "U Ne Win is Removed From Office in Burma," July 26, p. 2.

Hipwell, William T. (2005), "Re-Constructing Nature and Reterritorialising Alishan: Taiwan's Cou Nation and the Making of Danayigu," presented at the Association of American Geographers' 2005 Annual Meeting, Denver, Colorado, April 5–9.

Hirsh, Michael, and Ron Moreau (1995), "Risky Business," *Newsweek*, June 19, p. 10.

Hla, Lludu U. (1975), *Rice*, Mandalay: Kyipwaye Press.

Hodgson, Bryan (1984), "Time and Again in Burma," *National Geographic* 166 (1), 90–121.

Hoge, James F. (2006), "The Emergence of India," Statement at the World Economic Forum, Davos, January 25.

Hong, Ma (1990), *Modern China's Economy and Management*, Beijing: Foreign Languages Press.

Hornaday, John A. (1982), "Research About Living Entrepreneurs," in Calvin A. Kent, Donald L. Sexton, and Karl H. Vesper, eds., *Encyclopedia of Entrepreneurship*, Englewood Cliffs, New Jersey: Prentice Hall, pp. 20–38.

Hughes, Caroline (2006), "The Politics of Gifts: Tradition and Regimentation in Contemporary Cambodia," *Journal of Southeast Asian Studies* 37 (3), 469–489.

Hughes, Caroline (2009), *Dependent Communities: Aid and Politics in Cambodia and East Timor,* Ithaca, New York: Cornell Southeast Asia Program Publications.

Hughes, Caroline, and Kheang Un, eds. (2011), *Cambodia's Economic Transformation,* Copenhagen: Nordic Institute of Asian Studies Press.

Hull, David, John J. Bosley, and Gerald G. Udell (1980), "Renewing the Hunt for the Heffalump: Identifying Potential Entrepreneurs by Personality Characteristics," *Journal of Small Business Management* 18 (1), 11–18.

Huntington, Samuel P. (1996), *The Clash of Civilization and the Remaking of World Order*, New York: Simon and Schuster.

Hwang, Eui-Gak (1993), *The Korean Economies: A Comparison of North & South,* Oxford: Clarendon.

Iyer, Gopalkrishnan, and Jon M. Shapiro (1999), "Ethnic Entrepreneurship and Marketing Systems: Implications for the Global Economy," *Journal of International Marketing* 7 (4), 83–110.

Jackson, Karl D., ed., (1989), *Cambodia 1975–1978*, Princeton, New Jersey: Princeton University Press.

Jain, Anita (2006), "A Dramatic Change in Shopping," *Financial Times,* Wednesday, June 28, p. 4.

Japan Times (1999), "Bear Market," March 7, p. 11.

Jenkins, Richard (1984), "Ethnicity and the Rise of Capitalism in Ulster," in Robin Ward and Richard Jenkins, eds., *Ethnic Communities in Business: Strategies for Economic Survival,* Cambridge: Cambridge University Press, pp. 57–72.

Johanson, Jan, and Associates (1994), *Internationalization, Relationships and Networks*, Stockholm: Almquist and Wiksell International.

Johnson, Jo (2006), "Surging with Self-confidence and Ambition," *Special Report on the World's Fastest Growing Democracy,* London: Financial Times, January 26.

Kahin, George M. (1952), *Nationalism and Revolution in Indonesia,* Ithaca: Cornell University Press.

Kakar, Sudhir (1978), *The Inner World: A Psycho-Analytic Study of Hindu Childhood and Society*, Oxford University Press, London.

Kamei, Katsuyuki, and Léo-Paul Dana (2010), "Business Incubation & the Pursuit of Opportunity," *Journal of Asia Entrepreneurship and Sustainability* 6 (2), 3–18.

Kamei, Katsuyuki, and Léo-Paul Dana (2012), "Examining the Impact of New Policy Facilitating SME Succession in Japan: From a Viewpoint of Risk Management in Family Business," *International Journal of Entrepreneurship & Small Business* 16 (1), 60–70.

Kanitkar, Ajit, and Nalinee Contractor (1992), *In Search of Identity: The Women Entrepreneurs of India,* Ahmedabad: Entrepreneurship Development Institute of India.

Khatiwada, Yuba Raj (2002), "Banking Sector Reforms for Nepal: Implications for Corporate Governance," in John Adams, Bishwa K. Maskay, and Sugandha D. Tulandhar, eds., *Corporate Governance in Nepal,* Kathmandu: Centre for Development and Governance.

Khup, San (1996), "Macroeconomic Policies with Special Emphasis on Infrastructural Development," in Tan Teck Meng, Low Aik Meng, John J. Williams, and Ivan P. Polunin, eds., *Business Opportunities in Myanmar*, Singapore: Prentice Hall, pp. 69–79.

Kinyanjui, Mary Njeri (1993), "Finance Availability of Capital and New Firm Formation in Central Kenya," *Journal of East African Research and Development* 23, 63–87.

Kipling, Rudyard (1890), *Letters from the East,* New York: Frank F. Lovell.

Kirjassoff, Alice Ballantine (1920), "Formosa the Beautiful," *National Geographic* 37 (3), 247–292.

Kirzner, Israel M. (1973), *Competition and Entrepreneurship,* Chicago: University of Chicago Press.

Kirzner, Israel M. (1979), *Perception, Opportunity, and Profit*, Chicago: University of Chicago Press.

Kirzner, Israel M. (1982), *Method, Process and Austrian Economics*, Lexington, Massachusetts: Lexington Books.

Kirzner, Israel M. (1985), *Discovery and the Capitalist Process*, Chicago: University of Chicago Press.

Koster, Sierdjan, and Shailendra Kumar Rai (2008), "Entrepreneurship and Economic Development in a Developing Country: A Case Study of India," *Journal of Entrepreneurship* 17 (2), 117–137.

Kunstadter, Peter (1972), "Spirits of Change Capture the Karens," *National Geographic* 141 (2), 267–285.

Kyi, Khin Maung (1970), "Western Enterprises and Economic Development in Burma," *Journal of Burma Research Society* 53 (1), 25–49.

Lamb, David (2004), "Hanoi: Shedding the Ghosts of War," *National Geographic* 205 (5), 80–97.

Lasserre, Philippe, and Hellmut Schütte (1995), *Strategies for Asia Pacific*, London: Macmillan.

Lee, Byoung-Hoon (2003), "Globalization and Industrial Relations in Korea," *Korean Journal* 43 (1), 261–288.

Lee, Byoung-Hoon, and Seong Kyeun Kwun (2003), "Public Policy Toward the Innovation-driven Economy in Korea," *International Journal of Entrepreneurship and Innovation Management* 3 (3), 267–281.

Lee, Choong Y. (1998), "Quality Management by Small Manufacturers in Korea: An Exploratory Study," *Journal of Small Business Management* 36 (4), 73–76.

Lee, Joseph S., and Jiann-Chyuan Wang (2003), "Public Policies for the Promotion of an Innovation-driven Economy in Taiwan," *International Journal of Entrepreneurship and Innovation Management* 3 (3), 227–248.

Leong, Choon Chiang (2004), "Government Development Assistance Programmes (GDAPs) for Small- and Medium-sized Enterprises (SMEs) in a Knowledge-based Economy," *International Journal of Entrepreneurship and Innovation Management* 4 (2–3), 124–137.

Lewis, W. Arthur (1955), *The Theory of Economic Growth*, Homewood, Illinois: Richard D. Irwin.

Light, Ivan H. (1972), *Ethnic Enterprise in America: Business and Welfare among Chinese, Japanese and Blacks,* Berkeley, California: University of California Press.

Light, Ivan H. (1984), "Immigrant and Ethnic Enterprise in North America," *Ethnic and Racial Studies* 7 (2), 195–216.

Light, Ivan H, and Edna Bonacich (1988), *Immigrant Entrepreneurs: Koreans in Los Angeles 1965–1985,* Berkeley, California: University of California Press.

Light, Ivan H, and Léo-Paul Dana (2013), "Boundaries of Social Capital in Entrepreneurship," *Entrepreneurship: Theory & Practice,* 37(3), 603–624.

Lin, Carol Yeh-Yun (1998), "Success Factors of Small and Medium-Sized Enterprises in Taiwan," *Journal of Small Business Management* 36 (4), 43–56.

Loewen, James W. (1971), *The Mississippi Chinese: Between Black and White*, Cambridge: Harvard University Press.

Long, George W. (1952), "Indochina Faces the Dragon," *National Geographic* 102 (3), 287–328.

Long, George W. (1954), "Hong Kong Hangs On," *National Geographic* 105 (2), 239–272.

Lowdermilk, Walter C. (1945), "China Fights Erosion with U.S. Aid," *National Geographic* 87 (6), 641–680.

Luo, Jar-Der (1997), "The Significance of Networks in the Initiation of Small Businesses in Taiwan," *Sociological Forum* 12, 297–317.

Macaulay, R. H. (1934), *History of the Bombay Burmah Trading Corporation, Ltd., 1864–1910*, Colchester, London and Eton: Spottiswoode, Ballantyne and Co.

MacDonald, Don (2005), "China's Challenges to Growth," *The Gazette,* Saturday, October 1, pp. B.1–2.

Marx, Karl, and Friedrich Engels (1848), *Manifest der Kommunisitischen Partei,* London: J. E. Burghard.

Maung, Mya (1991), *The Burma Road to Poverty*, New York: Praeger.

May, Daw Khin San (1996), "Mandalay: The Handicraft Centre of Myanmar," in Tan Teck Meng, Low Aik Meng, John J. Williams, and Ivan P. Polunin, eds., *Business Opportunities in Myanmar*, Singapore: Prentice Hall, 47–52.

McClelland, David Clarence (1961), *The Achieving Society,* Princeton, New Jersey: D. Van Nostrand.

McClelland, David Clarence (1975), *Power*, New York: Free Press.

Medhora, Phiroze B. (1965), "Entrepreneurship in India," *Political Science Quarterly* 80 (4), 558–559.

Mill, John Stuart (1869), *On Liberty,* London: Longman, Roberts & Green.

Min, Pyong Gap (1984), "From White-Collar Occupation to Small Business: Korean Immigrants' Occupational Adjustment," *Sociological Quarterly* 25 (3), 333–352.

Min, Pyong Gap (1986–7), "Filipino and Korean Immigrants in Small Business: A Comparative Analysis," *Amerasia* 13 (1), 53–71.

Min, Pyong Gap (1987), "Factors Contributing to Ethnic Business: A Comprehensive Synthesis," *International Journal of Comparative Sociology* 28 (3–4), 173–193.

Min, Pyong Gap, and Charles Jaret (1985), "Ethnic Business Success: the Case of Korean Small Business in Atlanta," *Sociology and Social Research* 69 (3), 412–435.

Minniti, Maria, William D. Bygrave, and Erkko Autio (2006), *Global Entrepreneurship Monitor: 2005 Executive Report,* London: London Business School.

Mishra, Atul (2005), "Entrepreneurial Motivations in Start-up and Survival of Micro- and Small Enterprises in the Rural Non-Farm Economy," *Journal of Small Business and Entrepreneurship* 18 (3), 289–326.

Moore, W. Robert (1930), "Among the Hill Tribes of Sumatra," *National Geographic* 57 (2), 187–227.

Moore, W. Robert (1933), "The Glory that Was Imperial Peking," *National Geographic* 63 (6), 745–780.

Moore, W. Robert (1950), "Strife-torn Indochina," *National Geographic* 98 (4), 499–510.

Moore, W. Robert (1954), "War and Quiet on the Laos Frontier," *National Geographic* 105 (5), 665– 680.

Moore, W. Robert (1963), "Burma: Gentle Neighbor of India and Red China," *National Geographic* 123 (2), 153–199.

Moore, W. Robert, and Maynard Owen Williams (1951), "Portrait of Indochina," *National Geographic* 99 (4), 461– 490.

Moser, Don (1977), "The Philippines: Better Days Still Elude an Old Friend," *National Geographic* 151 (3), 360–391.

Mydans, Seth (2005), "In Aceh, Empty Spaces Won't Be Filled Soon," *International Herald Tribune,* Saturday-Sunday, June 25–26, p. 2.

Nafziger, E. Wayne (1971), "Indian Entrepreneurship: A Survey," in Peter Kilby, *Entrepreneurship and Economic Development*, New York: The Free Press, pp. 287–316.

Nevade, Sidram A., Sachin G. Lokapure and N.V. Kalyane (2011), "Study on Anti-solar Activity of Ehanolic Extract of Flower of *Hibiscus rosa-sinensis* Linn," *Research Journal of Pharmacy and Technology* 4 (3), 472–473.

Ngudup, Penjor, Jason C. H. Chen, and Binshan Lin (2005), "E-commerce in Nepal: A Case Study of An Underdeveloped Country," *International Journal of Management and Enterprise Development* 2 (3–4), 306–324.

North, Douglass (1990), *Institutions, Institutional Change, and Economic Performance*, Cambridge: Harvard University Press.

O'Driscoll, Gerald P., Kim R. Holmes, and Melanie Kirkpatrick (2001), *2001 Index of Economic Freedom,* New York: The Wall Street Journal.

Ong, Jeen Wei, and Hishamuddin Bin Ismail (2011), "Entrepreneurial Traits and Firm Performance: Is Gender a Matter?" *International Journal of Entrepreneurship and Small Business* 13 (4), 499–517.

Orwell, George (1930), *Burmese Days*, New York: Harcourt-Brace Co.

Outram, Frank, and G. E. Fane (1940), "Burma Road, Back Door to China," *National Geographic* 78 (5), 629–658.

Pandey, Ram Chandra (2009), "Rural Entrepreneurship through Electricity," *Hydro Nepal* 4 36–39.

Parnwell, Mike, and Sarah Turner (1998), "Sustaining the Unsustainable? City and Society in Indonesia," *Third World Planning Review* 20 (2), 147–163.

Parsons, Talcott (1951), *The Social System*, Glencoe, Illinois: Free Press.

Parsons, Talcott, and Neil Smelzer (1956), *Economy and Society*, Glencoe, Illinois: Free Press.

Passantino, Joseph E. (1946), "Kunming, Southwestern Gateway to China," *National Geographic* 90 (2), 137–168.

Patel, V. G. (1987), *Entrepreneurship Development Programme in India and Its Relevance to Developing Countries*, Ahmedabad: Entrepreneurship Development Institute of India.

Patric, John (1936), "Friendly Journeys in Japan: A Young American Finds a Ready Welcome in the Homes of the Japanese During Leisurely Travels Through the Islands," *National Geographic* 69 (4), 441–480.

Peng, Michael W., and Peggy Sue Heath (1996), "The Growth of the Firm in Planned Economies in Transition: Institutions, Organizations, and Strategic Choice," *Academy of Management Review* 21 (2), 492–528.

Perazic, Elizabeth (1960), "Little Laos Next Door to Red China," *National Geographic* 117 (1), 46–69.

Perlez, Jane (2006), "Women Caught in a More Radical Indonesia," *International Herald Tribune,* Wednesday, June 28, p. 2.

Pio, Edwina (2005a), "A Change Process Imbued with an Eastern Ethos Revitalizes an Indian Business," *Journal of Organizational Excellence* 24 (3), 3–10.

Pio, Edwina (2005b), "A Time to Sew: Work, Culture and Organic Cotton at Knitex India," *Management Case Study Journal* 5 (2), 69–82.

Pio, Edwina (2010), "Religious Merchants? Entrepreneurship in India," in Léo-Paul Dana, ed. *Entrepreneurship and Religion,* Cheltenham, United Kingdom: Edward Elgar, pp. 27–42.

Ponchaud, François (1977), *Cambodia: Year Zero*, New York: Holt, Rinehart and Winston.

Poon, Teresa Shuk-ching (2002), *Competition and Cooperation in Taiwan's Information Technology Industry: Inter-firm Networks and Industrial Upgrading*, Westport, Connecticut: Quorum Books.

Porter, Elaine G., and K. V. Nagarajan (2005), "Successful Women Entrepreneurs as Pioneers: Results from a Study Conducted in Karaikudi, Tamil Nadu, India," *Journal of Small Business and Entrepreneurship* 18 (1), 39–52.

Portes, Alejandro, and Robert C. Bach (1985), *Latin Journey*, Berkeley, California: University of California Press.

Portes, Alejandro, and Leif Jensen (1987), "What's an Ethnic Enclave? The Case for Conceptual Clarity," *American Sociological Review* 52 (6), 768–771.

Portes, Alejandro, and Leif Jensen (1989), "The Enclave and the Entrants: Patterns of Ethnic Enterprise in Miami Before and After Mariel," *American Sociological Review* 54 (6), 929–949.

Portes, Alejandro, and Leif Jensen (1992), "Disproving the Enclave Hypothesis," *American Sociological Review* 57 (3), 418–420.

Prasso, Sheridan T. (2001), "The Riel Value of Money: How the World's Only Attempt to Abolish Money Has Hindered Cambodia's Economic Development," *Asia Pacific Issues* 49, 1– 8.

Prud'Homme, Remy (1969), *L'économie du Cambodge*, Paris: Presses Universitaires de France.

Raghavendra, N. V., and M. H. Bala Subrahmanya (2005), "Collective Efficiency and Technological Capacity on Small Firms: Evidence from Two Foundry Clusters in South India," *International Journal of Management and Enterprise Development* 2 (3–4), pp. 325–348.

Redding, Gordon (1990), *The Spirit of Chinese Capitalism*, Berlin: de Gruyter.

Rein, Shaun (2012), *The End of Cheap China: Economic and Cultural Trends That Will Disrupt the World,* Hoboken, New Jersey: John Wiley & Sons.

Rigg, Jonathan (1997), *Southeast Asia: The Human Landscape of Modernization and Development* London: Routledge.

Roberts, William H. (1931), "The Five Thousand Temples of Pagan," *National Geographic* 60 (4), 445–454.

Robinson, H. W. (1923), "The Hairnet Industry in North China," *National Geographic* 44 (3), 327–336.

Rock, Joseph F. (1924), "Banishing the Devil of Disease among the Nashi," *National Geographic* 66 (5), 473–499.

Rock, Joseph F. (1930), "Seeking the Mountains of Mystery: An Expedition on the China-Tibet Frontier to the Unexplored Amnyi Machen Range, One of Whose Peaks Rivals Everest," *National Geographic* 57 (2), 131–185.

Rock, Joseph F. (1935), "Sungmas, the Living Oracles of the Tibetan Church," *National Geographic* 68 (4), 475–478.

Rodrik, Dani (2007), *One Economics, Many Recipes: Globalization, Institutions, and Economic Growth*, Princeton, New Jersey: Princeton University Press.

Rondinelli, Dennis A., and Jennie I. Litvack (1999), "Economic Reform, Social Progress, and Institutional Development: A Framework for Assessing Vietnam's Transition," in Jennie I. Litvack and Dennis A. Rondinelli, eds., *Market Reform in Vietnam: Building Institutions for Development*, Westport, Connecticut: Quorum, pp. 1–30.

Rosenbloom, Alfred, and Bijay K.C. (2005), "Management Education in Nepal: A View from the High Country," in John R. McIntyre and Ilan Alon, eds., *Business and Management Education in Transitioning and Developing Countries: A Handbook,* Armonk, New York: M. E. Sharpe, pp. 69–82.

Roth, Siobhan (2006), "Marrying Young," *National Geographic* 209 (5), p. 26.

Rothenberger, Catherine (1999), "Growing Pains: Management Challenges in an Emerging Financial Market," in Richard G. Linowes, ed., *Portraits of Business Practices in Emerging Markets: Cases for Management Education,* Washington, DC: Institute of International Education and US Agency for International Development, Volume 2, pp. 164–173.

Roy, Denny (2003), *Taiwan: A Political History,* Ithaca: Cornell University Press.

Ruane, Ma C. (2007), "Small-scale Business Enterprises in the Philippines: Survey and Empirical Analysis," *International Journal of Entrepreneurship* 11 (1), 1–25.

Samuels, Gertrude (1955), "Passage to Freedom in Viet Nam," *National Geographic* 107 (6), 858–874.

Sanders, Jimmy M., and Victor Nee (1987), "Limits of Ethnic Solidarity in the Enclave Economy," *American Sociological Review* 52 (6), 745–767.

Sanghavi, Nitkin (2002), "Franchising as a Growth Strategy in the Japanese Retail Market," in Dianne N. B. Welsh and Ilan Alon, eds., *International Franchising in Industrialized Markets: North America, the Pacific Rim, and Other Countries,* Chicago: CCH, pp. 269–286.

Say, Jean Baptiste (1816), *Catechism of Political Economy: Or, Familiar Conversations of the Manner in Which Wealth is Produced, Distributed, and Consumed by Society,* London: Sherwood.

Schaper, Michael, and Thierry Volery (2004), *Entrepreneurship and Small Business: A Pacific Rim Perspective,* Milton, Queensland: John Wiley & Sons.

Schive, Chi, and Ming-Wen Hu (2001), "The Evolution and Competitiveness of Taiwan's SMEs," in Chao-Cheng Mai and Chien-Sheng Shih, eds., *Taiwan's Economic Success Since 1980*, Cheltenham, UK: Edward Elgar, pp. 248–274.

Schumpeter, Joseph Alois (1912), *Theorie der wirtschaftlichen Entwicklung*, Munich and Leipzig: Dunker und Humblat.

Schumpeter, Joseph Alois (1928), "The Instability of Capitalism," *Economic Journal* 38, 361–386.

Schumpeter, Joseph Alois (1934), *The Theory of Economic Development: An Inquiry into Profits, Capital, Credit, Interest, and the Business Cycle,* Cambridge, Massachusetts: Harvard University Press.

Schumpeter, Joseph Alois (1939), *Business Cycles: A Theoretical, Historical and Statistical Analysis of the Capitalist Process*, New York: McGraw Hill.

Schumpeter, Joseph Alois (1942), *Capitalism, Socialism and Democracy*, New York: Harper and Row.

Schumpeter, Joseph Alois (1947), "The Creative Response in Economic History," *Journal of Economic History* 7, 149–159.

Schumpeter, Joseph Alois (1949), "Economic Theory and Entrepreneurial History," in *Change and the Entrepreneur: Postulates and Patterns for Entrepreneurial History*, Cambridge, Massachusetts: Harvard University Press, pp. 63–84.

Scidmore, Eliza R. (1910), "Mukden, the Manchu Home, and Its Great Art Museum," *National Geographic* 21 (4), 289–320.

Scidmore, Eliza R. (1914), "Young Japan," *National Geographic* 26 (1), 54–64.

Sebastian, Jose, and Sanjay Thakur (1994), *Not Born — The Created Entrepreneurs,* Ahmedabad: Entrepreneurship Development Institute of India.

Seglin, Jeffrey L. (1990), *The McGraw Hill 36-Hour Marketing Course*, New York: McGraw Hill.

Sein, Thaung (1950), *Problems of the Burmese Film*, Rangoon: Bamakhit Press.

Sharma, S.V.S. (1979), *Small Entrepreneurial Development in Some Asian Countries: A Comparative Study*, New Delhi: Light and Life.

Shi, Henry X., and Léo-Paul Dana (2013), "Market Orientation and Entrepreneurship in Chinese Family Business: A Socialisation View," *International Journal of Entrepreneurship & Small Business* 20 (1), 1–16.

Shinato, Teruo, Katsuyuki Kamei, and Léo-Paul Dana (2013), "Entrepreneurship Education in Japanese Universities," *International Journal of Entrepreneurship & Small Business* 20 (2), 184–204.

Shor, Franc (1960), "The City They Call Red China's Showcase," *National Geographic* 118 (2), 192–223.

Silcock, Thomas H. (1967), *Thailand: Social and Economic Studies in Development*, Durham, North Carolina: Duke.

Simon, Scott (2005), "Scarred Landscapes and Tattooed Faces: Poverty, Identity and Land Conflict in a Taiwanese Indigenous Community," in Robyn Eversole, John-Andrew McNeish, and Alberto D. Cimadamore, eds., *Indigenous Peoples and Poverty: An International Perspective*, London: Zed Books, pp. 53–68.

Simpich, Frederick (1926), "Singapore, Crossroads of the East: The World's Greatest Mart for Rubber and Tin Was in Recent Times a Pirate-haunted, Tiger-infested Jungle Isle," *National Geographic* 49 (3), 235–269.

Simpich, Frederick (1929), "Manchuria, Promised Land of Asia: Invaded by Railways and Millions of Settlers, This Vast Region Now Recalls Early Boom Days in the American West," *National Geographic* 56 (4), 379–428.

Singh, Manmohan (2006), "India's Economic Challenge," in George Skaria, ed., *India 2006: Taking India to the World,* London: World Link, pp. 12–14.

Singha, Komol (2013), "Infrastructure for Entrepreneurship in India's Trouble-torn State of Manipur," *Journal of Economic Philosophy* 1 (1), 12–16.

Sinha, Jai B. P. (1978), "Superior Subordinate Relationship and Alienation," *National Labour Institute Bulletin* 4, 209–223.

Sinha, Jai B. P. (1984), "A Model of Effective Leadership Style in India," *International Studies of Management and Organization* 14, 86–98.

Skaria, George, ed. (2006), *India 2006: Taking India to the World,* London: World Link.

Small and Medium Enterprise Agency, Ministry of Economy, Trade and Industry (2005) *The 2005 White Paper on Small and Medium Enterprises in Japan Structural Change in Japanese Society and the Dynamism of Small and Medium Enterprises*, Tokyo: Japan Small Business Reseach Institute.

Smith, A. W. (1930), "Working Teak in the Burma Forests: The Sagacious Elephant Is Man's Ablest Ally in the Logging Industry of the Far East," *National Geographic* 68 (2), 239–256.

Smith, Adam (1892), *Inquiry into the Nature and Causes of the Wealth of Nations*, Volumes I & II (reprinted from the sixth edition with an introduction by Ernest Belfort Bax), Covent Garden, London: George Bell & Sons, York Street.

Smith-Hunter, Andrea E. (2006), *Women Entrepreneurs Across Racial Lines: Issues of Human Capital, Financial Capital and Network Structures,* Cheltenham, United Kingdom: Edward Elgar.

So-young, Kim, and Shin Hae-in (2005), "176 public agencies to be relocated out of Seoul by 2012," *The Korea Herald*, June 25, p. 1.

Sochurek, Howard (1964), "Slow Train Through Viet Nam's War," *National Geographic* 126 (3), 412–444.

Soh-jung, Yoo (2005), "Jobless rate higher than official figure," *The Korea Herald*, June 25, p. 5.

Somavia, Juan (2006), "SMEs," Statement at the World Economic Forum, Davos, January 26.

Speece, Mark, and Phyu Phyu Sann (1998), "Problems and Conflicts in Manufacturing Joint Ventures in Myanmar," *Journal of Euro-Asian Management* 4 (3), 19–43.

Steinberg, David I. (1982), *Burma: A Socialist Nation of Southeast Asia*, Boulder, Colorado: Westview Press.

Steinberg, David I. (1959), *Cambodia*, New Haven: Human Relations Area Files Press.

Stewart, B. Anthony (1944), "Salt for China's Daily Rice," *National Geographic* 86 (3), 329–336.

Štulhofer, Aleksandar (1999), "Between Opportunism and Distrust: Socio-Cultural Aspects of the Underground Economy in Croatia," in Edgar L. Feige and Katarina Ott, eds., *Underground Economies in Transition: Unrecorded Activity, Tax, Corruption and Organized Crime*, Aldershot: Ashgate, pp. 43–63.

Swe, Myint (1972), *History of Burmese Printed Books*, Rangoon: Kayathuka Press.

Swerdlow, Joel L. (1995), "Burma: The Richest of Poor Countries," *National Geographic* 188 (1), 70–97.

Swierczek, Frederic William, and Somkid Jatusripatak (1994), "Exploring Entrepreneurship Cultures in Southeast Asia," *Journal of Enterprising Culture* 2 (2), 687–708.

Tambunan, Tulus T. H. (1992), "The Role of Small Firms in Indonesia," *Small Business Economics* 4 (1), 59–77.

Tambunan, Tulus T. H. (2005), "Promoting Small and Medium Enterprises with a Clustering Approach: A Policy Experience from Indonesia," *Journal of Small Business Management* 43 (2), 138–154.

Tan, Cheng Leong, and Terence S. Lim (1993), *Vietnam: Business and Investment Opportunities,* Singapore: Cassia.

Tan, Wee–Liang (2013), "Collectivistic Norms and International Entrepreneurship: A Tale of Two Clans, the Wenzhounese from China and the Chettiars from India," *International Journal of Business and Globalisation* 10 (3), 245–255.

Thai, Mai Thi Thanh, and Li Choy Chong (2013), "Dynamic Experimental Internationalization: Strategy of SMEs from a Transition Economy," *Journal of International Entrepreneurship* 11 (4), 370–399.

Thein, Myat (1996), "Socio-economic and Cultural Background of Myanmar," in Tan Teck Meng, Low Aik Meng, John J. Williams, and Ivan P. Polunin, eds., *Business Opportunities in Myanmar*, Singapore: Prentice Hall, pp. 17–24.

Thomas, Chithung, Mary Thomas, and G. P. Prasain (2013), "Problems of Entrepreneurship Development in Hill Districts of Manipur — A Case Study of Ukhrul District," *Research Analysis and Evaluation* 4(41), 16–18.

Torri, Maria Costanza (2013), "Traditional Jamu versus Industrial Jamu: Perceptions and Beliefs of Consumers in the City of Yogyakarta: What Future for Traditional Herbal Medicine in Urban

Indonesia?" *International Journal of Entrepreneurship and Small Business* 19 (1), 1–20.
Torri, Maria Costanza, and Andrea Martinez (2014), "Women's Empowerment and Micro-entrepreneurship in India: Constructing A New Development Paradigm?" *Progress in Developmental Studies* 14 (1), 31–48.
Turnbull, Constance M. (1977), *A History of Singapore 1819–1975,* Oxford, United Kingdom: Oxford University Press.
Turner, Sarah (2003a), *Small Entrepreneurs in Indonesia: Trading on the Margins,* London: Routledge Curzon.
Turner, Sarah (2003b), "Speaking Out: Chinese Indonesians After Suharto," *Asian Ethnicity* 4 (3), 337–352.
Venard, Bernard (1998), "Vietnam in Mutation: Will it Be the Next Tiger or a Future Jaguar?" *Asia Pacific Journal of Management* 15, 77–99.
Verver, Michiel (2012), "Templates of 'Chineseness' and Trajectories of Cambodian Chinese Entrepreneurship in Phnom Penh," *Cross-Currents: East Asian History and Culture Review* 4, 23–50.
Verver, Michiel, and Heidi Dahles (2013), "The Anthropology of Chinese Capitalism in Southeast Asia: From Culture to Institution?" *Journal of Business Anthropology* 2 (1), 93–114.
Vial, Virginie (2011), "Micro-entrepreneurship in a Hostile Environment: Evidence from Indonesia," *Bulletin of Indonesian Economic Studies* 47 (2), 233–262.
Wai, U Tun (1955), *Burma's Currency and Credit*, Calcutta: Orient Longmans.
Waldinger, Roger David (1984), "Immigrant Enterprise in the New York Garment Industry," *Social Problems* 32 (1), 60–71.
Waldinger, Roger David (1986a), "Immigrant Enterprise: A Critique and Reformulation," *Theory and Society* 15 (1–2), 249–285.
Waldinger, Roger David (1986b), *Through the Eye of the Needle: Immigrants and Enterprise in New York's Garment Trades*, New York: New York University Press.
Waldinger, Roger David, and Howard E. Aldrich (1990), "Trends in Ethnic Business in the United States," in Roger David Waldinger, Howard E. Aldrich, Robin Ward, and Associates, eds., *Ethnic Entrepreneurs: Immigrant Business in Industrial Societies*, Newbury Park, California: Sage, pp. 49–78.
Waldinger, Roger David, Howard E. Aldrich, and Robin Ward (1990), "Opportunities, Group Characteristics and Strategies," in Roger David Waldinger, Howard E. Aldrich, Robin Ward, and Associates, eds., *Ethnic Entrepreneurs: Immigrant Business in Industrial Societies*, Newbury Park, California: Sage, pp. 13–48.
Waldinger, Roger David, David McEvoy, and Howard E. Aldrich (1990), "Spatial Dimensions of Opportunity Structures," in Roger David Waldinger, Howard E. Aldrich, Robin Ward, and Associates, eds. *Ethnic*

Entrepreneurs: Immigrant Business in Industrial Societies, Newbury Park, California: Sage, pp. 106–130.

Walsh, James, and Philip Anderson (1995), "Owner-Manager Adoption/Innovation Preference and Employment Performance," *Journal of Small Business Management* 33 (3), 1–8.

Wang, Yueping. P., and Yang Yao (2002), "Market Reforms, Technological Capabilities, and the Performance of Small Enterprises in China," *Small Business Economics* 18 (1–3), 197–211.

Wani, V. P., T. K. Garg, and S. K. Sharma (2003), "The Role of Technical Institutions in Developing a Techno-entrepreneurial Workforce for Sustainable Development of SMEs in India," *International Journal of Management and Enterprise Development* 1 (1), 71–88.

Wani, V. P., T. K. Garg, and S. K. Sharma (2005), "Engineer as Entrepreneur: A Necessity for Successful Product Innovation in the Small-scale Industry Sector in India," in John R. McIntyre and Ilan Alon, eds., *Business and Management Education in Transitioning and Developing Countries: A Handbook,* Armonk, New York: M. E. Sharpe, pp. 39–57.

Ward, Robin (1987), "Ethnic Entrepreneurs in Britain and in Europe," in Robert Goffee and Richard Scase, eds., *Entrepreneurship in Europe: The Social Processes*, London: Croom Helm, pp. 83–104.

Ward, Robin, and Richard Jenkins, eds. (1984), *Ethnic Communities in Business: Strategies for Economic Survival*, Cambridge: Cambridge University Press, pp. 105–124.

Weber, Max (1904–5), "Die protestantische Ethik und der Geist des Kapitalismus," *Archiv fur Sozialwissenschaft und Sozialpolitik* (20–21); translated (1930) by Talcott Parsons, *The Protestant Ethic and the Spirit of Capitalism*, New York: George Allen & Unwin.

Weber, Max (1924), *The Theory of Social and Economic Organization*, New York: The Free Press.

Weber, Max (1958*), The Religion of India — The Sociology of Hinduism & Buddhism*, New York: The Free Press.

Webster, Donovan (2003), "Blood, Sweat, and Toil along the Burma Road," *National Geographic* 204 (5), 84–103.

Webster, Frederick E. (1992), "The Changing Role of Marketing in the Corporation," *Journal of Marketing* 53, 1–17.

Wei, Liu (2001), "Incentive Systems for Technical Change: The Chinese System in Transition," *International Journal of Entrepreneurship and Innovation Management* 1 (2), 157–177.

White, Peter T. (1961a), "Report on Laos," *National Geographic* 120 (2), 241–275.

White, Peter T. (1961b), "South Viet Nam Fights the Red Tide," *National Geographic* 120 (4), 445–489.

White, Peter T. (1967), "Behind the Headlines in Viet Nam," *National Geographic* 131 (2), 149– 193.

White, Peter T. (1968), "The Mekong River of Terror and Hope," *National Geographic* 134 (6), 737–787.
White, Peter T. (1982), "Kampuchea Wakens From a Nightmare," *National Geographic* 161 (5), 590–623.
White, Peter T. (1987), "Laos Today," *National Geographic* 171 (6), 772–795.
Williams, Maynard Owens (1919), "The Descendants of Confucius," *National Geographic* 36 (3), 253–265.
Williams, Maynard Owens (1935), "By Motor Trail across French Indo-China," *National Geographic* 68 (4), 487–534.
Williams, Maynard Owens (1942), "New Delhi Goes Full Time," *National Geographic* 82 (4), 465–494.
Williamson, Oliver E. (1985), *The Economic Institutions of Capitalism*, New York: Free Press.
Williamson, Oliver E. (1996), *The Mechanisms of Governance*, New York: Oxford University Press.
Wong, Bernard (1987), "The Role of Ethnicity in Enclave Enterprises: A Study of the Chinese Garment Factories in New York City," *Human Organization* 66 (2), 120–130.
Wong, How-Man (1984), "Peoples of China's Far Provinces," *National Geographic* 165 (3), 283–333.
Wong, Poh Kam, Finna Wong, Lena Lee, and Yuen Ping Ho (2005), *Global Entrepreneurship Monitor,* Singapore: National University of Singapore.
Wright, Nadia H. (2003), *Respected Citizens: The History of Armenians in Singapore and Malaysia*, Middle Park, Victoria, Australia: Amassia.
Wright, Richard W., and Malcolm Innes-Brown (2009), "Cambodia," in Léo-Paul Dana, Mary Han, Vanessa Ratten and Isabell M. Welpe, eds., *Handbook of Research on Asian Entrepreneurship,* Cheltenham: Edward Elgar, pp. 53–66.
Wu, Yuan Li (1983), "The Role of Alien Entrepreneurs in Economic Development: An Entrepreneurial Problem," *American Economic Review* 73 (2), 112–117.
Wulsin, Frederick R. (1926), "The Road to Wang Ye Fu: An Account of the Work of the National Geographic Society's Central-China Expedition in the Mongol Kingdom of Ala Shan," *National Geographic* 69 (2), 195–234.
Yan, Ho–Don (2013), "Entrepreneurship, Competitive Strategies, and Ascending Global Brands from Taiwan: Lessons for Emerging Markets," *International Journal of Business and Globalisation* 10 (3), 325–344.
Yang, Sung-jin (2005), "Beyond Dichotomy Between Growth and Distribution," *The Korea Herald* 16, 060, Saturday, June 25, p. 12.
Yap, Josef T., and Ruperto P. Majuca (2013), "Aspirations and Challenges for Economic and Social Development in the Philippines Toward 2030," Discussion Paper Series 2013–27, Makati City: Philippine Institute for Development Studies.

Yeung, Henry Wai-Chung (1999), "The Internationalization of Ethnic Chinese Business Firms from Southeast Asia: Strategies, Processes and Competitive Advantage," *International Journal of Urban and Regional Research* 23 (1), 103–127.

Yu, Junbo, and Roger R. Stough (2006), "The Determinants of Entrepreneurship Development in China," *International Journal of Management and Enterprise Development* 3 (1–2), 30–52.

Zainol, Fakhrul Anwar (2013), "The Antecedents and Consequences of Entrepreneurial Orientation in Malay Family Firms in Malaysia," *International Journal of Entrepreneurship and Small Business* 18 (1), 103–123.

Zainol, Vivi (2005), "Govt Okays Youths' Ideas For Change," *The Straits Times,* Wednesday, June 8, p. 1.

Zasloff, Joseph Jermiah, ed., (1988), *Postwar Indochina: Old Enemies and New Allies*, Washington, DC: US Government Printing Office.

Zasloff, Joseph Jermiah, and Leonard Unger (1990), *Laos: Beyond the Revolution*, New York: St. Martin's Press.

Zineldin, Mosad Amin (1998), "Towards an Ecological Collaborative Relationship Management," *European Journal of Marketing* 32 (11–12), 1138–1164.

Zingales, Luigi (2006), "Gods and Mammon," *Global Agenda: The Magazine of World Economic Forum Annual Meeting* 4, February, 228–229.

Index

D

E

F

M

N

O

P

Q

R

U

V

W

X

Y